# THE CATERER

*a novel*

AMANDA LUNDAY

www.amandalunday.com

ISBN 13: 9798991119009 (paperback)
ISBN 13: 9798991119023 (digital)

Cover illustration © shutterstock/istock
Designed by emmagraves.co.uk

Printed in the United States of America.

First Edition.

*To my family,*
*Thank you for helping me*
*find the courage to chase this dream*

# CHAPTER 1

ALICE DREW THE SHREDDED PORK from its marinade of blood oranges and red wine, slipping it into three homemade tortillas she'd pressed that morning. She turned to the prep table on the other side of the food truck, topping the pork with mango salsa and pickled red onion before handing it to Valencia, who sprinkled on the cilantro. The garlic and the onion of the meat hit Alice's stomach, making it growl. Valencia handed the lidless to-go box to the man outside the window, who commented on the variety of color. Valencia smiled and drew in a long breath before starting off on the flavors of a meal, the true experience of well-made food when all the flavors blended perfectly. She set her dark hand on the back of her hip, the other waving in front of her square face. Valencia became more animated when she talked about food. Alice knew the feeling. The mixture of unexpected flavors, how it would hit a person in waves. The way the texture complemented the hints and tones of a perfectly assembled dish. The right food could take a person on a journey, transport them to another place.

The man told them to have a good day before sitting with his friends in the park beside the food truck. Alice glanced at her watch; she needed to leave for her event in an hour and a half.

"Mi querida, the line is getting long. Switch with me." Valencia preferred to be on the grill juggling orders while Alice managed the front, probably because Val loved to talk, whereas Alice could take orders and call out numbers. Alice stepped to the side and let Val slip back to the cooking area. She wiped her forehead with the top of her sleeve and moved into position.

The next time she looked up from giving the customer his change, twelve people waited in line. Where did they come from? If she didn't leave soon, she'd be late to her event; Carver would kill her.

"Your event, mi querida." Valencia looked her way. "You're late."

"I can stay." Alice glanced at the sidewalk, the line almost gone.

"Go. Go. We're almost out of things anyway."

"I can't let you clean all this up by yourself."

Valencia put her hand on the counter and cocked her head.

"Go. Tell me all about it *lunes*. Go." She pointed to the back door.

Alice sighed and slipped off her purple apron. "Thank you."

"Believe in yourself!" Valencia called as Alice stepped out of the food truck. She unclipped her bike from the side and started to ride. After being in the food truck all day, the rush of air was a welcome relief. A rare, perfect D.C. summer day—warm but not overly muggy. She meant to leave enough time to take a shower and change, but now she'd arrive smelling like cilantro and sweat. If all went to plan, she would go unnoticed. Normally cooking dinner for ten people wouldn't be that big of a deal, except for the client: Delany Clare, former point guard for the Wizards. The team's top shooter for close to a decade until he tore his ACL one too many times. She attended Delany's last home game the month before, her father a season ticket holder. The idea of him not being on the court in the fall still felt odd. He'd been with the team since Alice was in high school.

2

She locked up her bike and went inside his apartment building. *Please let there be a bathroom in the lobby.* She did a quick scan, not seeing one.

"Can I help you, miss?" the man at the desk asked.

"Alice Gibson. I'm here for Delany Clare."

"Ah yes, his assistant told me to expect you." He did a once-over on her and her short red jumpsuit and forced a smile before handing her a key card. "He's on the top floor, and I'll need that back when you're done."

"Of course." Alice shifted her messenger bag and got on the elevator. *Please don't let Mr. Clare already be there.* Give her one break today.

The elevator opened to three doors. Alice found the one Mr. Clare owned and knocked. A woman her age answered, a few inches shorter with paprika red hair and eyes the color of limes.

"Ms. Gibson? I'm Katy O'Toole. Come in."

Alice stepped inside the apartment. The front area went down three steps into the living room with a long L-shaped leather couch and a massive TV in the corner by the windows that offered a panoramic view of The District from the Capitol all the way to Rosslyn, including The Washington Monument and Lincoln Memorial.

"What you requested is in the kitchen. Dinner should be ready to go around seven." Katy led her to the narrow kitchen, most of the appliances on the far wall across from a long and skinny island with a series of stools on the far side. A small dining table sat before a set of windows, a built-in coffee bar to the right. Carver forced a smile from the stove. God bless her business partner for covering her butt.

"If you need to change, there's a guest bath around the corner," Katy said.

"Thank you." Alice smiled weakly. Katy left them alone.

"You're late!" Carver whispered.

"I know, I'm sorry. Where are we?" She took the lid off the leg of lamb she'd left marinating for two days.

"I started that about twenty minutes ago. I'm washing the veggies now."

Fresh flowers and edibles waited on the counter along with the oils and dressings they needed. She washed her hands and set their food processor on the island to make the pesto.

Sensing a quiet moment, she reached for her messenger bag and found the bathroom Katy told her about. She took out her slacks and a polka-dot blouse. After being in the food truck her chocolate-colored hair laid flat, but some goo helped bring it back to something fun and whimsical. By luck, she grabbed some body spray that morning. Alice slipped into her flats, shoved her dirty clothes into her bag and went back to the kitchen. A purple apron rested on the counter alongside the appropriate wine for the night. Carver worked to finish accenting the tiramisu.

"You can go if you want." Alice leaned her hip into the counter. Carver glanced at her, a hint of annoyance in his gaze. She studied his black eyes and diamond face. He belonged in a Motown band, smooth darker skin, easy smile. He wore colored chinos with a white cotton, collared shirt, and a black chef's apron

"It's okay. My wife is taking the kids to a movie at the zoo."

"I can handle ten people."

Carver put the hand strainer on a paper towel to not get cocoa on the counter.

"It's a big night, Lil. I know you can do it, but we're in this together." If he was really irate, he'd call her Alice. Thankfully, he used the nickname only close friends called her.

"I don't want you to miss time with your kids, Carver."

"Let's see where we are after we get the main course out. You're doing cleanup, believe me."

"I figured that." Alice set the vegetables to roast in the oven. Katy came into the kitchen, asking if they needed anything else.

"Is this the wine for tonight?" Katy picked up a bottle.

"I was told Mr. Clare didn't have any alcohol preferences." Carver wiped his hands on his apron.

Katy put the bottle down. "He owns a vineyard in Napa. Let me grab you some of his stock to use." She walked to a wine fridge by the windows, Carver following to investigate.

"Does Mr. Clare have a full bar?"

"I'll let you answer that," Katy said, and they walked to the main room, Alice unable to hear their conversation. Carver came back into the kitchen, a wide smile on his face.

"This just got fun!" The last bit of annoyance faded as Carver got lost in concocting a fun drink to pair with the lamb. He brought a sample for Alice to taste. She didn't drink often but could help with flavors.

"Try rosemary." She went back to work as the door opened multiple times, and the conversation in the front got louder.

"Five minutes." Katy poked her head in. Alice ran her hands over her purple apron and looked at the tomato, aubergine, and mozzarella mini tarts with local flowers on top. Katy came into the room and gave her the thumbs-up, before sitting at the end of the island. Alice hadn't run food in years, but hoped her skills from her catering days would come back as she balanced four plates to deliver.

The table for ten sat against the full wall of windows with a view of the city all lit up. Alice kept her gaze down, desperate to steady her nerves. She started at the far end, slipping plates into places. Carver carried three more plates behind her. On the next trip, Alice grabbed two bottles of the drier red wine. She filled people's glasses, leaving the rest on the table. Back in the kitchen, she put a tarte next to Katy, who thanked her, looking up from her laptop.

"What do you do for Mr. Clare?" Alice asked.

"I'm his personal assistant, so I keep his life running, and yeah, whatever he asks."

"How did you get hired for that?"

Katy bobbed her head and finished her bite. "Ad in the paper. I moved here after college about five years ago and had no desire to work on the hill or rot in an office. Why not travel the world and have no social life?"

Alice laughed as Carver came in with dirty appetizer plates. The second course featured lamb shanks with locally sourced fingerling potatoes and mini carrots, topped with a pesto made from local edibles, including chickweed and dandelion leaves. Alice plated the lamb as Carver came back for the plates, not wanting them to get cold. He asked her to take the last three, grabbing the pitchers of rosemary margaritas he prepared.

"That last plate is for you," Alice said to Katy as she followed Carver back to the party. She set the plates down while Carver told the table about the drink and how it should hit their palate and interact with the lamb. She left two bottles of Mr. Clare's red wine on the table, doing a quick sweep of the party. Mr. Clare sat at the head, a beautiful Black woman with a long face and close-set dark eyes to his left. She touched his forearm as Carver talked. A heavier-set Black man sat on his right, drinking a whiskey, a skinny woman to his left. The rest of the party appeared to be couples, well-dressed, wealthier.

"Seriously, I normally just raid the fridge for leftovers," Katy said when Alice came back.

"Well, that's silly." Alice started to break down the pans, pulling together the last of the vegetables and extra edibles onto a plate. Alice ate a few pieces of lamb from the pan then started another pitcher of margaritas, asking Katy if she wanted one.

"Please!" She moaned. "God, the lamb is heavenly!"

"I run a food truck on K Street." Alice got a glass from the cupboard to fill.

"The Cuban food one? I love that place!"

She took the pitcher to the table, clearing bottles and plates.

Carver pulled his tiramisu from the fridge. Alice carried two carafes of coffee to the table. Delany stood and offered espresso drinks, three people going with him into the area by the wine fridge. Carver went to serve his dessert, the swooshing of steaming milk filling the air. The kitchen looked like children made the meal. Alice would never have left it in such a state if she knew Mr. Clare might see it. She tried to pull things together, hiding plates in the sink, and trying to stack the pans better. She wiped down the island, throwing the crumbs in the sink.

"I'll be right there," a voice said. "Hi, I'm Delany." He was shorter for a basketball player. Tailored, tan slacks showed off his slender frame, dark blue button-up rolled almost to his elbows.

"Alice Gibson." She ran her hand over her apron before shaking his.

"The food's delicious. I've never seen anyone put flowers on a quiche before." His eyes reminded her of the moonless nights at her parents' house near the Pennsylvania border. The well-kept beard on his rugged chin highlighted his full lips.

"They're local and completely edible. I hope that's okay."

"No, I liked it." He smiled and touched her arm, warmth flooding her body. "I didn't realize Carver had a catering arm."

"We're just getting going. A way for us to have fun with food."

"You certainly did that. The meal was delicious."

She smiled. Someone called Delany's name.

"It was nice meeting you, Alice." He walked away. Alice leaned forward on her tiptoes. Holy cheese puffs, he was hot up close.

"Yeah, I know, right?" Katy said from the end of the island. Alice froze, forgetting Katy was there. She came back down and went to collect the dishes. Katy laughed from her place.

# CHAPTER 2

TABBY TWITCHED HER FOOT as Paul rambled on about their children to the interviewer. She tried to stay in the moment, but her mind kept going back to the discussion with Mo Mo before she left that afternoon. Of course, he'd wait until Friday afternoon when she was running late and rushing to get out of the office before bringing up something as significant as selling his shares. The man was spineless, had been since college, but he was loyal. "Just let me be a coder," he'd said. He didn't want to be involved in board meetings and decisions on whether they went public. Well, she told him again, they weren't going public.

Paul touched her thigh, bringing Tabby back. She forced a smile, hoping she looked engaged and not bored. After six interviews that week, the process felt tedious. Yes, she appreciated the publicity, but couldn't one of them ask an original question?

"What you are on the brink of is remarkable." The interviewer glanced at her notes. "Already critics are hailing your website as a site to watch in 2009, calling it a game changer. Tell us more about Welcome Note."

"Welcome Note lets the little guy into the hospitality space by enabling people to rent out their basement apartments, extra rooms, or rental houses to paying guests. With the downturn in the economy, people are looking for additional income. Some can't afford a hotel or want more comfort when they travel. All we are doing is marrying a need with a resource." She put on the politician smile her mother taught her. The interviewer laughed.

"And you are the visionary and heart behind TabiKat. How did you learn so much about coding?"

"I'm self-taught. I played with BASIC when I was younger and hoped to study game design in college. For the last few years, I've stayed home with our twins and, well, needed something to do once they went to school. But like I've said, the push to get into it sparked when I realized I could connect two groups of people who were desperate to find each other."

"And there is an app coming out later this year? Is that what it's called?" She looked at her notes again. People were still figuring out how to code for Apple's new app store, the iPhone barely on the market for two years. Tabby already figured it out.

"Yes. Our app will be available for the iPhone by September, giving people easier access to renting and posting."

"Remarkable!"

She led the woman around the apartment as they got images for the story, her life painted as Rockwell perfection, with Paul a successful lawyer with the EPA. They lived in a modest apartment in Alexandria, just outside D.C., with their twins—a boy and a girl—straight out of a *Pottery Barn Kids* catalog. The twins, starting fifth grade in the fall, were spitting images of their parents. Only her little girl, Annie, looked like Paul with her curly mahogany hair and close-set sky-blue eyes. Their son, James, or Mac as he preferred to be called, looked like Tabby—narrower face, straight hay-colored hair that fell to his chin, dark blue eyes.

Paul reminded her to smile during the interview, to keep her features soft. She wanted to ask if a man ever got told to soften his appearance, but she knew the answer to that question. So what if some found Tabby's features stiff? Her chiseled chin, the lack of smile lines around her dark blue eyes or mouth, a hardness to her gaze. She preferred calling it determination to succeed in a male-dominated arena.

Finally, the camera lights went off and she could relax. Dozens of people milled around the apartment for the interview or to help prep for TabiKat's party that night. A thank-you and a celebration, the chance for Tabby, and the three friends from college who helped finance her vision, to bask in their accomplishment at the trendiest rooftop bar in D.C. Thank goodness sweet Alice got the owner to agree to close for the night. This was her moment, and Tabby spared no expense. She'd never admit it to Paul, but she felt more excited for the party than their wedding. Her mother utilized their big day at St. John's Church to flex her political muscle, so nothing quite aligned with Tabby's taste, whereas tonight everything was as she wanted it.

Tabby sat again in the dining room. The makeup artist moved in to adjust her look from camera-ready to powerful and in charge. Tabby closed her eyes when the woman told her to. Mo Mo's comments were not the first time someone mentioned going public. Bigger tech companies offered to buy them out, but Tabby would not hear of it. She loved her company, her "third child" as she called it, and wanted to keep it private to use its success to bring her tech firm into the forefront. She already started coding her next app, BackDoor, that let employers access their company's cell phone files from wherever they were. She wanted TabiKat to become an East Coast beacon for Silicon Valley. Her mother nitpicked all that time she spent alone in her room, learning to code. But it gave Tabby the competitive edge she needed to make her dreams succeed.

Alice opened the front door and called hello. Tabby glanced at her, huffing. Her sister needed to do something with that short mop of hair, and *please stop calling short jumpsuits appropriate work attire.* She wasn't a mechanic! *The Washingtonian* dubbed her a rising chef in D.C. only a few years before, but you'd never know it to look at her now. Someday life would demand her sister take herself more seriously and stop bemoaning how a man pushed her out of her industry. If anyone understood sexism's limitations, Tabby did, but she wasn't hiding away and wasting her talent in a food truck.

No one would doubt that her sister was a Gibson. Alice and their mother had the same green eyes and thinner lips. Before their father's hair went white, he and Alice shared the same dulled brown hair. She shared his build too, but instead of heft in her stomach, it seemed to all go to Alice's chest and thighs. Why she got all the form when she didn't appreciate or utilize it didn't seem fair to Tabby, who found herself tall and flat like their mother.

"Is the interview done?" Alice asked.

"We just finished. God, you smell like oil and onions."

"Why are you in a mood? I thought you'd be high as a cloud today."

Tabby started to tell her about Mo Mo, but didn't want to get riled up or risk the interviewer overhearing. She didn't need rumors of dissent making the news.

"I left you a dress for tonight, and the stylist said she can do your hair."

"I can dress myself, thank you very much."

Tabby glared. "This is a big night for me Alice, just do what I ask!"

Alice started to object, but walked away instead. Tabby thought about calling after her. Her sister's financial and employment status were the only reason she started the website for goodness' sake! Living in D.C. was expensive, and her sister needed income to relaunch her culinary career. Tabby suggested leveraging their parents' apartment in the city. They lived near the

Pennsylvania border now, and only kept the space in D.C. for Alice to live in. She needed the funds, but didn't want to advertise on less than credible websites with no way to track who people were. Tabby got tired of her little sister's bemoaning and so went to some friends from college and came up with WlkmNt—as in what hosts left for those staying in their homes.

Only, plans stalled for Alice's catering company. Another month and no business plan, no events. Carver gave Alice full access to his kitchen to work in, and yet all Tabby heard from her sister were excuses. Alice lived with them since the website became viable. The kids loved having their "Aunt A" close—but Alice was not supposed to be their au pair.

Get through the party and the website launch, and then she'd sit Alice down and make her pull things together. If Tabby could find time to create a website and launch a startup with two kids and a house to run, surely her little sister could find time between her work at the food truck and foraging with their father all over D.C.

TABBY TOOK A SIP of her drink and looked out over the rooftop bar. Just the right number of people there, conversation flowed. The servers were available, but unobtrusive with the menu of finger food Alice put together. Her cucumber mojito was heavy on the rum, not that she, or Paul, would mind later. The D.C. evening was hot without being excessive. She looked like a million bucks, and nothing was going to ruin her night.

Across the bar Paul spoke to Mo Mo, who still looked the part of a defensive tackle, still dressed like he did at USC—unruly black hair, oversized, short-sleeved plaid shirt. At least he'd replaced the board shorts with wrinkled brown pants. *Still, stop screaming IT for a moment Mo Mo!* Take a lesson from her husband who'd cut his curly toffee hair down again, just a small messy

Mohawk on the top with a nice fade. Clean-shaven, he wore a dark, well-cut suit, a tie that matched her yellow midi dress. Even from this distance his wide smile made her heart race, those sea-blue eyes. Maybe if Mo Mo stepped up his game, he could stop bumming dates off their old college friends.

Paul reminded her on the ride in that tonight was only about good things. Tabby could deal with Mo Mo on Monday. Still, something about their conversation nagged at her. If she knew how wishy-washy he'd be, she never would have given him part of the company. But funding was tight as they were getting going so there was no money to pay him; it felt like a fair trade. Sadly, he was the investor she worried about the least.

A hand touched her elbow. Carrie Beaumont, another one of the investors, stood beside her with a man Tabby had never met.

"Tabby, this is Delany Clare," Carrie said, her arm looped into his. God bless her best friend, fresh off her latest divorce. She'd hang onto any man who might keep her in the lifestyle her exes got her used to. She might be trying a bit too hard in her tight, low-cut red dress that did its best to revive the curves she flaunted in college. Kids changed most women's forms, as did time, and sipping champagne around the world while your latest ex-husband made his fortunes on the stock market. Not that Tabby didn't benefit from his investments that helped launch her company. Still, Carrie teased her blond hair a bit too much, her makeup a tad overdone over her lighter brown eyes. People often said they looked like sisters, though Tabby prayed she did not appear that exhausted. Maybe after the website launched Tabby could treat her best friend to a weekend in Mexico.

"Tabby Black. How do I know your name?" She shook Delany's hand, the motion causing him to drop Carrie's arm. He was attractive. Easily half a foot taller than her with skin like brown sugar. His dark blue blazer pulled on his T-frame, no tie, the top button undone on his white collared shirt. He wore pressed dark trousers, and a dark brown trilby. Wood-framed, square sunglasses hid his eyes. Here was a man who took himself seriously.

"I used to play basketball for the Wizards, ma'am." His voice was smooth and deep. He could read a menu and it would be interesting.

"Ah yes, my father has season tickets. Didn't you just retire?"

"Yeah, this spring."

Carrie slipped away to speak with someone else. Tabby kept a certain distance between them. Delany leaned sideways on the balcony railing, giving them more space. Tabby smiled to herself. Carrie might have to look elsewhere for a bedfellow that night as this man seemed to have a bit of discretion.

"What are your plans now?"

"Well, I am getting into the day-to-day at my holding company, hoping to be able to do more charity work."

"Using your time and talents well." Tabby did a quick scan for her sister. There was not a ring on Mr. Clare's hand, no woman appeared to be watching them. He was articulate and giving, sexy enough to melt a circuit board. It was time her sister went on a date again. She would never find Mr. Right hiding out in the apartment and that greasy food truck. Yes, her ex had been a mistake, as Tabby tried to tell her. One of these days her sweet sister would realize her life would run much more smoothly if she just listened to what Tabby said.

"I hear tonight is for you." Delany brought Tabby's attention back.

"Two years of hard work. The finish line is so close."

Tabby raised her hand, Paul coming toward them. She introduced him to Delany and scanned the crowd, her sister standing at the railing alone. Leave it to her to miss a golden opportunity to network for her business. At least she wore the dress Tabby left. The merlot color would bring out her pale green eyes; it showed off her form without being clingy. Tabby told the men she'd be back. Time for a gentle push.

# CHAPTER 3

ALICE ARRIVED AT THE PARTY as late as she dared. Coming off the elevator, she worked her way through the mass of people there until she found a spot to breathe, questioning if her sister would know if she left. Only Tabby would be looking for her. She made some comment walking out the door about Alice not hiding away with the kids. The sitter laughed quietly from the kitchen. Where did Tabby get off thinking Alice needed her to dictate her life?

She slipped a potato and chickpea samosa off a passing tray. She rolled the filling over her tongue, smacking her lips. A bit too much salt and store-bought filo dough. Disappointing. Hopefully they didn't over-salt the pan con tomate. She got in line for a drink, fighting the urge to mess with her hair. She resisted washing the makeup off after Tabby left. Why did women want to feel like clowns all day?

Her friend who ran the front of house for the bar said hello. Alice hugged him and asked how he was. She would never tell

Tabby the man thanked her for the party, preferring a private event to hill interns blowing off steam. Let Tabby think she did her one favor.

"How are you?" he asked. Alice shrugged, never sure what to say. She took her glass of wine, and they walked to the railing overlooking the city. She glanced toward the Old Post Office Pavilion. Just let her be sitting in its clocktower, watching the sunset.

"I ran into Carver the other day," he went on. "He told me about Hasty Pudding."

"Yeah, we're still getting going. I'm trying to figure out how to balance everything." Her usual line. Even after how well the dinner went, Alice still questioned if she could break into the catering world. She cut her teeth in catering, so had the experience, taught by the revered D.B. Cornelia himself. But she was still a disgraced female chef in a male-dominated industry. The fact that Carver partnered with her had to mean something. He was *the* baker for weddings and high-class events. So far, Alice had been able to pull a couple events from his bookings, not that she was being overly aggressive about it.

"It's good to see you back out there." He glanced at the party. "Stick it to Jonas."

"Jonas." She finished her sip. "Someday that man has to live and let live. No one would know what happened if it wasn't for his big mouth."

"You rejected him, Lil."

"He never should have been hired in that kitchen. I'm glad people in Hollywood don't know what good food tastes like, but I do!"

"We all agree. Listen, if you ever want a job as a saucier—I can talk to our chef." He touched her arm before disappearing into the crowd. Alice set her gaze on the building next door. How was she the pariah? It wasn't right.

Alice longed to finish her wine and bolt. She understood it was a big night for her sister and wanted to be there to celebrate all Tabby had accomplished to that point, but she'd be more comfortable preparing the menu and managing the food line, being able to duck into the kitchen and get a breather. She didn't know what to do in these situations. Her sister was the networker, the social one, the one who somehow found three friends from her college days with money and expertise to help launch what was already being heralded as the start-up of the year.

She looked over the sea of people for a friendly face. Why weren't the twins there? It was a silly question but again would give her a distraction. Back at the apartment, before Tabby and Paul left for the event, Alice had offered to bring the twins home if it got to be too late. Paul had simply laughed and taken the kids to eat their dinner. Tabby stepped closer and reached to adjust Alice's longer pixie cut, but seeing the amount of goo and hairspray the stylists put in, she pulled her hand back and rested her hands on Alice's arms instead.

"It wouldn't kill you to be an adult for one night," she said. Alice studied her dark blue eyes, tilting her head. Since Alice agreed to live with them while TabiKat got off the ground, her sister had become more maternal. She was six years older and lorded it over Alice, convinced she was filled with sage wisdom. Alice felt like a teenager again, only their mother had never been this overbearing.

"Come to the party." Tabby ignored Alice's glare. "Make some contacts. See if you can't get an investor for your catering company. Don't forget who I'm doing this for." She walked into the kitchen. Alice rolled her eyes. Her sister wasn't doing any of this for her. Her business was the cover Tabby needed to admit the stay-at-home, socialite mother role was as boring in real life as it looked to them growing up. Not that their mother was around much with all those donor events and working the campaign trail.

Tabby refused to admit that TabiKat was her dream—had been for years. No, make it all about Alice's catering company and use it as leverage to guilt her and treat her like a child.

She turned back toward the city, the uncertainty salt in a wound. She worked too damn hard in Cornelia's kitchen to be passed over for Executive Chef after he died. If she wasn't given the promotion, she should have at least kept her position as sous chef. But Jonas made it clear how she would keep her job. Alice told him not to burn himself on the béchamel and walked out. He'd smeared her name across D.C., calling her ungrateful and hard to work with. He thought she'd crawl back, but Alice had come too far to work for a man like that.

Tabby came her way with the look that said Alice messed up. Alice merged into the crowd, not in the mood for another of Tabby's pep talks/micromanaging guilt trips, aka tell Alice everything she did wrong. There had to be someone in this sea of people she could talk to.

Moe grabbed her arm and asked how she was doing before introducing his girlfriend. The woman was petite with black hair to her mid-back, and eyes the color of pure maple syrup that lit up when she looked at Moe. For someone who always appeared overworked, it was nice to see him relax. The fact he could survive working with her sister all the time, well, that should qualify him for sainthood.

"Hello, Alice." Harry stepped into the conversation. The last of "The Three Stooges," as Tabby called them, Harry—Carrie—and Moe, contacts from college who invested in her start-up. Harry always looked like he stepped out of an action film, tighter short-sleeved button-up, almost-too-tight slacks, aviator glasses.

"You look stunning." Harry gave her a side hug and kissed her cheek. "Doesn't she look stunning, Mo Mo?"

"Moe was telling me about his upcoming vacation to St. Lucia." Alice elbowed Harry to create some distance. *Rule number one when trying to impress a girl: don't call your supposed friend a name everyone knows he hates.* "Any fun plans while you're there?" Alice turned her attention back toward Moe, ready for Harry to move on.

"When's the last time you got a vacation, Lil?" Moe asked.

"Let's see—it's '09 so…maybe '96, when Tabby and I went to Europe for the summer."

"That can't be right."

Alice thought about it. "No, you're right. It was Mexico with my ex." Three years before.

"We could go somewhere," Harry said. "Your sister said you're not working much."

Alice forced a smile. "I'm working at my food truck and my catering company."

"That's with Carver Wright?" Moe's girlfriend asked. Alice nodded. "We got a cake from him for a friend's birthday last year. It was really good."

"Carver is the best. He's letting me use his kitchen and does desserts. I'm not a baker."

"Let me talk to my friend. There are some events she does for her clients. It's real estate people, but it could lead somewhere."

"Yeah, thank you." She twitched her nose. "How's the supermodel?" Alice looked at Harry. If he was going to leer at her, she was going to remind him of the bimbo he had at home.

"Cheerleader. We broke up. I'm apparently working too much."

"Do you work? I thought you were a silent partner." Moe took a drink of his beer. Harry chuckled. Alice waited; it was rare to see Harry Clarks agitated.

"Tabs needed both expertise and funding. You gave one. I gave the other." Harry flashed a smile that got him out of far too much, too bad it had no effect on those he was with presently.

"Still haven't seen you in the office since we started. Where have you been working?"

"My father's lobbying firm. Doll, do you want to go somewhere more private?" He turned his full attention onto Alice. His neck was red, his smile a little too forced. Alice opened her mouth to reject him when someone tapped a knife on their glass. Moe touched her elbow and told Alice to have a good night before moving into the crowd with his girlfriend. Tabby tapped her knife on the glass again, waiting for the crowd to quiet. Alice debated leaving. But if Tabby noticed, Alice would have to justify why. Better to not risk her sister's ire.

"Thank you for being here," Tabby began. "This is a night that has been years in the making."

Alice scanned the crowd. Across the way, Carrie stood with two men. One eyed her tight red dress without disregard, his black suit ill-cut for his bulky frame. It was the man from Delany's dinner, darker brown skin, a round face, and bald head. Next to him stood Delany Clare. Why didn't Tabby mention he would be there? He saw Alice and raised his hand, Alice waving back. Harry joined them, Carrie introducing him to the two men. Delany said something and moved out of the group. Alice stood straighter as he weaved through the crowd toward her. She slipped between those around her, meeting him at the bar.

"What are you doing here?" Alice asked.

"Bobbie heard about it. Listen, can I buy you a drink?"

"Now?"

He smiled. "If that works for you."

Alice glanced toward her sister. "A drink sounds lovely."

They made their way to the elevator, Alice letting out her breath. It felt good to get out of the crowd, except she was leaving to get a drink with Delany Clare. Of course she was in a dress she'd never pick out for herself, and her hair probably resembled a mohawk. *Just play it cool.*

They end up in a basement bar near Lafayette Square. Delany got a sidecar. Alice asked for the first drink she could think of: a Cosmo.

"My friends loved your food last night." He undid his sleeves and rolled them back.

"Good. It's what I love to do." She sat on the booth side of their table, Delany in a chair.

"What did you do to the pesto? Elle was trying to figure it out."

*Elle must be the woman sitting next to him.* Alice debated whether to tell him his friends consumed leaves and weeds. "Dandelion leaves."

"Like the weed?" He leaned into the table between them.

The server came back with their drinks, forcing Delany to sit back. Alice took a longer sip, remembering she hated Cosmos due to the triple sec. She'd found a way to all but eliminate it from the cocktails at Hasty Pudding. She put it down and forced herself to swallow.

"There are a host of things around us we can eat, goldenrod, sumac, chickweed. Did you know you can eat cherry blossoms?"

"As in what blooms around here in the spring?" He tilted his head.

"Yeah." She took another sip. "You can use it for tea, or it's good with mochi. I infused a jar of vodka with them."

He set his elbow on the table and rubbed his forehead, his brow pinched. Here came the time for him to make an excuse to leave. Well, she could say she had a drink once with Delany Clare.

"How did you figure all this out?"

"My father got into foraging during college. It's how we bonded growing up. How is retirement going?" She sipped her drink again, ready to get the attention off herself.

"Good. Do you not like your drink?"

"Why do you say that?"

"You just grimace every time you take a sip."

"Oh god." She put her head in her hands. Delany chuckled and reached for her hand to get her to look at him again.

"Take mine." He pushed her drink her way. "Does it taste like cough syrup? That's why I never get one."

"You don't have to," she started to say, but he sipped her drink and rocked his head. "Thank you. I forgot I hate triple sec. So, your retirement." She sipped his sidecar. He laughed, seeming to remember there was triple sec in it as well. "I can finish this, it's fine."

"Alice, we can get you something you like." He touched her wrist before flagging down a waitress.

"Can I get a gin and tonic?" She asked, grateful the low lighting kept Delany from seeing how her face probably matched the Cosmo he finished before asking for another sidecar. He turned his attention back to her, his eyebrows raising as he wet his lips. "My retirement is going well. Working at my holding company, getting into philanthropy more."

"You didn't take that much time off."

He laughed. "No, I guess not."

"Well, I'm just glad someone of note took interest in the women's team here."

"You're a Mystics fan?" He leaned into the table again.

"Misty Barber came into the restaurant I used to work at. I got to know some of the players. My niece loves them, wants to play in the WNBA someday." She caught his gaze, and her cheeks flushed. She leaned in to ask another question when his cell phone rang. Delany held up his finger and leaned back.

"Hey Bobbie....Having drinks with a friend....I didn't sneak off anywhere." He looked over the restaurant, his other hand drumming the table. "I will see you Monday....No, Katy has the weekend off. Goodbye." He hung up and shook his head. "Don't know why I answered that. Are you hungry?"

"Like, for dinner?"

"That is what people normally eat after drinks." He winked. The server came back with their drinks, Delany asking for menus. Alice reached for her drink and sipped. Maybe the evening wasn't going as badly as she imagined.

# CHAPTER 4

TABBY DRUMMED HER FINGERS on the railing in the elevator while it made its slow crawl to the seventh floor. *Three days.* Three days and the WlkmNt would be live, and then she could breathe. The party Friday night had been what she needed to refocus her attention. Nothing would derail this moment. Failure was not a word Tabby understood. She had never failed at anything. Her mother taught her how to work hard and plan for every contingency. Never get caught off guard. She didn't ask for the hype around her website, but was not going to shy away from it.

TabiKat's offices shared the floor with an investment firm and a real estate agency. Both had glass doors leading to their offices, while TabiKat looked like the entrance to a closet. People missed it all the time. She asked the landlord if they could paint the door red or put their logo on it. The man had yet to get back to her, which was fine. Fine. Just a few more days and TabiKat would be the talk of D.C., and they could move somewhere better.

The office featured an open floor plan with cubicles in the center. She had an office, Mo Mo had one, the head of finance had one. A conference room and break area backed up to the inside wall. She humored the impersonal off-white paint and a sad bluish-gray carpet. After the launch, she'd spruce up the place. Until then, every dollar went into hiring the best coders and marketers. No point having a gorgeous office space if their products didn't do what they needed to.

She'd pulled her best two coders off WlkmNt to help with BackDoor, unwilling to let the press die away before launching her second project. It took all her restraint not to jump into BackDoor full-time, but as Mo Mo reminded her—she needed to keep her eye on the prize.

"Spying on my sister again?" Tabby walked into her office where Harry stood at the window, Alice's food truck barely visible at the end of the street.

"Have you ever eaten there?" he asked.

"I don't like cilantro. Why are you here?"

"Just wanted to check in…"

"Harry, you're a silent partner. Silent. Isn't there some college girl in Miami you can be hitting on right now?" She sat and turned her computer on.

"Now I know why your sister hates me." He parked in the chair across from her, putting his left foot on his right knee.

"My sister is discerning without my help. Why are you here?"

"We want to talk about going public—"

"We're not going public! For the love. I didn't do all this work to turn control of my company over to a bunch of stock people."

"This could be the biggest opening since Priceline. The revenue, Tabs…"

"I don't care about the money." She stopped and took a deep breath. Yes, the idea of making an easy couple million did appeal. It would restock her family's budget, get Paul to stop worrying about their lack of a rainy day fund. It would set the firm up to do what she wanted. But it would also be losing control of her company. She didn't want to muddy the waters more, or worse, risk someone else buying them out.

"I think you're being shortsighted," Harry said. "The attention we're getting…"

"And I think you see my company as a way to bypass having to be an adult. If you hate being a lobbyist, put that law degree your dad paid for to use and go be an ambulance chaser."

Harry scoffed. "You're not the only voice in the company, Tabs."

"I am the majority one."

"The three of us together out own you and I think we should get a say in our future."

She only owned 46 percent of her company. The other three held 18 percent each. Maybe she should take Mo Mo up on his offer, at least get over the 50 percent mark. But this was her paranoia sneaking up again. She was the brains behind things, The Stooges knew that. Without her, TabiKat did not exist. What incentive did they have to oust her?

"Give it a year," she said. Harry groaned. "We'll launch the apps, increase revenue and work on other projects. We get $100 a share now, give me a year it could be $200, easily." She leaned into the desk. "Have you thought about what going public means outside of the money? The hassle of shareholders and more voices? We wanted this company to build apps that help people. You think a bunch of money-hungry investors care about quality over what makes a quick buck?"

Harry studied her. The wildcard. Paul told her to think long and hard about bringing Harry on. But he brought access to his father, and endless money. The fact that Mr. Clarks funded her at such a level and his entitled son only held 18 percent of her company was a stroke of luck.

"So you won't even discuss it?" he asked.

"I didn't come this far to let someone else take all the credit. If you want to sell, give me six months, and I'll buy you out for what you paid."

"My shares are worth more than that now." He gave a slight laugh.

She shrugged. "I'm not selling my company."

Harry stood and walked to the door. A GQ model to the core down to the messy light brown hair, full lips, coffee-brown eyes. It drew her to him in college. Now she knew looks only went so far and after she met Paul, the dimwit before her didn't spark much of anything.

"I'm going to go see if I can reason Alice into helping you see the light."

"Please, my sister is even less impressed with you than I am." She turned her attention to her computer.

"World must look pretty nice from your glass castle. I hate to think what happens when you can't dictate those around you anymore." He left. Tabby kept herself from calling after him. *Get through the launch and buy him out.* The less control he held over her company, the better.

To take her mind off the encounter, Tabby went to work with the coders. She reread every piece of feedback from the beta testers and tried to test for every contingency. *Please let this thing work on a larger scale.*

Moe and Carrie walked across the office toward the elevators together, Carrie waving hello. Tabby raised her hand, finding it odd they were going to lunch. Mo Mo probably wanted to vent about her. Men and their feeble emotions. If only Alice got how much Tabby understood double standards and sexism. If Tabby wanted a Bloody Mary lunch to vent about her meeting with Harry, she'd be emotional. But for Mo Mo to do it with Carrie was just letting off steam. She'd take the kids to the pool after work, get a cucumber mojito and vent to Alice. Her mother taught her discretion in who one let into her inner circle. After twelve years together, Paul should know where her deep-seated mistrust came from. Try having a mother who controlled the House with an iron fist for seventeen years.

MO MO CAME BACK two hours later. Maybe it was time to patch things up. Paul told her to get through the launch, but after Harry's comments and Carrie's surprise appearance, Tabby needed to get a hold on things. Mo Mo saw her coming and tried to leave the cubicle he stood in. Tabby followed him into his office and closed the door.

"I thought about your offer," she said. "I'll buy part of your shares."

"That offer is gone." He fidgeted with the pen in his hands.

"You made it to me Friday."

"And you told me to take my boyish insecurity to a bottle of whiskey. So I did." He shook his head, seeming to debate something. "And you were right, I looked a year into the future, and losing shares is not what I'm interested in."

"That's great. You can enjoy that position with 13 percent as much as 18."

Moe chuckled sadly. "I know you're the vision behind TabiKat, no one will deny that. But maybe Carrie's right, and there's something about keeping you in line that feels good."

"What does that mean?" She told herself to not overreact. Her best friend could be catty when she needed to feel better about herself. Take out her fears as a single mother with three failed marriages out on Tabby instead of doing some basic self-reflecting. Tabby was about to give Carrie access to a whole new world of wealthy men and Carrie chose to bash her reputation. What had Carrie done but marry well to deserve the benefits of Thursday?

"We know we're a means to an end for you. But you still need us."

"As long as we're in this together." She stressed the last word. Moe held her gaze and nodded once.

"Together," he said slowly. Tabby scoffed and walked out of the office. Let Paul tell her she was being paranoid now.

# CHAPTER 5

THE PARK OUTSIDE THE FOOD TRUCK was quiet, the lunch rush coming soon enough. Alice unwrapped the toppings for the street tacos: cilantro, pickled red onions, various salsas and slaws, chopped mango, and sliced lime. The fresh loaves for the sandwiches sat ready next to the panini maker. Valencia sang "America" from *West Side Story* in Spanish as she sliced the steak they'd need later. Pork shoulders left to marinade all night now cooked slowly in a pot on the griddle.

Alice oversaw the "front" of the truck: the prep and steam tables, finishing touches, and the window. The back half of the truck—the stovetop, fryer, and griddle, were Valencia's domain. Somehow over the last few months they learned to dance around each other. At first, Alice did not get the small cut out near the window, shouldn't every available surface area be utilized for counters? The alcove became a kind of oasis, a place for her to be out of the way. The inside of the truck was the pale red of Cuban clay, Valencia's father's favorite color from his home country.

They worked together at Cornelia's restaurant before Val left to take care of her ailing father and they lost touch. She ran into Val the year before at a mutual friend's birthday. Valencia at the time was trying to process the death of her father. Alice faced yet another executive chef who offered to hire her as a station chef if she slept with him. She was thinking of moving on from the industry altogether and might have if she had not seen Val that night. They sat on the back porch and complained about the closed doors before them. Offhandedly Alice mentioned the idea of the food truck, the trend just starting to take over D.C. Something clicked, a light filled Valencia's date-colored eyes, and she pulled up her swing skirt to sit on her knees. For the first time in years, a smile graced her square face. They launched their food truck at the Drag Queen Race near Dupont just before Halloween. The excitement that night told Alice maybe they were onto something.

Alice leaned toward the window, scanning the park across from the food truck. She sucked her lips, thinking about her date with Delany. Was it a date? They got dinner at the bar and then dessert. He made her laugh, something unassuming about him. They talked about why they loved D.C. Delany told her about playing in the Beijing Olympics. They stood on the sidewalk after, Alice delaying getting a cab.

"This was a fun, unexpected night." Delany slid his hands into his pockets.

"Can I see your cell phone?" Alice didn't know why she felt so bold, except the three drinks helped. He slid it from his pocket and unlocked it. Alice keyed her number in, Delany smiling to himself. "Call me sometime." She leaned in and kissed his cheek before stepping back and hailing a cab. Tabby asked about her night the next day at breakfast, Alice saying she'd been with Val. She wasn't ready to tell her sister about what happened. He had yet to call, Alice trying not to drive herself crazy figuring out if she did something wrong.

"Mi querida," Valencia said from her place at the cutting board. "I found her."

"Her?" Alice stood fully and leaned on the counter.

"Mi mamá."

"Where?"

Valencia had been trying to find her mother since before her father passed away. He gave few details on how or why he ended up a single father.

"She's in Spain, married with another family. I emailed her over the weekend. She asked me to come see her."

"When?" Maybe Valencia could go in the winter. Alice should be able to manage the truck by herself, things quieter during the winter months.

"She asked if I could come this summer." Valencia sucked her bottom lip. Even without makeup, Val turned heads. Delicate features, pomegranate lips. Her curly black hair usually tucked under a wrap. "I can tell her no…"

"Hello?" A man's voice broke into the moment.

"Let me think about it." Alice faced the man and got his order. Steak sizzled on the grill, the air permeated with garlic and onions. Alice looked over the man to the mostly empty park behind him. What would it mean if Valencia left the food truck?

The chaos of the lunch rush kept her from thinking. She diced more cilantro and jalapeños, refilled the items in her prep table. They were just starting to get a following, people recommending the food truck to their friends. Alice kept their Facebook and MySpace pages up to date, used Twitter to tell people where they were. A year from now, she might be able to hire help. But how could she deny her friend the chance to meet the one person she'd been looking for all her life, the last family member she could have, because it was an inconvenient time for their business? Valencia processed her grief via cooking, one reason the food truck was doing so well, but what if getting to know the other half of who she was helped Valencia heal and feel less alone?

When things quieted, Alice went to update the board out front with what they still had available. They painted the outside of the food truck an ocean-blue with various colored hibiscus. Valencia's father brought her to the U.S. as a little girl to escape the regime. He got a job cleaning at the local community college, but his true passion was food. He taught his little flower everything he knew.

Alice could not work the truck by herself. They were only able to make it work now because Val had her inheritance, and Alice lived at Tabby's for free. One word, and Valencia would cancel her trip. Wait a year, save some money, and then go be with her mother's family. Only Alice could never ask her to do that.

"You okay?" Harry touched her shoulder causing her to jump.

"Val's leaving." She stopped, unwilling to lament to Harry Clarks. "I'm fine. What are you doing here?" She stood fully, the motion causing Harry to pull back his hand.

"I was in the area. What do you recommend?"

Their menu featured street tacos, sandwiches, and traditional Cuban rice and meat dishes, all with a reimagined twist.

"Everything Val makes is amazing." She raised her voice in hopes that Valencia might pop her head out, but either she couldn't hear her or was content to avoid the frat boy as much as Alice wished she could.

"I just saw your sister." Harry looked over his shoulder at the building that held Tabby's office. "She's wound tight."

"Well two years of your life, your reputation, and the financial security of your family might leave you a bit stressed out."

He laughed. "I'm not as bad as you think, Lil."

"I'm not as naïve as you hope. Are you eating? The second

rush is coming." She headed for the back of the truck, her culinary reboot dead before it ever began. Harry reached for her arm.

"I want to talk to you about your catering company." His grip eased. Alice's breath caught in her throat. "I want to invest. My dad can get you booked solid for a year. I believe in what you're trying to do, Lil."

On paper, it looked like an ideal offer. It would give her the money to cook what she wanted— have fun with food. But nothing Harry offered came without conditions, and it would give him a reason to be around more. Besides, she hated his father, disagreed with everything his lobbying firm pushed through Congress. A perfect opportunity she could never look at herself in the mirror for taking. There had to be another way.

"I don't think that's the best idea."

"How do I get you to trust me?" An edge of pain filled his voice. She studied his eyes, barely visible under his aviator sunglasses, unsure why he cared about her opinion.

"Do right by my sister." Alice tilted her head and went into the truck. Valencia took Harry's order and got to work. By the time Alice returned to her post, two more customers waited. The second rush had begun.

Two hours later, she helped put away leftovers and wash the dishes.

"I think you should go." Alice leaned on the counter and crossed her arms. "I know how important this is to you. I'll figure something out."

"Are you sure, mi querida?" Valencia closed the small refrigerator before she faced Alice and put her hands on her arms. "I can stay."

"Go. Meet your mom and your half siblings, enjoy Spain and if you come back—bring some ideas for this place."

"I am coming back."

"Or you'll travel the world and meet some lovely French girl and settle down." She tried to hold back her emotion. Her brain screamed at her to beg for more time, to ask Valencia to wait. "I want you to do this." She put on her most convincing smile. Valencia hugged her, thanking her over and over. Alice held her and closed her eyes. What if she couldn't make it on her own? What if she had to close the food truck and go back to being a station chef? She hugged Valencia tighter, unsure how to handle having a dream she just started to appreciate pulled from her.

"I'll send you pictures and recipes." Valencia's smile took over her entire face, her cheeks wet. "Thank you, Alice."

She could only nod. Valencia went back to cleaning, singing to herself.


Alice opened the door to Tabby's apartment, ready for a long bath and some quiet. Just let her have a bit of time to process what changed. She set her bag on the bench by the front door. Tabby hated clutter, but life with two kids taught her to have places for things to go. Each of the twins, plus Alice, had a bin for their items in the bench by the door. A spot between the bench and the wall to the dining room waited for Alice's collapsible bike. Paul negotiated the concession after Alice refused to risk her bike being stolen from the rack outside, and Tabby refused to have the dirt on the carpet in the bedroom.

Across from the bench was Alice's bedroom door. She shared a bathroom with the twins, who were now in bunk beds in Mac's room. Just beyond their room was Tabby's office, then the kitchen and living room. The extra space beyond the faux industrial kitchen was supposed to be the dining room, but Tabby loved to entertain and have a designated place for the kids to be. They could run around the island with its chairs and watch TV and confine their chaos to a room with everything the sitter could need, while the adults got to talk and sip wine in the private living, now, dining room. The master bedroom sat off the kitchen. The only bedroom with windows, the other side of the apartment an inward facing wall.

The darker oak accents contrasted lighter paint and clear glass light coverings. Off-white subway tiles filled the kitchen and bathroom walls, lighter hardwood floors throughout. Tabby tried to fill the bland space with paintings of colorful flowers or photos of Aruba from their honeymoon.

Alice's bedroom was soft pink. Annie picked the color when she was five and now pleaded to change it, maybe once Alice moved out. The space was barely bigger than the queen bed and bedside table in it. Alice left her furniture in her apartment; most of it from IKEA held little meaning to her. When she moved home, she'd figure out what to do with it all.

Alice sat on the bench and slipped off her Keds. Tabby's high-pitched shout floated out of the kitchen. The twins sat at the dining room table, banished so their parents could talk. Annie sighed from her place.

"What happened?" Alice put her hand on Annie's head, who looked up from her book, her overly curly date colored hair pulled into twin knots on the back of her head. She had Paul's sky-blue eyes and was built long and thin like her mother.

"Mom's in a mood," Mac said from the other side of the table, where he played on his console. With his shaggy almond-colored hair down to his chin, he was a spitting image of Tabby growing up, not that Alice told him that. Somehow, Mac convinced his father to help lobby the private school they attended to veto their hair policy. Mac's long locks were his form of rebellion against the micromanaging tendencies of his mother. Still, he had Tabby's long face and button nose and the same dark blue eyes.

"Do you know what's going on?" Alice put her knee on the chair beside Annie and leaned on the back. She hoped to talk to Tabby about the food truck. Maybe it was hasty to turn down

Harry's offer, but it didn't sit right with her, and she wasn't willing to admit she was that desperate.

"Moe reneged his offer to sell his shares." Annie said, most likely quoting her mother.

"Did he say why?"

Annie shook her head.

"Harry and Carrie were there too. Mom's all freaked out." Mac added.

They were probably there to see if they could help. Her sister was notorious for making something out of nothing. They could all breathe easier over the weekend.

"Hey, Lil." Paul came into the room. Tabby must have started her rant before he could get changed from work because Paul rarely wore a suit outside the office. He cocked his head and widened his eyes, and Alice laughed to herself.

"I'll tell you what, if you and your sister never learn to trust anyone, you'll both go through life alone. Not everyone is out to get you."

"What do I have to do with this?" She stood and crossed her arms, her heart racing. Paul laughed and undid his tie with tiny lemons on it.

"Not every restaurant owner is Jonas."

"You're right, but some idiot decided to hit the one exception on his bike and leave him on the side of the road in Rock Creek Park."

"What happened?" Mac's gaze shot up from his game, his eyes wide.

"Nothing, play your game. Why did Moe revoke his offer?"

"Ask your sister. Do you all want pizza for dinner?"

"Angelo's?" Mac asked.

"Let me change and we can go." Paul walked toward his bedroom.

"Are you okay, Aunt A?" Annie asked. Alice nodded and

decided to risk her sister's ire to find out what happened. The island filled the space on the left, stainless steel appliances along the two walls in front of it. A gaudy chandelier hung above the stainless sink in the island. Pantry cabinets filled the wall between the entry and the door to the bedroom. There were windows on either side of the fireplace along the far wall, an L-shaped leather couch in front of it.

Tabby leaned against the dishwasher studying the window, a bottle of white wine open on the island. At least she hadn't reached for Paul's whiskey, things could not be that dire. News played on the TV above the fireplace. Alice reached for the bottle and dragged it on the island. Tabby did a once-over on her.

"Did you get all of your crops harvested?"

"What got you in a mood?" Maybe she should find the whiskey.

"Mo Mo's acting all jittery. Offered me his shares Friday, holding them with an iron fist today."

"Did you ask Carrie about it?" Alice poured herself a glass of wine and sat on the island. Tabby started a rebuke, but then sighed. Alice smiled to herself.

"No. She and Mo Mo went out for a two-hour lunch. It's weird because she didn't come to see me. But I guess she met some imbecile with half a brain at the party Friday night and thinks it's love."

"It's never love with her; it's a warm bed and money." Alice finished her glass. She angled down the counter and refilled Tabby's glass. Her sister leaned on the island close to her and took a long drink.

"Paul tells me I'm being paranoid. The launch is Thursday and I want it to go well."

"It will. Moe is good, Tabs. Don't read into things. He's working twenty-hour days right now."

"I guess you're right."

The kids poured into the kitchen, both talking about Angelo's. Alice slipped off the island and raised her hand over her head as she walked to her room. Her sister's blue heeler, Taco, trailed after her. *Please let whatever's going on with Moe and the others be all in Tabby's head.*

# CHAPTER 6

VALENCIA SANG A SONG from *Moulin Rouge* in Spanish as she prepped food for the day. Alice finished chopping the cilantro, glancing in the direction of her sister's office. Two days. If they could all make it two more days, they could breathe easier, and Tabby would stop reading into every little thing as a sign someone planned to stab her in the back. Alice wanted to tell her about Valencia leaving and ask for advice, but Tabby wasn't in a place to be supportive or reassuring. She would lecture Alice about how she told her to start networking and that she needed a plan. Alice didn't need to hear, "I told you so."

"I bought my ticket today." Valencia pushed a tray of corn tortillas into the warmer. "July 14."

"That's soon." Alice tried to keep her tone light. Five weeks. Carver kept pushing her to get out there, Tabby too, Alice running out of excuses and time.

"I spoke to my landlord, and I am going to be out at the end of the month. If you want any of my things," Valencia offered.

"If only I had a place to put things." She laughed. A man came to the window, Valencia starting on his order while he gave it. Alice rang up his purchase, hoping by the time he left the conversation could move on, but sensed Valencia bookmarked her last comment in her head. Alice took the to-go box and handed it to the man, glancing at the tiny park in front of their truck with its man on a horse statue, collection of benches, and a few patches of grass.

"How long are you with your sister for?" Valencia asked. Alice leaned her hip on the counter and crossed her arms loosely.

"For the summer, I think. Even only being in beta, my apartment is almost booked solid through August."

"I can ask my landlord if you can sublease for a few months."

"Going from no rent to paying rent defeats the purpose of living with Tabby." She wiped the counter around her. Her cell phone rang. Alice slipped out the back, letting Valencia help the small group coming up to the truck.

"Alice? It's Delany, how are you?"

"Oh, hey. I'm hanging in there. You?" She scrunched her nose.

"Still getting used to office life. I wanted to see if you're available to cook for a party we're having for our staff next week. I know this is last minute…"

"No, it's okay. My schedule just opened." No point in telling her only repeat customer she did not need to check her schedule, any time would work.

"Great. It's at the Hillsburg Gardens in Rosslyn."

Alice tried to pull it up in her head, unsure where the gardens were. "So, you're thinking dinner?"

"Appetizers, dinner, and dessert. The event is planned for four hours. And you all can do drinks?"

"Of course."

"Great. Listen, I wanted to call before, but things are busy this week."

"It's okay. I wasn't counting the minutes or anything." Yes, she was.

He laughed. "When things calm down maybe we can get dinner again."

"You have my number." She smiled.

They talked for a bit more before Delany told her how much the budget was, asking if it was enough. Alice tried not to laugh. It was more than she would consider charging. She played it cool, not wanting to do what Carver always accused her of and lowball the deal. She just wanted to cook. Delany told her to have a good day and hung up the call. Alice did a happy dance on the sidewalk. *Please let this be the start of good things.*

#

TABBY OPENED THE DOOR TO TABIKAT, fresh off another interview about WlkmNt. She glanced up from her BlackBerry, almost running into her favorite coder. The girl waited in front of the cubicle area, frowning. Something happened with the website, they discovered a glitch or, heaven forbid, it crashed.

"Ms. Beaumont is here." The girl failed to keep back her eye roll. "I'm sorry."

Tabby presumed she meant to apologize for her eye roll and told her it was okay. She went to her office. Carrie stood at the window, her hand loose around her neck. She wore a blue pantsuit, her dirty blond hair pulled into a high ponytail. Tabby had known Carrie since college where they pledged and lived together for three years. She had been her maid-of-honor in two of three of Carrie's weddings. Tabby didn't realize Carrie still owned anything deemed professional. She hadn't had to work since her second husband, a surrealist sculptor, swept her off her feet.

"Finances really so bad you have to go to work?" Tabby put her purse on the desk. Carrie looked at her and forced a smile. "Are you okay?"

"Yeah. I fired the nanny yesterday; Pettie was extra clingy today."

Tabby remembered life with a four-year-old. She logged into her computer.

"Why are you here?"

"Can't a best friend just stop by?" She raised her head. Harry sauntered across the office, lifting his hand in the direction of Mo Mo's office. "I thought maybe we could get an early lunch."

Tabby laughed. "You both might not have anything better to do with your day, but some of us do work."

"We need to talk, Tabatha." Harry leaned in the doorway to her office, his hands in his pockets. Moe waited behind him, refusing to meet Tabby's gaze. Apparently, Harry still held onto the idea of taking TabiKat public. Did this have to get settled today?

A car waited on the street. Tabby kept trying to ask where they were going, but Harry told her to be patient. Moe seemed extra quiet, but it could be the grind of the last few weeks and staying late to get things ready. Tabby pulled out her phone, a string of emails from coders with questions. There was too much going on for them to take a two-hour lunch. Harry and Carrie had nothing to do all day, but she and Mo Mo did. They were within forty-eight hours of going live. The discussion could wait.

The car pulled up to an office building in Rosslyn, a man opening the door for them. Tabby followed The Stooges into the lobby and onto the elevator. Her heart raced, and she found herself unable to take more than shallow breaths. It felt like a bad dream. Something told her to walk away, refuse to go in. Force the three people who never shut up, and yet barely said three words since they left the office, to tell her what the hell was going on. Instead, she felt out of her body. The elevator opened onto an office.

"What's going on?" Tabby started to ask when a petite younger woman with curly red hair and striking green eyes walked toward them.

"I'm Katy O'Toole, Mr. Clare is this way." She motioned toward a large conference room where Delany Clare stood waiting.

"You were at the party last week." Tabby shook his hand.

"Yes, Mrs. Black, I was." He motioned for them to sit. The redhead closed the door to the conference room and sat at Delany's side.

"I know this is a busy time for you all. Thank you for agreeing to meet so quickly," Delany said.

"Well, Welcome Note launches in two days. No time like the present," Harry answered. Carrie chuckled nervously as Mo Mo looked at the table.

"I hope this can be the start of a great partnership. Not that much will change for you all day-to-day, though I guess now, Mrs. Black will have the time and money to pursue projects she loves." Delany smiled at Tabby, who tilted her head and scowled.

"What's going on?" she asked.

Harry leaned forward into the table and looked at her. "We sold our shares of TabiKat to Macon."

"You did what?" She looked between those she came in with, her heart racing. Surely it must be a joke; she waited for one of them to laugh.

"It's best for the company, Tabby," Carrie said. "We were going to tell you, but you've been so focused on the launch."

"Should we give you all a minute?" Delany asked.

"You sold me out," Tabby said. "That's why you wouldn't sell me your shares!" She turned her attention to Mo Mo. "I can't believe…" She paused and pursed her lips. The bubble that kept reality from reaching her brain shattered and Tabby's body filled with a sense of encompassing rage. But as Maryanne Gibson's daughter, theatrics had never been her style. Maybe she should try some—stand and shriek, call her so-called friends what she'd been holding back for months. "And just how much is *my* company worth?" She set her jaw and met Delany's gaze. Mo Mo was right—they were means to an end. Only not the path to everything she wanted but the end of her dreams. Two years of time, blood, sweat, hard work, nights away from the kids, straining her marriage, to be left out in the cold when it mattered most.

"The details are all laid out in the contract." Another man in the room motioned for the contracts. Delany handed them to him, his gaze still on Tabby.

"Mrs. Black, I was assured all the partners would be aware of the sale."

"Well, obviously not." She snapped the contract away from the man and looked at it. "I want my husband to look at this before I'll sign."

"Of course." Delany talked over a Black man lurking further down the table, who seemed to start to say that wasn't how things worked. The man scoffed and rolled his eyes like a rebuked puppy. She had no idea who Delany or his muscle thought they were dealing with, but she knew what she built and would demand a fair assessment for their treachery.

"Tabs, we only did what we thought was best." Carrie signed her contract and pushed it back toward the redhead. Given how fast The Stooges signed their forms, there must have been discussions about things before today.

"I'm sorry, Tabby. Carrie told me she'd…"

"Not here, Mo Mo. Okay?" Tabby clung to her last bit of restraint. Please let her wake up now.

"Can you excuse us, please?" Delany said. The others in the room cleared out before the scoundrel stood and walked around the conference table, sitting two chairs down from her. Her heart raced. Surely he knew about this when they met Friday night. How casual he had been. Why was he even at the event? He must have come to gloat! Did they all toast her ignorance after? How long had this been in the works?

"This is not how I expected things to go, Mrs. Black." He sounded remorseful.

"How did you expect the takeover of my company to go?" She dabbed beside her eye and met his gaze. She always heard Delany Clare was a good guy who cared about others and gave back to the community he grew up in. For some reason, she associated his business with charitable deeds. He didn't tell her who he worked for when they met, just said he ran "a holding company." A lie. Other people might be taken by his good boy persona, but Tabby would not be duped.

"I was assured all four shareholders knew of the sale and approved." He looked where the other man had been, the one who followed Carrie around like a puppy at the party. She said she'd met someone new. Was it possible Carrie was sleeping with someone at Macon? She'd rip into her supposed best friend later, for the moment, she needed to deal with this two-faced SOB.

She took a longer breath and channeled her mother. How would The Queen take being stabbed in the back for money? She refused to lose the last two years of her life to some good-for-nothing sports star who thought she would just lie down and let him take what she'd built.

"What you're offering is more than generous. But I won't sell my shares."

"I can't make you. But if you wait to sell later, it will be for less than I'm offering now."

"Why is that?" She looked at him. Delany leaned back more, his arm on the table. His fingers reached for the pen at his original place, Delany starting to spin it between his thumb and first finger.

"Well, we're changing the name and merging it with another tech firm we bought, so you'd own almost half of TabiKat, but less than a quarter of the new company." This had been in the works for a while. Her gaze shifted to the glass walls, the area beside the elevators empty, The Stooges gone. Which one sold her out? Who led this scoundrel to her baby?

"I see," she said flatly. "And it's this new company you expect me to work for?"

When he didn't answer right away, she pulled her gaze off the front windows. His dark eyes almost appeared bereft. He was a damn good actor, she'd give him that.

"Mrs. Black, I would love for you to stay on. Mr. Manuel is going to stay as CEO. If you wanted to work for him…"

"Work for Mo Mo?" A small laugh escaped. "Do you know what I did to get this company going?"

"It's an impressive idea, ma'am. You should be proud of Mr. Manuel and his team."

"You think…" She studied him. "Of course, you think a man coded this. You're all the same." She stood and shoved the contract into her purse. She refused to reason with someone so small-minded. She'd talk to Paul and come up with a plan. Tabatha Gibson Black never went down without a fight.

"I will not work for Mo Mo, and I will not work for a man so shortsighted as to presume only men warrant a place in the tech world. I have put too much into this company to be reduced to a worker bee. I hope you are proud of yourself, Mr. Clare."

She opened the door, the redhead barely having enough time to move. Tabby held her head high as she waited for the elevator. Inside, she let her shoulders droop. What the hell just happened? On the first floor of the building she paused, disoriented. She should go back and check on the website. She should call Paul. She needed to do something, but her world felt off, something vital gone.

"Are you okay, ma'am?" An older Black gentleman in a security uniform approached her. "Can we call someone for you?"

"No. I'm okay." Her voice shook. She sniffed back her

emotion. Tears would get her nowhere. Tabby adjusted her purse, dabbed by her eye, and squared her shoulders. "Thank you for checking on me." She forced a smile and walked onto the street. Getting around the corner she leaned on the building and found her cell phone. Her hands shook while she tried to dial the number. She cursed and pressed each button deliberately. The phone went to voicemail. No surprise, her former best friend lacked the courage to take her call. How had Tabby underestimated them?

# CHAPTER 7

**B**OBBIE WHISTLED AS HE WALKED through Macon's mostly empty office. It was Friday, the end of a good week, and he planned to celebrate. He stopped and shook his tush, still riding high off getting rid of Tabby Black and bringing TabiKat under Macon's control. The woman brought in her resignation midweek. A diva to the last. Upset someone realized what an unoriginal prima donna existed under her off-putting exterior. Bobbie did his homework and used his keen business sense to sniff out her pretending. Now she was gone, and they could take her pathetic vision to the next level.

He planned to whisk Carrie away for the weekend to thank her for bringing him the score of the decade. They met at a party over the spring. He almost didn't go, but his friend told him to make an appearance, the guy who owned the house could be a valuable contact later. Bobbie went because he could appreciate a contact but was no one's sucker. He would not be at this man's beck and call.

Carrie stood across the room with another friend. Blond hair, ideal frame, nice ass, healthy rack—probably fake, but what did he care? He knew her type: divorced, used to a certain lifestyle, unsure how to be alone. He finished his Scotch, noticed she drank a martini, and got two fresh ones from the bar before sauntering her way. Her friend did a once-over, brushing him off. He knew he retained a bit of a baby face, that many passed off his ability to enjoy the finer things as overindulgence. Most only saw him as Delany Clare's best friend. But he made sure people like that regretted the day they underestimated him.

"Your drink is empty." He stopped beside Carrie and held the fresh one out for her. Her weary brown eyes sized him up. The hand that held her drink also held his Cartier ring. If this broad worked as he suspected, she'd understand what it cost. She saw it, a flirty smile filling her face.

"Thank you, Mr. ..." She reached for the martini.

"Dunn, Bobbie Dunn."

They chatted before Bobbie asked if she wanted to come back to his place. She shrugged and left her latest drink on the counter in the kitchen.

They met for dinner later that week, Bobbie jonesing for a repeat. When the meal came, to pass the time, they got into what the other did. He ran a holding company. She recently divorced and hoped to reestablish herself in D.C. Over dessert, she told him about TabiKat and WlkmNt. The stupid names made sense once he learned one of Carrie's girlfriends ran the company. Something about the website stayed with him.

Carrie introduced him to Harry; now he was dealing with someone serious. He knew all about Harry's father, supported much of what his firm lobbied through Congress. If Gene Clarks saw value in this pithy venture, maybe Bobbie had underestimated it. Harry wanted to sell, but Tabby was shortsighted, unwilling to let anyone challenge her. Both men understood TabiKat could be huge. Bobbie became obsessed with bringing it under Macon.

He walked into the lunchroom on the top floor to the wine fridge in the corner with its collection of white wines and champagnes from a vineyard Macon owned outside Napa. The stock was reserved for special occasions and this week qualified as one of those. He reached for a bottle of their best champagne, taking two glasses out of the cabinet above it. Get Bulldog focused on what the acquisition of TabiKat meant for Macon and their plans for the tech space, and he'd forget about what happened.

Carrie mentioned the rooftop event as a great way for her and Harry to meet Delany. The night had to be done with caution as Bobbie could not risk Delany realizing not everyone knew about the sale or perhaps talking to Tabby and saying something. Then Carrie found him at the event and stole him away for a quickie. His heart stopped when he came back and found Delany talking to Tabby. Carrie warned him about Tabby's paranoia and how she'd guard her hand at the first hint something might be amiss. Bobbie watched the encounter and found Tabby to be a frumpier version of Carrie. She didn't take care of herself; everything sagged. Carrie still held tenacity and fire; Tabby came off antiquated and vanilla. Carrie believed her bestie could code something so complex, but women were not that smart. Tabby had to be feeding her ideas to Moe, the one doing all the real work.

He called to see why Delany left the party early, hoping to go out after and celebrate, but Bulldog said he was with a friend. *Please.* Bobbie had been Delany's best friend since middle school and Bobbie came up with the nickname Bulldog. "Friend" meant a woman, but who? Delany hadn't mentioned anyone to him, so maybe it was nothing.

Bobbie went to work Monday and finished modifying the boilerplate contract they used for most of their acquisitions. He wrote himself a bigger bonus, since he'd done all the work to get Carrie to show her hand and let him in. Then Bulldog announced he planned to be at the meeting. Bobbie told him he had it. Delany didn't need to be bothered with a run-of-the-mill acquisition, let him handle it. But Delany insisted. He came early and asked for the contract. Bulldog found the fee and took it out, giving the papers to the lawyer before Bobbie could object.

He looked toward the empty conference room. For the last three years he had overseen acquisitions at Macon without Bulldog ever being at a meeting. He did not get why Delany refused to let him handle things, why he insisted on taking the lead. Tabby's reaction surprised him, Bobbie expecting her to fold. He tried to stay when Delany told everyone to clear out. The dowdy mess would not walk out with the contract. *You never let an acquisition leave, never let them look at alternatives.* The companies they acquired should be grateful Macon offered them a chance to expand their pathetic horizons.

If anyone other than that redheaded pipsqueak stood outside the door, he would have muscled his way back in and demand Delany let him handle things. Something in Delany's face told Bobbie he had questions. It would be better if he laid low for a few days. But fate did it for him, taking Delany out of the office all week. Carrie had been sulking since the merger, not receptive like she should be. He told her it was business, and friendship had no place in it. Hopefully, she got over it soon.

Bobbie looked around, Delany's office empty. Where was Bulldog?

#

DELANY LOOSENED HIS TIE, the elevator clicking through the floors. Friday night. Things should be quiet at the office. Maybe now he could figure out what went wrong with the TabiKat deal. Nothing Delany said could get Mrs. Black to consider staying on when she brought back her contract and resignation letter, telling him to wait and see how all the vision within her company was walking out the door. When he went to meet with the coders and Mr. Manuel, it became clear Bobbie underestimated who was who in that building. The marketing team shifted gears to keep the merger from hitting the papers. The story became about minimizing Mrs. Black's departure and lifting Mr. Manuel up as the new CEO.

The elevator doors opened to the top floor. He'd spent most of the day bringing Mr. Manuel and the other TabiKat officers in to meet with Chip-Pixel and start discussions of how the firms could work together. He needed to check his email and see what Katy left him to do, still trying to figure out how to balance things since his retirement. Ultimately, he hoped Macon could be a part-time gig. He wanted to give more to his philanthropic endeavors, especially his nonprofit, but the board chair asked that Delany give Macon his full attention. It had been a second priority while he balled, but as his mother reminded him, he could only be as generous as he wanted with Macon thriving. Delany got it and cleared the next eighteen months to be present at his company. He wanted to get to know those they partnered with, go see some of their businesses outside of D.C. Macon Enterprises grossed over three billion annually, mostly because of those they invested in.

"There you are!" Bobbie smiled wide and lifted the bottle in his hands. "I brought the good stuff."

"Since we own the vineyard, I hope you did." Delany walked into his office, passing two empty bookcases between the door and his desk. The space was long and narrow. Two walls of windows provided an unobstructed view from Georgetown to the Lincoln Memorial. Sometimes, he would sit at the conference table at the far end and pretend he wasn't locked inside all day. Someday he'd figure out how to make the space feel like more than a rectangular cage. Pick a paint color. Hang something on the walls. For now, the "I just retired" line seemed to work well.

Bobbie sat on the dark leather couch between the conference table and his desk and took a drink. "Damn that's good."

Delany chose one of the chairs opposite him and waited while Bobbie poured champagne into a second glass before he sat back and rested the glass on the arm of his chair.

"Do you know why Mrs. Black was so upset the other day?" He hadn't had time to ask Bobbie how the entire fiasco happened.

"Ah, come on, Bulldog, water under the bridge. She's a control freak who wanted to keep things simple. Her vision was small, the other shareholders saw it. Hence why they came to us."

"It still feels like she was taken out of left field."

Bobbie pulled the glass away from his lips. "Mr. Clarks assured me he would tell her. Carrie told me Harry was unreliable. I should have listened, instead I trusted him to uphold his word. I won't make that mistake again."

He thought Bobbie mentioned meeting with all four investors on Monday, but maybe something came up. Perhaps Tabby couldn't make the lunch, and Harry promised to tell her; that wasn't on Bobbie.

"You really think it's the best idea to date her?"

Bobbie laughed. "Nothing happened until after the sale. She approached us at the party, remember?" He finished his glass. "Listen, I know you're Mr. Want To Do The Right Thing, but this isn't on you. Trust me, it will all work out. You'll see."

Delany took a drink, something about it not adding up. Bobbie was closer than a brother and practically grew up at his house. He watched the fakes hound Delany for time and money, only wanting to use his name and image to sell their products and get rich. Delany's high school coach told him to "remember where you came from." Outsiders would only use him, but those who had been there since the start had his back. Bobbie always had his back.

# CHAPTER 8

ALICE WALKED THE APARTMENT, things eerily quiet since the family's departure to Europe the day before. They would be gone for most of the summer, Paul hoping the distance would help Tabby deal with what happened. For the first time since Alice moved out of her apartment so Tabby could post it on her website, she could do as she pleased. She could leave her cereal bowl in the sink, her bag on top of the bench. She could watch what she wanted and shower without locking the door, *got to love sharing a bathroom with two ten-year-olds.* Taco lounged on Tabby's bed, a place strictly off-limits, and sat on the floor beside Alice, who fed her scraps and rubbed her ears. They all needed the break.

She got a paper from the front desk and folded it into her messenger bag before getting onto her bike and starting the ride toward Chinatown, debating taking her apartment off WlkmNt. On the one hand, it felt wrong to use the website that ousted her sister. On the other, it provided money she needed. She kept the calendar open until the weekend before Tabby and her family got home and would decide then whether to leave it up. For the next seven weeks, it helped with her income as things were about to get tight with Valencia leaving for Spain. One thing at a time.

She crossed the Potomac and rode beside the Jefferson Memorial, the Washington Monument rising on her left. As she turned onto Pennsylvania Avenue, she stopped to look at the building on the corner, her favorite in all of D.C.

The construction fencing had gone up over the spring. Someone bought the old beauty. Ten stories tall, the marble exterior featured a clocktower that rose into the sky. Built in the late 1800s, the building's center opened to the top floor, flooding the space in natural light. For years it sat underutilized with a sparse food court on the bottom floor, only a few of the offices in use. Just blocks from the White House, Alice wondered how The Old Post Office Pavilion stayed two steps from vacant for so long.

In high school, she thought about becoming an architect so she could save the building and restore it to its heyday in the 1920s, when it was the city's premiere apartment complex. But her mother helped her see how impossible that dream was. Then she met Cornelia and never looked back. She talked to him about opening a restaurant in the space. A restaurant by D.B. Cornelia could bring in the D.C. elite, which would attract others, and bring the building back. They started talking about it when he passed away. Another dream that died with him.

The fencing around the building felt like the wall around her dream of a white linen restaurant. Maybe she could let go of both dreams and find a way to be happy with what she had.

She opened the back door to Carver's bakery and put her collapsible bike in his office, taking a moment to run her fingers through her hair and cool down from her ride before going to find Carver, who chatted with a customer at the front counter. Alice got a muffin and a cup of coffee and went to find a table. They needed a plan for the Macon event on Friday. She wanted to do deluxe charcuterie boards with locally sourced meats and vegetables, complemented with a variety of Chardonnays and specialty drinks at the bar. Carver played with how to manage a sorbet bar with a variety of berries for dessert.

Knowing Carver would be in his meeting for a bit, Alice opened the paper. On the third page, below the fold, was a story on Macon Enterprises' acquisition and merger of TabiKat and Chip-Pixel. Moe Manuel, the new CEO, called it a bold step forward. Alice reread the name of who acquired her sister's company. *Oh, cheese puffs!* Tabby never told her who bought her out, only calling it a holding company, or "the scoundrel." It felt like one more sign to get out of the industry with Jonas blocking her from every credible kitchen and Valencia leaving for Spain. Try as she might, Alice could not cook as well as her friend and working the truck alone was impossible. Now the one legit, non-wedding or family-based event she'd booked was for the company that just screwed her sister. Maybe her mother was right, and she needed to try an industry that had not kicked her in the teeth for the last four years.

Carver sat across from her, asking what was shaking. Alice slid the paper his way. Carver finished his raspberry croissant while he skimmed the story.

"Huh." He looked at Alice. "And?"

"And what? I can't cater this event."

"How much is this man paying us?"

"That's not the point."

"It is the point, Lil. Listen, I get they did your sister wrong. But it's a job like any other. Macon owns dozens of businesses across D.C.; there is a high chance you will do an event for this man sometime." He sat back and chose his words. "I am behind you, 100 percent, you know that. My kitchen is here for you to use. I am happy to be in this business. But I need you to decide if you want to be in this business."

"What does that mean?" She tried to sound incredulous. Carver sat back and said hello to a regular. They chatted. Alice's gaze turned on the article. *Either commit to the catering company or don't.* The idea of losing her own kitchen hurt. But Alice could either take the catering company seriously and let it be an outlet for her dream, or she needed to close it down with the food truck and move on. This was her chance. The Macon event opened the door. For all her lectures and micromanaging, Alice could only hope her sister would understand the decision.

"So?" Carver asked after the customer moved on.

"Maybe we could do charcuterie boards."

"That's my girl." Carver folded the paper and put it on the table behind him. Alice reached for her laptop. If all went according to plan, by the time Tabby got home in the middle of August, the Macon event would not matter anymore. She finalized the menu and sent it off to Katy.

Her cell phone rang. Alice answered it and sat back, a polite voice on the other side asking where the rest of her menu went. Alice asked Katy what she meant, putting the phone on speaker.

Katy laughed. "This is not just an office party. This is the event of the year. It's Mr. Clare celebrating his retirement and casting a vision for his next phase. We're talking board members, investors, the leadership of dozens of companies Macon owns in the area, not to mention the boards of nonprofits and philanthropic endeavors Mr. Clare is connected to—easily four-hundred people. I think cheese and meat boards are a great start. But what else do you have? We were thinking appetizers, a meal, some kind of fun dessert or three."

Alice closed her eyes and latched onto the first vision she thought of. "Based off the board, we could add in locally sourced oysters…"

"Shucked as people ordered," Carver whispered.

"Shucked fresh on hand. We could do spit-roasted meat, and a variety of shot-sized gazpacho. I know Carver will add in more desserts."

He nodded, adding it to the list he'd started.

"I can modify the drink menu to match. How does all that sound?" Alice held her breath.

A contented sigh came through the phone. "We can't wait to see how you pull this all together." Katy hung up. Alice reached for Carver's notes, unsure how to pull off her vision.

# CHAPTER 9

ALICE PASSED UNDER THE WROUGHT IRON, vine-covered arch into a secret garden. Japanese wisteria, redbud and dogwood, rows of hydrangea bushes, and various colored azalea lined a perfectly kept lawn. She resisted the urge to kick off her shoes and run and spin. On the far side stood a two-story structure with windows along the back wall and a winding staircase to the second story inside, a magnificent chandelier in the upper windows.

Closer to the main estate people hung lights in the trees as men carried off-white picnic tables to supplement the collection of tables on the back patio, while others worked to erect a stage off on the grass. Katy watched it all with a clipboard in hand, ensuring every detail met her elite standards.

"Hey, Katy." Alice said, causing Katy to turn. "This is an impressive space."

Katy faced the lawn area with her, a proud smile on her face. "Don't let it slip, but tonight is Mr. Clare's 35th birthday. His best friend sold it as a vision casting event, but really it's a party for him."

"I see." Another pressure added to the evening.

"It's going to be so fun." She beamed and squealed. "Let me know if you need anything. I'll have my cell with me all night."

"Thank you, Katy."

Somehow Carver assembled an army of students from various culinary programs across the city to help ensure the event went off without a hitch. He schmoozed the partygoers and worked to keep the front end going, identifying what the servers needed to refill. Alice stayed in the kitchen, working with two of Carver's best chefs to keep the trays restocked and refills ready. A collection of top hits played on the speakers. Alice hummed along, trusting that some of the 'beautiful girls' looked 'glamorous' and hoped there would be no need for an 'umbrella.' Judging from the music and conversation that flowed into the side building, it was a good thing she ordered extra of everything.

Sending the next round of gazpacho shots out, Alice went to lean on the back door to the service kitchen. The lights in the trees, coupled with the strands across the back patio, cast the scene in a magical glow. People danced close to the stage, children laughing and running in the grass. Around the space men stood in button-down shirts with no ties, women in shorter dresses and neon-colored leggings or oversized accent belts. The lines at the food stations were decent, but not too long. Closer to the house, the two sorbet bars were well-patronized. Another staffer rushed by with a crate of dirty dishes for the van. Alice sensed she'd be doing dishes at the bakery for a week.

She walked back into the kitchen and opened the transport cabinet. Hopefully the party would wind down soon; they were about to run out of charcuterie boards. But people should be transitioning to the desserts. She reached for one of the remaining trays.

"I hoped you'd be here tonight." Delany's voice caused her to jump. Alice barely missed whacking her face on the cabinet door, almost dropping the tray of charcuterie boards. "I'm sorry." He took the tray so she could find her feet again. "I didn't mean to startle you."

"It's fine." She drew in her breath, still not sure what to do. She'd avoided his call since putting two and two together. She wanted to hate him, take on some of Tabby's anger over what he did. But then she thought about their date and all she knew about him, unable to get the requisite emotions to stick.

"Your food is a big hit. The staff can barely keep it stocked."

Alice reached for the tray. "I can tell them to go faster if you…"

"Not what I meant." He touched her arm. Her body flooded with warmth, her legs feeling weak. A server came for the charcuterie boards. Delany stepped back and waited while Alice unloaded four more trays to servers who took them to tables throughout the garden.

"I hoped maybe we could get dinner sometime."

"I can't, Delany. Things are busy for the summer."

"Lunch? I'd take a coffee, Alice."

She wanted to be near him, but after what Macon did to her sister, there was no way. Carver came to ask a question. "I should go. Happy birthday." Alice went to check on things, needing to get out of the kitchen.

Holy cheese puffs, he was attractive. His smile could melt an ice sculpture, and the way his shirt sat undone over the top of his chest. That man could bat his eyes, and any woman would be putty. Based on what she'd seen and heard she always believed he was a good guy, but after what happened, she questioned if he got by on his charm. Maybe he was more like Harry than she wanted to believe.

Across the way the other man from Tabby's party stood with his arm around Carrie, his hand grazing her ass, Carrie in a skintight blue dress. Maybe all her dresses featured zippers down the front to make things easier later. Alice refused to say hello and pretend things were okay. Instead, she started to collect the empty dishes off a banquet table, the staff merging things down to two lines as people's focus shifted to Carver's desserts and the frozen yogurt bar. They were not responsible for the drinks so could leave once the tables were cleared.

A man's voice replaced the music.

"Thank you all for being here tonight. My name is Bobbie Dunn," said the man whose arm had been around Carrie. "I'm CIO at Macon and Delany's best friend since we were kids." He lifted his glass in the direction where Delany stood in a group with several other men. Alice kept working, ready to go. "Our guy is pretty great, right?" Cheers filled the air. Alice rolled her eyes and carried another tray of dishes to the van. The audio cut out on the side of the building. Servers ran in and out of the kitchen, working to shut things down. Carver walked back with her to the lawn, Delany now on the stage beside Bobbie. Alice stepped back and waited while two of the staff carried the cake onto the stage. Delany smiled while everyone sang "Happy Birthday".

"I can stay until dessert is done," Carver said. "If you want to head back and start cleaning up."

This was why their partnership worked.

"I just need the check." She found Katy and slipped through the crowd toward her.

"It's been a great year," Delany said at the microphone. Alice touched Katy's elbow.

"We're almost all packed and ready to head out. Carver and a few servers will stay until the dessert is done. If that's okay with you."

Katy looked at Delany. "Mr. Clare has your check. He asked me for it a minute ago. This shouldn't take too long."

Carrie saw Alice and dropped her jaw, her hand on her heart. She started to move through the crowd.

"You can mail the check, it's fine."

The crowd cheered again as Alice walked toward the catering van.

"Lil," Carrie called out. Alice met Carver's gaze and debated what to do. Music started on the speakers again.

"Lil." Carrie touched her arm. "What are you…"

Alice faced her. "If you think I have anything to say to you after the stunt you three pulled…"

"Lil…"

"It's Alice, Carrie. We're not friends. You used my sister and discarded her for your financial benefit. Did you sell her out before or after you started sleeping with Delany's best friend? God, how do you look at yourself in the mirror?"

"There is more to things than just…"

"No. There's not. My sister built that company, and you sold her out for financial gain. We aren't friends. I want no part in your plastic life." She walked back to the kitchen. Hopefully, after tonight, she would not have a reason to interact with Delany Clare or Macon Enterprises ever again.

# CHAPTER 10

ALICE LEANED FORWARD on the counter of the food truck, still riled up about the weekend. Valencia told her to stop playing it over and move on.

"It's done, mi querida, let it go." She started to sing "Tomorrow" from *Annie* in Spanish. Easier said than done. She studied the edge of her sister's old building knowing it was wrong to take the job. But how could she know Carrie would be there? Knowing her sister, Carrie had already been deleted from her contacts, removed from her social media. Tabby would be just as inclined to pretend her best friend for over a decade did not exist. There was no way for Carrie to make things up to her. No way for Carrie to tell Tabby about the event. It amazed her that Carrie would cling to Delany's best friend, unless they both filled a need.

"Can I get some tacos?"

Alice snapped up, Delany waiting on the sidewalk. "What are you doing here?"

He smiled, his hands resting on his hips. "Katy loves your food. Plus, you left before I could pay you."

"Hello, guapo." Valencia slid up next to Alice doing a long, deliberate once over on Delany. "What brings a tall drink like yourself our way?"

"Do you practice these lines at home?" Alice lowered her voice.

Valencia tickled her side and leaned into the counter by the windows.

"Something tells me you know how you like your Cuban food."

"I know how they do it in Puerto Rico," he said.

"Mama or papa?"

"Mom. My dad was never around."

Valencia spoke in rapid Spanish. Delany smiled and answered back. They started a conversation Alice could not understand a word of. At one point Valencia tilted her head toward her and said something. Delany glanced at her and smiled, his reply making Valencia laugh. Alice wanted to slink down the wall. They weren't mocking her, but the playful look in Valencia's eyes did not quell the dread over what they were discussing.

"I'll have your lunch in a moment, mi querido." Valencia stood fully. "Go talk to the man outside," she said to Alice.

"What did you say about me?"

"Learn Spanish, and you'd know." She smiled wide and went to cook. Alice slid her apron off and squeezed past Valencia to get to the back door. Delany found her a moment later.

"For you." He gave her the check. Alice slid it into the pocket of her short mustard colored jumpsuit. "I like your tattoo." He bent slightly as she pulled back her shorts to show off the two peonies with a collection of leaves around it on her mid-thigh.

"Thank you. They're my favorite." She found it hard to breathe.

"I didn't realize who you were." He stood and crossed his arms loosely. Alice shook her head, not sure what he was talking about. "I overheard what you said to Carrie Beaumont."

"Lovely." Alice stepped back. "I never meant…"

"I didn't want to push your sister out." Delany said over her. Alice studied his eyes, a dark night she wanted to get lost in. They appeared honest, not taking her in and thinking about other things like Harry's always did.

"Do you know how many hours and sacrifices my sister made for that place? Those three are nothing without her. I—" She shook her head. Going off on this millionaire would do nothing. It was just another acquisition to him. "Thank you for the money and the opportunity. If you will excuse me…"

"Are you free this weekend?" Delany asked when she turned toward the truck. Alice faced him again, ready to ask if he was serious. "My sister's getting married, and her caterer canceled." Alice cut off her smart-ass reply. "She was at both events. Loved your food…"

"She'll do it!" Valencia said from the back door of the truck. "Your street tacos, mi querido. Do come back now." She winked and went back into the truck. Delany chuckled to himself.

"I really don't think…"

"It's at his parents' house on the bay. A hundred people. She loves charcuterie and food like this. She said to tell you to have fun."

Alice took a deep breath. It was one thing to say yes before she knew who Macon was, but agreeing to an intimate family event. But if the caterer did call to cancel six days before any other credible caterer would be booked, or charge them a fortune, not that he couldn't afford it. If his sister loved what she did on Friday—her mind raced with ideas.

"I can pay whatever you need to pull this off. I have access to food suppliers…"

"Don't tell me you own a local farm or something."

"Would it help if I did?" He smiled, Alice's heart racing. Oh, he was good. See it as another job, another chance to prove her moxie and maybe get some work. She could not take Carver's disappointed sigh if he found out she turned down a gig. The clock was ticking on Valencia leaving. She hated to say yes, but the benefits outweighed her hesitation. As long as Tabby never found out.

"Okay," she said.

Delany smiled before he caught himself. "I'll have Katy send you the info." He paused. "Any chance I can get you to eat lunch with me?"

She laughed. "Don't push your luck, Mr. Clare. Tell your sister I'll see her Saturday." She went back into the truck. Valencia shook her head from the window.

"Girl, why aren't you pursuing that?" She cocked her head and let out a low moan. Alice sat on the stool they kept under the counter.

"Come with me this weekend, maybe he has a girlfriend you can chat up."

"You went on a date with him, right?"

"Yeah, I guess." Alice tried to forget how lovely the night had been.

"Must have been some damn good drinks."

# CHAPTER 11

**D**ELANY SAT ON THE BED. His sister stood before the mirror, her maid-of-honor helping to zip up her sleeveless dress. It hit just above her chest, straight cut, with a ruffle at her knee and almost no train. Olive swayed and beamed. How was his little sister getting married? The entire thing didn't seem real. Most days he still thought of her as a levelheaded teenager with her head in the books, ready to change the world like their mom did. She'd graduated from Howard Law a decade before, been making a name for herself doing immigration law. She never dated, as far as Delany knew, yet when she met Zed, something changed. He did family law for lower income families, treated his sister like a queen. Delany had no reservations.

Everyone knew he and Olive were Coretta Clare's children from their coarse black hair and dark eyes. Olive's face was long like their mother, but she got her wider nose and fuller lips from her dad. She was petite like her dad, who was smaller in stature from the little Delany remembered about him. Delany's father had never been in the picture. Delany was four when Olive was born. His mother said she wore newborn clothes for six months whereas Delany, based on his length, was almost too big for them from the beginning. Once her father left, it had always been the three of them.

His mother came in with Helene, who smiled when she saw him and ran toward him, her off-white dress flowing behind her.

"Be careful," his mother said. "You have to stay perfect for the wedding."

"It's okay, Mama." He collected his six-year-old daughter and stood. "I got her."

His mother scoffed playfully and asked Olive how she was doing. At sixty-two, Coretta looked like she was in her forties. Her cropped hair accented her long face, bringing out defined cheekbones. She had a wide smile and a kindness to her dark eyes.

Delany slipped out of the room with Helene and walked to the bottom floor. Through the full wall of windows, he watched his soon to be brothers-in-law put the final touches on the arch by the water, a hundred chairs set up to face it.

Helene rested her head on his shoulder. He had her for the last week while her mother went on some trip Delany did not ask about. Fortunately, the dates overlapped with the wedding. It would be nice not to have Nadia included in the memory, who would have guilted his sister into inviting her. Their mother would tell her kids they were being petty, to think of Helene or the families where the parents hated each other. Remember how hard that was on the children?

He remembered. And he didn't hate Nadia, how could he? But he could not say he entirely agreed with her decisions. It made sense she was Helene's primary custodian while he was playing and gone so much, but now? He tried to figure out how to chance the conversation. Nadia could jump to conclusions, and a simple question would be taken as his trying to steal their daughter. He wasn't trying to steal anything, but he could give Helene a better education and a more stable home. Nadia always bemoaned the things having to care for their daughter did not let her do. But somehow offering to let her recreate her twenties in her mid-thirties would not be seen as giving Nadia the freedom she hinted at.

None of that was for today. He told himself to forget the fight when he picked up Helene the weekend before. One saving grace in all of this was they were never married. He couldn't imagine adding alimony on top of what he paid in child support.

The side door opened, Delany glancing over his shoulder. Alice carried in a box of supplies. She wore a looser cut, floral print minidress, her hair styled into a messy bob. The mother of the groom showed her where everything was and what she could use before they went over the schedule one more time.

"Dad, you're staring," Helene said. Delany turned back and asked if she wanted to see the water. They went outside and walked down the pier, staying until the four-piece orchestra started to play. He found his sister alone in the bedroom.

"Where's Mama?" He motioned for Helene to come over, so he could add bows to her thick braids. Most days her black hair was pulled into twin buns. She had his dark eyes, her mother's square face and thin lips. She smiled more than Nadia did, seeming to not have inherited her mother's serious disposition. She could find something in any situation to laugh about, her curiosity helping him see things he'd otherwise miss.

"Chatting with Zed's mom. You okay?" she asked.

Delany looked at Helene and rolled his eyes. His sister nodded and looked at the mirror again.

Olive's dad left when she was only two. Delany's dad had never been there. Their mother raised two kids while working at legal aid in Anacostia. They went to church every Sunday. His upbringing showed him the importance of community and staying connected, giving back. Delany knew people expected him to make the neighborhood better. No way he was going to make it big and forget where he came from. Coretta taught him to treat people right, help where he could, and never forget those who shaped him.

His mother ducked her head in. It was time. Delany walked with Helene down the stairs, Coretta helping Olive with her dress. At the base of the stairs, his mother kissed Olive's cheek and went to walk down the aisle with one of the groomsmen. Delany asked Helene if she remembered what he told her. She nodded and started down the aisle, dropping rose petals as she went. Alice watched the processional from the kitchen, her arm on the counter, a sadness to her features. His sister pulled his arm, and he took a step with her.

The service went by with Delany watching the water. His mother slipped her arm through his, tears on her cheek. Everything she sacrificed for her kids, and yet could never find love herself. He wanted to ask what was happening with the head of the community center. They'd been each other's late-night call for decades. He heard the man's voice in high school, a creak on the stairs. To ask would be admitting he knew what was happening, but it wasn't that hard to see how they looked at each other. He never understood why his mother refused to let herself be happy, to trust someone else again.

Olive leaned in to kiss her husband, the crowd cheering. They faced those assembled, the local band Zed hired starting to play "If I Ain't Got You." Delany stood with everyone else, unsure what to make of his mood.

While the guests mingled and the brothers brought out tables for the guests to sit at, Alice and Valencia worked to get food into the buffet pieces. Delany took another drink of his beer as Helene ran around with the other kids. His mother sat with the groom's parents, their laughs filling the day. A slight breeze filtered through, aided by just enough clouds to break the heat.

Bobbie took a drink back to Carrie, her gaze locked on Alice. Bobbie said something, and she pulled her gaze, smiling politely.

When Alice slipped in during the Macon event to speak with Katy, Delany guessed what they were discussing. He asked for the check as a reason to talk to her again. He hoped to catch her before she left, to thank her again, to ask what changed. Then he came around the corner and saw the tautness of her body, the aggression in her eyes, and approached slowly, not wanting the women to hear him. At least now the change in Alice's attitude made sense. He hid himself until Carrie passed him and let Alice leave. On Monday, he asked Bobbie again if he tried to tell Tabby about the acquisition.

"Come on, Bulldog, you know I wouldn't lie to you!" Delany had to believe him. Realizing he still had the check, he asked Katy where the food truck parked and went to get lunch. Her coworker was hilarious. He decided to be bold and asked if Alice was dating anyone. She told him Alice enjoyed their date but had a chip on her shoulder. Maybe that was why she looked so sad earlier.

Bobbie stopped next to him, taking a drink of his beer.

"Come sit with us." He motioned toward the table he was at with Carrie and some of the guys he still talked to from Anacostia. "Carrie has a friend for you to meet."

"Oh yeah?" He studied the blond playfully sparring with the one of the men at the table, the others eyeing her low-cut dress. She shifted her torso to give them a better view. "I don't know if she's my type." He rested his elbow on the top of Bobbie's head, his best friend swatting him away. It drove Bobbie crazy, which was why he did it. They were opposite in so many ways—tall and short, thin and well, not. Delany wanted to hang out with a few friends where Bobbie loved a crowd. He went for girls with natural beauty, whereas Bobbie believed being hot was all that mattered.

"Nah, come on, Bulldog. If her friend is anything like her, she'll be a freak in the sheets. Trust me on this." He gave him a playful smile. If he hadn't known Bobbie since he sounded like he belonged in the Jackson Five, his attitude might bother him. But he knew where Bobbie came from, knew his father and the shoes Bobbie was desperate to fill. It was his job to keep Bobbie humble. Without him, Bobbie would likely buy into his own hype.

"Are you sure you know how to keep her happy?"

Bobbie's eyes went wide, as he looked ready to hit him. Delany started to laugh. It was far too easy to rile Bobbie up. "At least I'm not afraid of women."

"Discretion, Bobbie. It's called discretion."

"Whatever." He took another drink. "So, I'm going to tell Carrie we're on for next week."

"Sure." He did a look around the yard, not seeing Helene. "Let me know when." He left Bobbie standing there, unsure what happened to his daughter. She sat inside on the kitchen counter talking to Alice with an empty spoon in her hand and her eyes closed. Alice saw Delany and gave him a closed mouth smile. Helene tapped her tongue like she did when she was trying to identify a flavor.

"Is it lime?" Helene opened her eyes.

"Yes," Alice said.

"And coriander?"

"Wow, you have a better palate than some chefs I've worked under."

"I've never heard of Cuban tabbouli, but I like it." Helene handed Alice the spoon and jumped off the counter.

"Then maybe we'll keep it on the menu." Alice said with no hint of sarcasm. "I hope that's okay." Alice slid her hands down her back. Seeming to realize there were no pockets she started to cross her arms, but then settled for slipping them into her purple apron.

"I thought you all wore white coats." Delany tried to hide his smile.

"Old stuffy men wear white coats. We get to bring some distinction to the role." She looked at Helene. "She said you took her on a cooking tour in France."

"That's when I wanted to go to Le Cordon Bleu." Helene slipped her hand into his.

"That is a very lofty school."

"Where did you go?"

"GW."

"They have a culinary program?" Delany asked.

Alice rested her arm on the counter. "No. I got my degree in Biology. I was trained by the best in the industry, D.B. Cornelia."

"He ran Marigolds."

Alice nodded, pain behind her forced smile.

"I hate to interrupt. But we need more chifrijo," Valencia said from the doorway. Alice pointed toward the lawn and went to help. Delany found two seats with some other friends, where he abandoned his jacket and rolled up his sleeves. The reception progressed around him. During the speeches, he glanced at Alice who stood beside the cut wedding cake with Valencia, who got her to smile. There was an ease about her, Alice in her element. When the next speech started, Alice went back into the house for more coffee. She set the new dispenser on the drink table and took the old one back inside. Music started again.

Delany took Helene to sit with her grandma. Inside the kitchen, Alice laughed while she talked to Valencia who packed up the last of their leftovers. Valencia motioned toward Delany and started to stack their dirty dishes.

"I came to settle up," Delany said.

"I can invoice you."

"It gives me a reason to avoid the reception. I'm kind of peopled out."

Alice found her bag and dug out a notebook. She started to flip through the pages. The hesitancy in her gaze hurt but something about her drew him in. She was kind, easygoing, daring, simple in the best way. Why did the first woman he'd been attracted to in years have to be connected to a botched acquisition he still did not understand?

"What all are you involved in at the moment?" He broke the silence.

"Well, the food truck is ending mid-July, Valencia is leaving to see the world. I am in the process of getting my catering company off the ground." She folded the receipt book to a page and put it on the counter close to him. Delany picked it up and pretended to skim the invoice.

"How is business?" He looked at her.

Alice leaned on the counter opposite him and looked out of the backyard.

"Slow, to be honest. But hopefully that will change soon. My sister hoped Welcome Note would help me get some funding by renting my place. I'm debating how long to leave it on the site."

He reached for his checkbook and started to write, adding in a generous tip. Her cooking was worth more than she charged. He tore out the check and gave it to her.

"Thank you for the opportunity. I hope your sister is very happy." She pushed off the counter and went back to the reception. Delany stayed where he was. Maybe her anger was justified. To her, he was the man who screwed her sister out of her dream. He swept in and now reaped the benefits of her sister's years of hard work. If he could redo the week he would have gone with Bobbie to the lunch, approached Tabby himself. But he presumed Bobbie had it. Bobbie had overseen the acquisition of a dozen companies and never had an incident like this. But how was Bobbie to know Mr. Clarks would not follow through? Still, he never wanted to hurt Tabby, never wanted her to feel pushed out or like she had to walk away. Something about Alice drew him in and yet how would she ever see him as something other than the man who killed her sister's dream?

"WHO'S THE GIRL?" His mother asked on the drive back to Anacostia. Delany did a quick check over his shoulder, Helene passed out in her car seat.

"What do you mean?" He tried to play it cool.

His mother laughed. "The caterer. You were watching her for most of the afternoon."

"She's a business contact."

"If you say so." She looked out the side window.

They pulled into the community center. Delany put the front windows down and went to unload the leftover food from the wedding. Coretta started talking to the night manager, one of those she'd helped at her law office. Everywhere Delany went in Anacostia, he ran into someone who knew his mother, went to church with his mother, or was helped by his mother. Growing up he hated it. The few times he dared to misbehave she knew before he even got home. The threat of someone calling her was enough to keep Delany from doing anything. Now, her presence in the community comforted him.

Coretta got back into the car and Delany started for her home. The two-story dark brick house had changed little on the outside since she bought it back in the late 70s after Olive's dad left. A front porch with an overhang, bars over the windows. He'd offered to buy her a new house after he made it, but she refused to leave what she bought for herself. She let him update the inside. New hardwood floors, updated kitchen, a layout that better suited her life as an empty nester with an office on the main floor. His mother didn't entertain at home much. To her, home was a sanctuary where she recharged. He talked her into taking out one of the bedrooms upstairs and putting in a proper master bath with a deep tub and adequate closet space. At first, she called it extravagant, but now admitted it was her favorite room in the house. There was a room upstairs for Helene. Photos of her family were in frames on the fireplace mantle and the bookcases. The art on the walls was a collection of Black artists, some friends, others she wanted to support. He kept telling her to get the works appraised, Delany sensing she had quite the nest egg in the collection she'd cultivated over the years.

"If you need another reason to see your new friend, I can ask if anyone has any events coming up." She looked at him as he pulled in front of her house. "Or is Katy already doing that?" Delany stumbled over what to say. His mother laughed and kissed his cheek. "You are so transparent." She got out of the car. Delany waited until she was safely inside before he pulled away. Maybe if he could make it up to Alice, her sister would realize he never meant to hurt her. If he could prove to Alice he wasn't what his sister thought, maybe she'd look at him with anything but betrayal. An idea formed in his head. One Alice might just say yes to.

# CHAPTER 12

ALICE CHAINED HER BIKE to a hook on the back of the food truck and went inside. Valencia called good morning, working to slice a series of limes on the cutting board. Alice asked about the rest of her weekend while she washed her hands and pulled her apron on. Two days later, she was still on a high from the wedding. Working an event without Carver showed her she could do it on her own. She had set the menu, coordinated with the host, and talked to the guests. It was easier to let Carver do those things, but Alice could do them too. The wedding Saturday gave her a whole new level of confidence, something Alice didn't realize until she got home and thought about the event outside of Delany.

"Who was the little girl you were talking to?" Val asked as she sautéed veggies on the grill.

"Helene, I think. Delany's daughter." She scrunched her nose, hoping she had that right.

"And she wants to be a chef?"

Alice faced the prep table again. "Okay, you can stop now."

"I'm just saying…"

Alice didn't hear the rest of Val's sentence; the air sucked out of the food truck. Jonas stood in the park with his signature smirk and crossed arms. Even with his sunglasses on, she could feel the gloat in his eyes. She could be working at a (formerly) premiere restaurant in the city and instead she stood chopping jalapeños for street tacos.

He reminded her of the cliched image of a chef: overweight in all respects, arrogant, oblivious to what people wanted versus what he thought. A conniving dough boy with a baby face who lost all joy. Poke him and you'd get yelled at and degraded. She never understood how he got by considering his extreme lack of a palate. Her mother told her to look at the doofuses in Congress. People could be blind when they wanted to be.

"What is he doing here?" Valencia growled a bit. Jonas stepped to the window, taking off his sunglasses. His close-set, pale eyes reminded her of the hazelnut syrup they used at Marigolds. Those eyes lingered, telling her she'd never be good enough, and who was she kidding? The joy she'd felt over the weekend faded under the disapproval of the man who took everything from her.

"Are you going to take my order or talk about me?" It always sounded like he had marbles in his mouth, his words tending to flow together.

"Don't you have a restaurant, or did you get tired of that bland goop you pass off as food?" Valencia's hand rested on her back hip. "If you need a hint, Betty Crocker is great for beginners."

Jonas laughed. "Three of your carne asada, please, dearie." He winked at Valencia who started to reach for a knife.

"Just cook," Alice whispered. Valencia went to the grill,

muttering in Spanish. "Is that all for you?" *Get him in and out and pray for another customer.*

"Thought I'd come see what you were doing now, overheard some locals talking about your cute little truck. I heard you stole the Clare wedding. I didn't think that was your style." He gave her some cash.

"I didn't steal anything. The caterer canceled on her…"

"Is that what we call it when a client dumps you the week before an event? Word is her brother said their food was too unoriginal and bland."

"If it's anyone you're talking to that might be a valid assessment." Alice gave him his change and closed the window. Jonas slid his sunglasses back on and stepped back. Delany told her the caterer canceled, but what if they didn't? It wasn't her fault his sister tasted real food and decided she wanted better. Any chef who would be complaining to Jonas either wanted favor with him or was on par with his cooking. Either felt like enough of a reason for Alice to write them off. The fact he came to check up on her was unsettling.

"As if that imbecile knows any seasoning outside of salt. Maybe he'll choke on the pineapple salsa." Valencia gave Alice his order. Alice called his name. Jonas took an envelope out from his jacket and slid it onto the counter before taking his box.

"I give your catering foray six months. When you fail, you know where I am." He walked away, dumping the box in the garbage. Alice exhaled, grateful Valencia couldn't see from her place beside the grill.

"I can stay, Alice. I don't want to leave you in a lurch. Spain will be there a year from now." Val deflated, her eyes sad. Alice refused to let that man destroy anyone else's dream.

"With you living in it. I won't hold you back, Val. You're going." If things kept going as they were, she might be eating tapas and drinking mojitos on the beach with her.

She told Val she'd see her in the morning and started on her bike toward Tabby's apartment. Soon it would be too muggy to be out this time of day, D.C. miserable in the middle of summer. Even if it wasn't too hot, the humidity made one feel like they were melting. She rode on the side streets and did her best to avoid the tourists around the Tidal Basin.

A few people milled around The FDR Memorial. It lingered over several acres, highlighting the country's changing situation from the Dust Bowl to WWII. There were several water features, with quotes from the president etched in granite. And in the middle, tucked into an alcove, easily overlooked, stood a statue of Eleanor in a dress and knee-length coat, her hands clasped before her.

The bench before it became Alice's escape in middle school when the pressure of being the Minority Whip's daughter got to be too much. When she needed an escape from the meetings at the house, or her mother being on the phone at all hours, or yet another fundraiser in Maryland the girls just had to attend, she'd find her father. He'd laugh and tell her to get her coat and they would drive to the memorial. He would wander while Alice sat before Eleanor's statue.

It wasn't until high school Alice realized her father came for the same reason. He liked the sound of the waterfalls. They both appreciated the lack of people there at night, the memorial a bit removed from the main thoroughfare. Her father would sit beside the Tidal Basin and close his eyes. He grew up on a five-acre plot halfway between D.C. and Annapolis. He felt at home outside, loved nature, and the quiet. Her mother's job in Congress kept them in D.C. If her father had his way, they would have lived in the country full-time. But his wife's job was once in a lifetime. So, her father took a job at George Washington University, teaching biology and tried to cultivate nature wherever they lived. When her parents bought some acreage near the Pennsylvania border, her father finally had the land and space he craved. He only came into The District now to guest lecture or visit the girls. She missed having him close. They used to see each other all the time, Alice not realizing how special those moments were until they were gone.

Alice slid onto the bench and took off her helmet before running her hand through her hair to try to bring any sense of life or style to it.

"I don't know if I can do this."

This woman heard far too many of her confessions. To be strong like Eleanor. Steadfast. To choose to persevere with everything stacked against you. To be faced with a cheating husband, a world war, and a society that only wanted to hold you back. And yet, to still take a stand for what was right, to fight for the equality of others, to not let men tell you how to behave. Alice never found a way of connecting with her mother, but she did so with Eleanor. Alice always felt a tie with the former first lady as they shared a birthday. She named her catering company after Eleanor's favorite dessert—Hasty Pudding.

She pulled Jonas' envelope out of her backpack. Valencia told her to throw it away. Alice wished she could. Let it be a truce or his admitting he was wrong and apologizing for massacring her career. More likely it was a rebuke for stealing the Clare event, a list of her deficiencies. What did she care what this imitation chef thought of her? She put her hands on it to tear it in half. Nothing this imbecile had to say she cared to hear. *Tear it up and throw it in the garbage.*

She sighed and opened the envelope, hating her weakness. Inside were torn out pages from a magazine, an article on the woman her ex got pregnant. The bottom of page two featured a photo of her ex, Chase, still dressed like a J.Crew ad, the woman he left her for, and their two kids.

Her ex came into Marigolds one day. They chatted, waiting for Cornelia to come up. At the time, Chase was a wine rep for his parents' vineyard in Virginia. He came back a few days later and asked her out. It was extravagance meets simplicity. She rode her bike around the city. He drove a red Beamer. She shopped at thrift stores. He only wore J.Crew and Ralph Lauren. Alice preferred to eat at hidden gems (if she ate out at all). Chase called them greasy and gross. Tabby asked what Alice saw in him. Well, he was interesting and easy to be around. They had fun together. Her wardrobe became plaid dresses and patterned pants, wedges. She started brushing out her bob, letting it grow out.

They saw each other whenever he was in town on his sales route. He took her to expensive restaurants, fancier events, even up to New York City. He pushed to sleep with her, Alice not in any hurry. From the start, she questioned what he saw in her, Chase so unlike her last boyfriend who was a homebody like her. Chase refused to stay at her basement apartment near the restaurant, called it dingy and off-putting. He insisted she come to the apartment he rented near Dupont, even though it was further from the restaurant than she felt comfortable riding late at night. Two years in, he proposed in Mexico with a massive 2-karat halo ring. Her breath caught in her throat, were they there yet? But she said what she had to: yes.

Alice went to work and wore the ring around her neck, always remembering to put it on when Chase was in town. She shifted her dream of running a white linen restaurant to the bistro on his vineyard. As things progressed toward the wedding, she moved into his apartment with his decorations, his art, his sheets, his taste. Her stuff barely made a dent. He found it childish and simple. She had money now and could afford better. Alice always had money; she didn't choose to spend it on stuff.

Alice had been engaged for months when her mother asked about a dress or flowers or a venue. Alice hadn't thought about it, but her menu was set. Her ex had opinions about the flowers (black dahlias, which she hated), the bridesmaid dresses (yellow, her least favorite), and their first song ("Fooled Around and Fell in Love"). The one thing they could agree on was having it at his parents' vineyard in Virginia. Alice kept waiting for her mother to take charge like she did with Tabby, but instead, her mother said it was her day and she wanted Alice to be happy. Then came the day she was sitting in his apartment (it never felt like hers) with a list of things to do before the ceremony that weekend. A knock came at the door, the woman there. The woman worked at a local historical estate that also did events. Chase suggested maybe she could help Alice with the wedding since it wasn't her strength. Alice didn't know if she would call them friends, but when it came to her big day, the woman became indispensable. Alice tried to remember if the woman had agreed to help with the dozens of things on Alice's list that day. Before she could ask, the woman dropped her bombshell: she was pregnant, and it was Chase's.

He came in on cue. It was simple; he didn't love Alice. She was a fun pastime, but it was time to move on. The woman told her to be gone by the time they got back from Jamaica on what was supposed to be Alice's honeymoon. The affair started before Chase ever introduced them. Alice asked why he proposed, asked her to move in, pursued her at all.

"I guess I thought I could have both. She is so voracious, and well, you do entertain me. But with our little one coming, I realized it was time to follow my heart."

"I have nowhere to go." Alice's tears started to build. She swallowed back the panic and pain. Her mother taught her to not let bullies see you cry.

"Well, I guess you have two weeks to figure that out."

Just like that, they were gone. Alice stood in the apartment she hated, blindsided. Nothing about the last twenty minutes made sense, only she knew she'd been played for a fool.

Cornelia saw through her ex and told Alice to figure out *her* dreams for *her* life. He took her back without question. Alice hid at Marigolds and moved in with Tabby and Paul until she could find an apartment she liked. Mostly she stayed with the twins (now seven) or went to work. Then her parents offered Alice their place to live. Her father was almost always at the other house, her mother could stay with her or Tabby when she came into the city. Alice moved into their apartment, the silence overwhelming. She felt alone and wondered how she could have been so blind and stupid.

Shortly thereafter, Cornelia told her he wanted Marigolds to go to her. For the first time Alice stepped into the space her fear held her back from. Six months later came the story in *The Washingtonian*. Alice felt like she'd finally found the missing ingredients. Four months after the article, Cornelia died. She still remembered the frantic call from another chef at the restaurant. Was Alice watching the news? She saw the downed blue trek bike and knew. The phone slipped from her grasp as Alice watched what she'd been promised scald into nothing.

# CHAPTER 13

ALICE LATCHED HER BIKE to the food truck the next morning, almost half an hour late. Valencia said good morning, washing what she'd used to slice and shred the meats.

"Do I want to ask what you did last night?" Val leaned against the back of the driver's seat and crossed her arms. Was Alice that transparent? Slowly, she reached for the envelope out of her backpack. Seeing Val wouldn't take it, Alice set it on the edge of the cutting area of the prep table.

"What if he's right, Val?"

Valencia waited while she rambled on about all the questions and fears the article unearthed, before asking if Alice was done and reaching for the article, tearing it in half, and dumping the scraps into the trash. "They only have power over you if you let them."

"It's easy for you to say…"

"Easy? I work in the same industry you do. I left before Jonas came, but that man is a complete hack. Why do you care what he thinks?"

"Because he's the reason I can't get things going."

"Is he?" Valencia crossed her arms. "Or is he an excuse?" She talked over Alice's objection. "Just like your ex. You let him define you, so you don't have to try again. I was there this weekend, mi querida, that man is attracted to you."

"It doesn't matter. Don't you agree he's the one man I can't date now?"

Valencia looked at her and put her hand on her hip. "So if it wasn't for what happened with Tabby, you'd be interested?"

"Yes. Very. But it doesn't matter, because what happened with Tabby happened."

"I see how that man looks at you, Alice. Are you going to hide behind your sister like you hide behind Jonas?" Valencia smiled wide and leaned on the counter toward the open window and batted her eyes. "We really must stop meeting this way."

Delany's laugh filled the space, Alice content to hide out beside the grill.

"Lil." Valencia tilted her head toward the window.

"No," Alice whispered. "Ask if he has any single girlfriends. When is the last time you went on a date?"

"Mi querida, I am not going to bother that tall drink with something I can figure out on my own." She smiled at Delany and told him Alice was coming. "Do you know how far this is from his office?"

"Why is he here?"

Val scowled. "I'm not even going to answer that."

"His best friend is Bobbie Dunn. Don't forget what kind of man he is, Val."

"Even you don't believe that." She shooed Alice out with her hands. Alice sighed and slipped out the back door. Delany waited in the shade of a nearby tree. Against widespread belief, she was not oblivious when it came to men. Delany had to be at least curious about her, but there was no way Alice could let something happen since he screwed her sister out of her dream.

"Who's getting married now?" She slid her hands into her back pockets. Delany laughed.

"I was hoping maybe we could get drinks, talk about your catering company."

"What about it?"

"I'd like to finance it, open my Rolodex and take Hasty Pudding from your food truck to the top catering company in D.C. We can build you a premiere kitchen…"

"I don't need a premiere kitchen. I don't need your dirty money either. I'm fine." She turned to leave, Delany grabbing her arm.

"What happened with your sister was a misunderstanding. I never wanted it to go down like that. I was told she knew." He waited. Alice looked at Valencia, who told her to let it go. "I just want to help." His grip softened.

Alice sighed. In two weeks, the food truck would be gone. Then she had less than a month before Tabby got home, and in that time, she had seven gigs. If things went on at this rate, her catering company was over before it began. This was the opportunity she'd been praying for, but she could not take his money. After everything Tabby had done for her, this was not how Alice was going to repay her sister. She would find some other way to get her company off the ground.

"I can't, Mr. Clare." She walked past the food truck and toward the rows of shops across the way to buy herself a water, hoping when she came back that man would be gone. Maybe now he'd get the hint and stop thinking his charity toward her made up for stealing her sister's business.

#

BOBBIE LEANED INTO THE SHORT WALL of Katy's cubicle outside of Delany's office. Bulldog's calendar was empty, so he should be there. If Bobbie's office was closer, he could keep an eye on things, but he'd been relegated down the hall with the other executives. He wasn't another exec. He was Delany's best friend and right hand. Since he cleared out the previous COO two years before, he'd run Macon with an iron fist. No one bothered Delany without his okay. The plan was for Delany to retire and go to work with his ridiculous charity while Bobbie ran Macon. Only something changed and Delany announced he would be in the office full-time. Katy started working there, people coming to her instead of him, and he became just another exec, getting left out of meetings, not being asked about decisions.

"Can I help you, Mr. Dunn?" Katy didn't look up from her computer.

"Do you know where Bulldog is?"

"Mr. Clare had some errands to run. I didn't ask for details."

"Isn't it your job to know where he is?" Bobbie eyed her and snorted.

Katy sighed and glanced at him, her green eyes impatient. But they usually were when she looked at him. "He told me he would be back by two. I don't have to keep tabs on Mr. Clare anymore." She went back to work, brushing him off.

"You realize you work for me, right?"

Katy caught the laugh a bit too late, trying to play it off by clearing her throat. "I work for Mr. Clare."

"As CIO, you work for me. I'm the silent leadership of this organization. Delany hired me to oversee things."

She stood and reached for one of her business cards on the front of her cubicle and read it before turning it to him.

"Until this says Executive Assistant to the CIO, I answer to Delany, not you." She sat again and went back to work. "I can tell him you stopped by."

He'd hate her if he could muster the energy. Why Bulldog kept this pipsqueak he'd never know. She had been a mild nuisance as his personal assistant, now she was a pain in the ass. If she just got how things worked, they could both spare the other a lot of frustration. Nothing he tried worked on her—flattery, intimidation. It often felt like she looked through him, Bobbie unsure what her issue was.

"The chick you got to cook for the company event…"

"You mean the woman whose company catered our event."

"Whatever. Do you know how she ended up at Olive's wedding?" He put one hand on his hip. Katy stopped working and looked up at him.

"Delany told Olive he thought the other caterer they hired was boring compared to what Alice could do. Did you like the food?"

Bobbie flexed his jaw. Yeah, he did. The dirty rice rivaled his mother's, and no one made dirty rice as good as his mother. The fact that Alice added in shrimp and pulled pork made his mouth water just thinking about it.

"She's Tabby Black's sister, right?"

Katy drew in a deep breath. Bobbie was bothering her— good. She thought could blow him off; he might just stay there until Delany got back.

"Your new girlfriend would be the better person to ask. Now if you don't mind, I have work to do."

Bobbie thought about staying, but instead, stepped back and bowed. Katy rolled her eyes and reached for her earphones. Bobbie walked back toward his office. He knew the caterer was related to Tabby. Carrie found him the night of the office party all upset because Tabby's sister was there and had been rude to her. He offered to take care of it, but Carrie told him not to. Then they were at Olive's wedding and Carrie gasped out of nowhere.

"What's wrong?" he asked, not caring.

"Alice is here." She pointed at the woman refilling the buffet bar. She was younger with a fuller form, shorter hair. That was the dowdy fraud's sister? Carrie told him Alice used to work at Marigolds before some hack took it over. Bobbie didn't bother telling her he loved Jonas' food and would have recommended him for the wedding if Bulldog told him something went awry with the original caterer. He watched her and her coworker refill the buffet line. Anytime he glanced at Delany, his gaze was on the caterer.

Something about the way Delany looked at her told Bobbie he was interested. Bobbie could list all the women Delany had dated, starting with that ungrateful gold digger Nadia. Outside of her, Delany tended to go for plain women, looking through the supermodels and drop-dead gorgeous women who flirted with him. Bobbie had no idea why Bulldog would be attracted to someone who had no idea how to make herself attractive. If Tabby was dowdy, her sister was boring. They were six years apart, if he heard Carrie right. He asked Jonas about her, who laughed and said he fired her because she had no talent and could not take basic feedback. Just like the dowdy mess.

Delany had offhandedly mentioned the caterer in a half a dozen meetings for people to use for their events. If he got close to Alice and figured out that Bobbie lied and intimidated his way into the deal, he might be toast. Best to find a way to nip Delany's crush in the bud.

#

ALICE WENT TO SEE CARVER after work. With a line almost to the door, she found a table and sat with her back to the front windows. The front door opened to a series of café tables, faux hardwood floors leading to a big island in the center of the space with two larger, oval pendant lights above it. A pastry case on either side displayed the day's offerings. Behind the island was a full coffee bar, mugs and plates resting on open shelving to the right. The other side held the double doors to the kitchen and office. With white shiplap walls and lots of natural light, the entire thing felt like an open concept kitchen.

Carver walked by and left the paper on her table, along with an iced coffee. On the page was a photo of the wedding from the weekend. The article talked about Hasty Pudding and how Delany Clare called it the best food he'd ever eaten. She looked up, Carver sitting there.

"Nice press. How was it?"

She set the paper down. Before Jonas' appearance, she would have gushed about the event. Now she didn't know how to feel. "Lovely house on the Bay. A hundred people. Nothing too exciting." She sat back. "Delany Clare offered to finance the company."

"How much did you ask for?" His black eyes went wide.

"Nothing. I am not taking Delany Clare's money. I won't be his absolution."

Carver's breath came out in a short huff.

"Did you snort some of Val's hot peppers? Our little venture is in the red. We need the money—not to mention Clare's connections. I get family loyalty, but this could be our chance!"

"You don't need the chance, Carver. You're already a baker to watch. Your waiting list for cakes is a yearlong. What do you get…"

"I love my wedding gigs. They made my name and sustain this place. But I want to have fun, Alice. I want to be creative and do more." He leaned into the table. "Do you remember what you told me when we talked about this? Do you remember how you set this up?"

"Let's have fun with food."

"Fun with food—get away from the cliche and overdone. The Macon event, what we did, that's what I want more of. You're the chef, I'm the baker. We are in this together." He drew in a deliberate breath, fisting and unfisting his hands. Alice never remembered seeing him so riled up. "You're not some lost puppy to me, Lil. I'm not here out of pity. What happened to that woman they wrote about in *The Washingtonian*? Where is the culinary genius who is going to revamp the food industry in this town? That chef—oooh, I miss that chef. She wouldn't be hiding out, feeling sorry for herself, waiting for an opportunity, while not realizing they are all around her! I am sorry your sister got her company taken away. It is unfortunate. But stop wallowing on her behalf. Get beyond who this is and see what he's offering you." He walked into the kitchen. Alice closed her eyes, wishing Carver would try to see things from her point of view.

# CHAPTER 14

DELANY CALLED NADIA when he got outside of D.C., who yelled to Helene that her father was coming and to get a move on. Delany hung up the phone and looked out the window, ready for the long weekend. He was getting Helene a day early, allowing Nadia to go to Charleston with the girls for the Fourth.

They grew up in the same neighborhood, went to the same schools, Delany one year ahead of her. With three brothers, Nadia knew how to hold her own. At fourteen, she walked into high school with confidence beyond her age and dared anyone to look at her wrong. For some reason, she set her sights on him. Delany was pudding. They started sleeping together his junior year. He felt ten feet tall with a girl like that on his arm. Nadia made sure every other girl knew better than to try anything. He overlooked her possessive nature because, damn, she was hot and at the time, the sex was pretty good.

Nadia talked about taking the ride with him, Gucci bags and vacations at the Four Seasons. He always sensed it was a high school thing. They broke up after his graduation. He went to UMD and dated other women, coming to understand what he wanted, the traits he held as important. She went to Bowie State, and they lost touch.

One day he ran into her at his favorite take out place in Anacostia. She asked if they could get lunch. There, she said she was getting older and wanted a child. If Delany wanted nothing to do with them, that was okay. She wasn't a gold digger. She wanted a baby, but not from some random stranger at a sperm bank. Given their history, he agreed. She didn't want to mess with in vitro, the pills, and the doctors. They slept together on and off for a year before she got pregnant. She played it off as they were dating to the press, not wanting to damage his reputation or give other women ideas.

At the time, Delany thought he would walk away. Then he got to thinking about how he never knew his father, the pain and questions that gave him. Nadia sent him pictures every now and again, the baby with bows in her hair and wearing frilly dresses. Not Delany's preference, but Nadia always was a bit over-the-top. He looked at his little girl and realized he couldn't just be the sperm donor. He took Nadia out to lunch and asked if he could be there for Helene. Nadia smiled.

"Of course, Bulldog." She put her hand on his wrist. "Your little girl is going to love you."

"How was Olive's wedding?" Nadia opened the door, her brown hair pulled into a messy ponytail. Delany couldn't remember ever seeing her square face without makeup. Not that she needed it with her big brown eyes and pouty lips. She had an ideal form, Nadia's version of religion was her time at the gym. He watched men fall over themselves to get her whatever she asked for. Some days, Delany fell into that group. Nadia commanded any room she entered. She knew her influence and scanned her surroundings for any potential threats. She was almost impossible to get close to. He prayed cynicism was not genetic, wanting his daughter to see the good in others.

"It was fine. How was your trip?" He stepped into the rowhouse, staying just inside the front door.

"Don't change the subject. Why wasn't I invited?"

"You were out of town." Delany glanced toward the stairs and called for Helene.

"Stay for a drink." She smiled playfully.

"I don't want Bear up that late."

Nadia laughed. "The implication was you'd stay here. You still that oblivious?"

"That was a long time ago." He cleared his throat.

"About seven years, if time serves me right." She called for Helene and walked to the back part of the house. His daughter came down the stairs, lugging a gym bag.

"How long are you planning on staying?" Delany took it from her, guessing she packed more than a few books.

"I want to figure out how to make that Cuban tabbouleh."

"Who's the chef?" Nadia came back with a glass of red wine. "Helene can't stop raving about this girl's food. Wants to cut her hair short now."

Delany tried to play it off, not needing Nadia to get worked up over nothing. "Do you have cookbooks in here, Bear?"

Helene nodded. Delany knelt and started to go through the bag.

"Daddy!"

"I have cookbooks, and this won't tell you. It's by taste, remember?"

Helene sighed overdramatically. Delany told her to take the books back to where they went. Not that it would matter, the chaotic state of Nadia's rowhouse never seemed to change.

"She must be cute." Nadia took a drink. "What's the plan—

use Helene to get a private lesson?" She tsked. "She only wants your money. You know how many gold diggers would be around if not for me?"

"Between you and Bobbie I am more than protected." He stood and called for Helene to hurry up.

Nadia glared. "Don't trust outsiders, Bulldog, they only want one thing. I'm serious about that drink." She batted her eyes. Helene came back and Delany opened the door, not bothering with a goodbye. He waited while Helene climbed into her seat. Even without turning around, he knew Nadia would be stalking them from the window. He needed to be careful. His daughter could be a little parrot, and now Nadia had an inkling something might be going on. She could sense another woman a thousand feet away. Not that she had any claim to things. He gave Nadia their daughter, that was supposed to be it. He loved Helene. Some days, he wished there wasn't a tie back to his ex.

"Daddy," Helene said after Delany buckled her in. He paused leaning out of the car. "I thought the chef was nice. I think you should go for it."

"Thanks, Bear." He kissed her forehead. "I think she's just a friend."

Helene giggled. She didn't believe him either. Great. He closed the door and got into the front seat. One thing at a time.

# CHAPTER 15

ALICE CALLED FOR HER MOTHER, setting her bag on the couch in the front room. It always felt like she was breaking the bliss of a B&B when she came to her parents' house. Built in the 1800s, the front foyer opened to the second story which held five bedrooms. Dark hardwood floors ran throughout, mostly covered in antique rugs. The formal sitting room stood to the right, an office beside it. The formal dining room waited on the other side, the opening to the kitchen before her. Family photos and shadow boxes of her mother's accomplishments in Congress covered the muted blue walls. Alice called for her mother again as Taco set to sniffing the house; surely her father left something out for her to enjoy.

"She's at her tennis game." Her father came out of the kitchen in his well-loved overalls, covered in paint and dirt. "This is a surprise."

"We didn't open the truck today with the long weekend, and nothing is going on that I need to be in town for. I thought I might crash up here for a few days."

"You're free to stay, though we got invited to the Capitol dome for the fireworks tomorrow." Her dad rubbed his chin with his broad hand, leaving a trail of dirt on his skin. How opposite her parents were. Her mother—The Queen as she became known on The Hill—always perfect and presentable. Somehow, she'd come back from tennis looking like a magazine ad. Then there was her dad, Dr. James Gibson, renowned horticulturist, disheveled and easygoing. Her father taught her about edibles and led her into a world too many overlooked, cultivating Alice into the chef she became.

"I can go." So much for her relaxing weekend in the country. "How are things growing this year?"

"Come see." He started back for the greenhouse, walking through the kitchen, which her mom remodeled into something from a hotel. Hilarious, considering her mother only knew how to cook soup. Alice soon realized her mother wanted her to feel comfortable cooking for her mother's parties and other get-togethers. A fireplace sat in the center of a full wall of windows, providing a view of the valley around them. The loose pages of her dad's latest book waited on the table against the far wall.

The greenhouse was her father's addition to the house. Two steps down into another world. Fresh earth and herbs replaced the floral of her mother's candle in the kitchen. Plants covered the various laboratory tables, grow lights pulled against the beams in the ceiling until they would be needed again. The glass panels stood open for the summer. Alice took a deep breath and relaxed. She picked a mint leaf and slipped it on her tongue. The family bloodhound slept in the corner, who raised her droopy eyes to Alice before going back to sleep.

"It's the heat of the summer," her dad said. Alice set her fingers on the tomatoes vining in the corner, the black strawberries starting to poke their heads out of the earth. A collection of snap peas climbed up a trellis near the back windows.

"What's going on, Birdie?" Her dad tended to the vegetables around him. Alice studied the peas.

"I got an investor for my catering company…"

"That's great!"

"Delany Clare."

He tilted his head. "How do you know Delany Clare?"

"His admin hired me to do an event before everything went down with Tabby. I-I can't turn him down, Dad."

"Why would you?"

Alice paused. "Because of what happened with Tabby."

Her dad passed it off with a wave of his hand and went to find his spray bottle.

"She won't understand." Alice leaned on a workbench.

"You cannot make your choices based on your sister. What would your mother say? This is business. Your company is not TabiKat. Is that your only holdup?"

The only one she was going to tell her father about. He indulged her schoolgirl crushes when she was younger. It hardly seemed a viable reason to turn down Delany's offer. Alice glanced at her father who watched her, waiting for an answer.

"If your sister can't be happy for you—that's hers to figure out. I know you, not cooking is eating at you. Clare is well-connected. This is your chance to prove Jonas and the others wrong."

"What if they're not wrong?" Alice tried to swallow her emotion. "What if I take this money and Delany's Rolodex and I fail? What if Cornelia was wrong, and I'm not meant to be an executive chef?"

Her father took a moment to finish spraying the chard before he set the bottle down and came to stand before Alice. She couldn't bring herself to meet his gaze, the tears a little too close in her eyes.

"What did we tell you growing up—people only bullied you because you highlighted something they didn't like in themselves. Jonas' want of talent is not a secret. Those men trying to hold you back are using you to mask their insecurities. If you do your best, this company will not fail."

He wiped the tear off her cheek, leaving a trail of mud. He started to apologize, but Alice shook her head. It was fine. The grit on her skin reminded her of her childhood and the promise her dad would always be there for her.

"I'm scared, Dad."

"I get that. You should be. A healthy bit of fear never hurt anyone but don't let that keep you from what you want."

She went to collect honey from the combs, the bees buzzing around her. Alice focused on what she needed to do before she reset the top cover and undid her suit at the bin her father kept near the hive boxes on the edge of their property. The only way her mother agreed to let him keep bees around was if they never interfered with one of her parties or made their guests feel uncomfortable. A chicken run surrounded her father's outdoor garden, a series of raised beds in perfectly formed rows. Alice collected the eggs before heading back to the house.

Her mother's voice floated out of the screen door. Alice drew in a deep breath and got ready. Inside, her mother waved and pointed to the phone in her other hand. Alice checked the sun tea brewing in the window before slipping out of the kitchen. She went to the bedroom she always stayed in with its antique four-post bed and vintage floral wallpaper. Her father's books lined the top shelf of the hutch on the secretary desk. She reached for the one on fungi and sat against the wall by the bed. She'd read it half a dozen times but always got new ideas of things to try. Knowing her mother had boxes of the books in the basement and that she encouraged guests to take them, Alice found a pen in the bedside table and started making notes. Taco curled up on the bed beside her.

"I'm sure you have at least two marked-up copies of that in your apartment." Her mother's voice filled the room. She stood with either hand on a side of the doorway, her white tennis outfit perfect even after an hour at the court. The glow brought out her emerald eyes and full lips. Her mother's skin chapped from being in the sun. They were the same height, Alice always feeling disheveled around her mother.

"But those are in a box in town, and I am here." Alice smiled. Her mother laughed, using her hand to pull her tapered dirty-blond hair out of her eyes.

"It's good to see you. I told your father we can do Charlie's for dinner tonight, watch the sunset over the ridge. Lovely story they did on you in the paper." She paused. Alice slid her finger into the book and waited. "Your dad told me about the offer…"

"Please don't side with Tabby for once." She didn't need her mother's guilt trip on top of her own.

Her mother sighed. "I was just going to say, let me know once you get going. I'm a bit miffed you held back those charcuterie boards from me." She walked away. Alice dropped her head. A lifetime of not measuring up reared its head at the worst times.

HER MOTHER CAME INTO the bedroom the next morning, setting a shorter pink dress on the bed. Alice kept herself from asking if the designer felt inspired by messy frosting. After the previous night, it would be better to not upset her mother. Most often her mother would be hurt for a few days and then act like nothing ever happened. Alice learned long ago to keep her head down.

"I was hoping you might be available to cater your father's birthday in October."

"Of course."

"It'll be here. Thirty, forty people. I need food for the whole weekend. I will pay you. Run it through your business and treat it like another event."

Alice started to laugh and say she couldn't, but seeing her mother's serious expression all she could think to say was, "Yes ma'am."

Her mother set her hand on the tall railing of the bed, choosing her words. Alice studied the oversized pearls on her mother's right wrist, matching ones on her ears and neck.

"Have you thought about Mr. Clare's offer?"

Alice closed the book around her hand and took a deep breath, preferring the conversation with her father. He might not understand any better, but he'd be gentler.

"I don't see how Tabby would ever understand."

Her mother nodded a few times. "Do you have any other prospects?"

"For backers? No." Except Harry, and Alice might be getting desperate enough to take him up on his offer. Not that Tabby would understand that decision any better.

"And Valencia leaves in two weeks?"

"Yeah." She hoped to keep the frustration out of her voice, not sure what her mother was getting at. Maryanne cleared her throat.

"We agreed to let you live in the apartment, Birdie, not sublease it to strangers. If you are not going to be there…"

"It's just until Hasty Pudding gets going." She dropped the book and sat up more. "I asked you and Dad if you cared."

"Yes, I remember. And in the spring, it felt like you had some momentum." She looked out the window and flexed her jaw. Alice's heart rate picked up. She started to tell her mother about the potential events she could have, to ask for more time. But her mother lifted her hand. "I took your sister out to lunch after she got back from college and told her the free ride was done. I would only support her as much as she put in the effort. I never thought I'd have to have the conversation with you."

"Mom." Alice's skin felt clammy. Her mother shook her head.

"If you want to go back to a basement apartment in Georgetown and be a junior chef and live in the past, that is your choice. But we both know you are more than that." She stood fully. "You have until the start of September to show me you intend to do something to make your company go. You know your father and I will do whatever we can. But I will not allow you to hide out at your sister's and jot ideas in books while there is a real opportunity out there for you to do what you want. It's time to find some gumption, Birdie. It's time for you to be proactive for what you want."

ALICE FOLLOWED HER PARENTS up the stairs to the balcony on the Capitol dome. No matter how many times she climbed these steps, the view still left her breathless. The latest country semi-star crooned from the lawn below for the televised event. The people looked like ants, and the city felt like a play set she could pick up and rearrange if she wished. It was her favorite place to watch the fireworks fill the skyline she loved.

She pulled at the high neckline of the dress her mother left. The Queen had standards for how the girls looked and behaved at The Capitol. After the exchange at the house, Alice was desperate to get on her good side again. She didn't want to believe her mother's ultimatum came because of what she said. A slip of the tongue, an indication she felt second to her sister. Her mother could remember offenses. *Don't get her started on how people stabbed her in the back in Congress.* Yes, it was ten years ago and neither one worked there anymore, but her mother loved to turn any conflict within these hallowed halls into a gladiator battle. If Alice didn't play things right, her mother would use the "well, you just think I love Tabby more" line against her any time Alice tried to stand up for herself. She wanted to ask her father if they were serious. Would they really kick her out of the apartment and sell it? But her parents tended to be in lockstep when it came to the girls.

Her mother chatted with some donor for the party, her father laughing with another representative's husband. The National Symphony Orchestra started to play on the lawn below. The fireworks were close. She pulled at the high collar of her dress, feeling like an Easter egg in the pink shift dress that barely fell to her mid-thigh. She hated heels but indulged her mother. She could leave it all in the closet at Tabby's house. For one night, just make her mother happy.

"I wouldn't have guessed you owned anything so frilly." Delany stopped at the rail beside her.

"What are you doing here?" She glanced back at her mother.

"The rep from Virginia invited me. Can you say hi, Helene?" He put his hand back over his daughter's shoulders as she pressed into him.

"You cut your hair!" Alice knelt to her level. Her tight black curls were cut to chin length now. "It's so cute."

"We can't figure out how to style it right though, huh, Bear?" Helene shook her head.

"Well, I love it. I wish my hair was curly like that." Alice winked at her. Helene giggled and looked up at her dad.

"It's Delany, right?" Maryanne said behind her. Alice stepped back while her mother introduced herself. "I'm Alice's mother."

"We've met before, ma'am. I didn't realize you all were related."

"It's rather fortuitous that you're here." She forced a smile.

"I think Rep. Duncan is trying to get me to move the Mystics to Arlington," Delany said.

"Would you?" Alice asked.

"And take it out of where I grew up? Not a chance." He introduced Helene, prompting her to say hello to Mrs. Gibson.

"How old are you?" Her mother bent down.

"I'm almost seven." Helene stood a bit straighter.

Her mother chuckled. "Lovely to meet you. Enjoy the show, Mr. Clare." She looked at Alice and walked away. The first firework burst into the night, Helene covering her ears. Delany picked her up and told her it was okay.

Alice swallowed her fears and prayed Tabby might someday understand her choice.

"Is your offer still good?" Alice asked. Delany looked at her and nodded, trying to hide his smile. "I'm in. But it's business. That's it."

He leaned in close, Alice's heart rate picking up. Another firework exploded overhead.

"Come by the office and we can work something out. You won't regret this, Alice." He leaned back and smiled with his mouth closed. Even when he didn't flash that million-dollar smile, he was still attractive. Alice looked ahead and cursed to herself. It was business. B-U-S-I-N-E-S-S! There was no time for a crush here, no place for emotion. Delany Clare was a means to an end. That was all.

# CHAPTER 16

TABBY SET HER PURSE on the kitchen counter and studied the pristine apartment. Not one dish was out of place, one pillow where it shouldn't be. No dust anywhere. Alice must have called their cleaning company. Like her whimsical hair, Alice could not be bothered with the tiny details that, all put together, led to her life being chaotic and messy. Somehow, she pulled it together for her cooking, but disarray was the name of her sister's life everywhere else.

Just to be sure, Tabby checked Alice's room. There was the chaos she knew—clothes on the bed, a coffee cup on the bedside table, another on the dresser. She hoped her sister was still there. They all enjoyed having Alice close. The twins missed her. They had a host of stories to tell her, mementos to give her. Finally, Tabby told them to take pictures. Her sister didn't need a trinket from each city they went to. She missed her sister too. Maybe they could do a mimosa lunch and catch up. After almost two months away, they were all ready to sleep in their beds and not be eating out.

Paul sorted through their luggage in their bedroom. She kissed his shoulder and took the pile of dirty clothes to the laundry bin in the closet. She started to undo her blouse. Paul pressed up behind her, his kiss on her neck.

"I can help." His hand went to the button of her slacks.

"The kids are too close and wound up with energy."

"Come on, Tabatha."

She moaned. The trip had been like a second honeymoon for them. As much of a honeymoon as one can enjoy with two curious, over-energized ten-year-olds. It had been too long since they stayed up and talked at night, enjoyed a shower together, saw each other. She loved Paul. He kept her sane and brought her so much joy. With his career and her trying to launch her company and the kids—it all got lost so easily.

"Mom!" Mac's voice rang through the apartment.

"Told you." Tabby laughed, Paul taking a step back.

"I got it." He went to see what Mac needed. Annie's joyful scream filled the apartment. Alice must be home. She followed the sounds. The twins spoke rapidly, Alice on her butt against the main door. Taco barked around the scene, her tail frantic.

"Let the poor girl stand up," Tabby said. Alice pushed herself up and hugged her sister, Tabby hit with a wave of sweat and cumin. "You smell disgusting!"

"But you missed me." Alice pulled herself closer. Tabby told her to get off her. Alice hugged Paul hello before turning her attention back to the twins. "What was your favorite part?" Both kids started talking at once. Alice laughed and stood. "I can take them to dinner if you want to unpack and be alone." Alice winked. Paul agreed before Tabby could respond. Alice sent the kids to get their shoes. "Welcome home."

It felt good to be back.

TABBY TOOK A LONG DRINK of her coffee as she walked into her office a few days later. Paul went back to work; Alice took the kids to the pool for a bit. For the first time in seven weeks Tabby found herself alone for more than a moment. She reached for her phone to call Mo Mo for an update. Her finger hovered above the green button before she remembered.

She glanced at her closed laptop. There'd be no emails from coders or beta testers. It was all spam and messages of curiosity masked as sympathy. She didn't know where things stood with Macon and their planned merger with that other tech company. The trip to Europe saved her sanity, but now the grief and questions hit her like a virus in the software. On her desk sat an oversized chip they gave everyone when TabiKat first started with the logo of a cat's paw on the top side, *'Stay Hungry, Stay Foolish'* by Steve Jobs on the other. It was her promise to those standing in the room she'd take TabiKat to the highest places it could go. She failed.

After two years of going nonstop, she found herself with nothing to do. Her days were back to being open blocks on her calendar. The silence of the apartment felt overwhelming. She could go for a walk. But at ten a.m. it was already ninety degrees and humid. The kids needed new clothes for the school year. Maybe her mother was in town, and they could get lunch. She could download the photos and work on an album. Maybe get a new photo for above the fireplace.

She turned on the business channel, two analysts discussing the latest market report and some company's less-than-projected earnings. Tabby sat at her desk and opened her laptop. Under all the junk and PTA updates for the twin's school, she did hate the PTA, waited a message from Mo Mo. *Just an FYI.* She clicked the email. "Thought you'd want to hear it from me. I hope you know I am sorry. Moe." Below was a draft press release for TabiKat— now Array—going public.

"It's expected to be the biggest release since Google," the male voice on the TV said. Tabby looked up. "For Macon to be in control of two tech companies is a sign Delany Clare wants to make a move into the tech space."

"Watch out Silicon Valley. Arlington, Virginia might become the new tech capital." The woman on the show laughed. Stock images of Delany flashed on the screen while the pundits talked including an image of Moe at an office Tabby didn't recognize. The screen changed to the timeline of events, the stock set to open at $123 a share.

"Array is set to release three projects, including two apps in the next year." The female reporter came back on the screen. "Their second app would enable employers to create digital backups of their employees' cell phones."

"That's my idea!" Tabby stood. "I thought of that. How in the…" Mo Mo! All her ideas, her work, her intellectual property stayed with TabiKat—which meant it now belonged to Delany Clare. In all the emotion and chaos off her departure, Tabby forgot about the projects she started before she left.

"You okay?" Alice asked from the doorway, Annie's laugh filling the apartment.

She turned the TV off and faced her little sister. "I hate Delany Clare and those lying jackals that kicked me out of my company." She walked past Alice, determined to think about anything else. She made the kids lunch and tried to forget the news. Alice called goodbye as she left for work, the front door closing. Tabby told the kids to keep their shoes on. Maybe if she focused on them, she could ignore the fact she felt stabbed in the back all over again.

#

CARVER SAT TALKING to some clients when Alice got to his bakery. She lifted her hand and went to find something sweet to eat. On the wall in Carver's office hung a calendar for the rest of the year, his bookings in blue, Hasty Pudding's in green. They were almost booked solid, mostly by businesses Delany owned. So far, he hadn't asked her to take any events tied to Array, a small consolation. In the chaos of things, Alice forgot about Tabby and how she might react. But her outburst brought back all the uncertainty Alice somehow managed to forget. How was she going to justify this to her sister?

Alice checked her email, the food truck was ready. The old girl got a facelift and new appliances. Carver thought they could use it for events, give them more of a home base and something else to drive their unique feel. She pulled up the images. The water blue paint and hibiscus were replaced with a pale-yellow base and the D.C. skyline mirrored on both sides with a hand-drawn serving of hasty pudding from above as the moon. A silhouette of Eleanor's statue stood beside the order window. In homage to its roots, they kept a grayed hibiscus over the back doors. Alice still went to K Street when they didn't have an event during lunch, taking a new trainee with her.

Carver came in, asking Alice about her night. She turned the monitor for him to see the redo on the truck. Carver whistled and sat on the edge of his desk.

"Looks good. Can you believe the last few weeks?"

"Doesn't feel real. We might break even this year." She crossed her arms and tilted her head. Carver laughed and set his hands beside him.

"We are going to do more than break even, Lil."

She looked at the food truck again and nodded a few times.

"Two separate worlds." He seemed to read her thoughts.

"How do I tell her?"

Carver sighed. "When the time comes, you'll know how."

Alice opened the door to the apartment, the twin's laughter filling the air. She found them in the living room playing video games. Taco saw her and barked, pulling their attention. Annie dropped her controller and ran to hug her. Mac paused the game and waited.

"Mom's in a mood," Annie whispered.

She had been avoiding her sister since they got back. If only Tabby would give her the chance to explain, to tell her why she took the deal. But with nothing else going on, Tabby was fixating, her anger growing. If Alice only mentioned the subsidiaries of Macon, Tabby might not connect that Delany owned most of her bookings. She hated lying, but needed to keep the peace until she could move home, her apartment booked until mid-September.

"Hey, Mac, want to make pizza for dinner?"

He left his controller and met her at the stove, wanting to recreate a pizza they had in France. Something about the crust, the simple flavors. Alice suspected a lot stemmed from the wood burning stove and local ingredients. While they worked, Mac asked how flavors blended, what gluten did, why she chose certain spices.

Paul came in as the pizza cooked in the oven, asking Alice about her day. It was the first time she'd seen him since the family got home. He was working some big case that when they left looked like it would settle, but now seemed headed for a trial. He couldn't say much about it.

After dinner, Mac went to play his console, Paul retreating to his bedroom to watch TV. Who knew what her sister was doing? Alice got a book to read. Annie sat close to her on the couch, sliding her notebook under her leg.

"What's going on?" Alice asked.

"I want to make a game."

"What kind of game?"

"A computer game. I was watching Mac play Zeds earlier..."

"You beat it already?" Alice smirked.

"Yeah, but don't tell him. And I was wondering, why can't there be a girl? Why is the princess just a person to come in later? Why couldn't she have this adventure?"

"What are you thinking?" Alice loved her niece's curiosity, her sense of what was possible.

Annie opened her notebook to a list of ideas, drawings for characters. "What do I do now?"

"Why not ask your mom? She's the coder."

Annie sighed. "She's not easy to talk to right now. Dad's working all the time."

It must feel like all the adults in their lives were too busy. Alice skimmed over what was there.

"I think we need a storyboard."

"A what?"

Alice took the notebook and drew a grid of six squares on the page. "In a film they do things shot by shot. Well, let's do the same with your game. How do you want the story to go?" She waited while Annie thought about it. Annie reached for the notebook and started to draw. Alice's cell phone rang. The 703 number wasn't in her contacts, but she got calls from a lot of people she didn't know. "Alice Gibson, Hasty Pudding."

"Alice, it's Bobbie Dunn. How are you?"

"How can I help you?" Alice scooted out from beside Annie and made her way to her bedroom, closing the door.

"I was hoping you were available for a party Friday night."

"To cater it?" She crossed her other arm across her chest and looked at her socked feet. "Mr. Dunn, not to sound rude, but I'm not…"

"It's my girl's birthday, and she loves your cooking."

Alice laughed. "Mr. Dunn, I am not…"

"Maybe you don't get how this works." The previous ease in his tone disappeared. "This isn't a request. The dinner is Friday at

6 p.m. I'm sure you know what Carrie likes. Katy will email you directions. Plan on twenty-five people, full course. Also bring some dandelion wine, Carrie said your dad makes it." He hung up. She sighed, not sure what he could want. Since starting she did her best to avoid interacting with him. The few events he attended for Macon, he seemed content to either look through her or dictate things. He hovered sometimes; his scowl set as if he sucked a lemon. Once he rebuked her at a board meeting for talking to a member of the board, but Alice knew the woman from a different Macon event. Delany encouraged Alice to be present, but to Bobbie she was to be unseen and not heard.

Alice was not a Macon employee and would not be at Mr. Dunn's beck and call. She had no desire to see Carrie. And Carrie meant Harry and probably Moe. The chance of her working with Delany undetected would decrease once the three of them knew. Only Carrie knew, and if she knew, surely the guys did.

With Delany out of the country until Saturday, she thought about calling Katy and asking for her advice, but knew what good friends Bobbie and Delany were. Keep it simple, beg Carver to go, make herself scarce. Hopefully Bobbie Dunn did not think Alice was there to be his private chef.

# CHAPTER 17

TABBY KNELT AND TOLD the twins to be good for her
friend taking them to the zoo. She waited for the front door to
close before she pulled herself off the floor. How long until they
were back in school? She went to the office ready to find a job.
Surely, she could parlay the success of WlkmNt into an interview.
After leading her own company, the idea of working under
someone sounded less than appealing, but she refused to stay at
home and wallow. The best way to show Delany Clare who ran her
company was to enable another one to compete with Array.

She wanted to study web design in college. One summer she
interned with a gaming company, and that was enough. The
costumes, the pathetic storylines, the lack of true representation.
Women were there as props for men to look at, possessions to
fuel their quests, or instruments for their sexual release. Her
mother taught the girls to stand tall, to take up space, to not accept
any man's BS. Tabby tried to push back, but then the harassment
got directed at her. Why did a woman having an opinion scare

men so much? She changed her major and studied communications. After graduation, she got a job doing marketing for a beef association, hating almost every day.

While she was pregnant, she and Paul decided that she would not go back to work. The cost of paying for daycare for two children would take almost her entire paycheck. They lived in The District then, this bleak two bedroom near Logan Circle. Once she got over her fears of trying to manage two infants in public, Tabby would put them in their stroller and walk the National Mall from The Capitol to The Lincoln Memorial and back again. She set up a collapsible playpen, getting the twins used to napping on a blanket. It taught her children to sleep anywhere.

That winter, Tabby was stuck inside with two kids in their terrible twos and a neighbor who banged on their ceiling all day. Her mother told her to hire a nanny and do something for herself. Tabby couldn't get over how pretentious that sounded. Instead, they reworked their budget and moved out of The District. Tabby started to teach herself HTML while the twins napped and at night. Her curiosity grew. Then the recession hit, and they prayed Paul would keep his job, government agencies taking a huge cut. Around that time, a friend needed a place to stay in D.C. and hated hotels. Alice had space and needed funding while she wallowed in her fears. Tabby put two and two together and TabiKat was born.

She stood and went to make another cup of tea. Two hours and she'd found three jobs that were beneath what she could do. She called her mother. Maryanne Gibson knew everyone worth knowing in the D.C. area, maybe she'd have a lead for her.


THEY MET AT HER MOTHER'S favorite hotel restaurant close to the White House. The Willard had been a D.C. staple for over 150 years. Inside featured tall marble columns, ornate ceilings, red drapes, and the best mimosa brunch in town. If someone wanted to reach her mother, the best first step would be suggesting they dine there. Maryanne was a sucker for their Bellinis and fromage tray. Regardless of where else Alice tried to tempt her to, their mother always went back to The Willard. Something about the low lighting, quiet alcoves, oversized furniture. It was Tabby's favorite place to spend an afternoon sipping cocktails.

"How goes the job search?" Her mother asked after they got their food. Tabby already told her all about their trip and how excited the kids were for school to start again.

Tabby shrugged and took a bite of her salad. "I was hoping maybe you could help me."

"Well, I don't know anyone who does IT, but I can ask around…"

"I don't do IT, Mom." They'd had this conversation before.

"You work on computers…"

"I write code for websites and apps on your phone."

Maryanne looked at her blankly. God bless her mother. Somehow the BlackBerry revolution went right past her, her father reminding her to check her email. They were still working on not getting her to send marathon texts. It was okay to abbreviate and not use proper grammar. No wonder her mother had no idea what Tabby did all day.

She reached for her water and told herself to calm down. "Not IT, Mom." Maybe this wasn't the best idea.

#

ALICE FOLLOWED CARVER onto the elevator at Bobbie's apartment. She thanked him again for coming as he pushed the button for the top floor.

"Not a big deal, Lil. The wife and kids are at my in-laws in Ohio for the week, and believe me, uninterrupted college football tomorrow sounds pretty great. Besides, we have that fundraiser on Sunday."

She could only nod. Her stomach twisted in knots, and she couldn't take anything but a shallow breath. Already she felt covered in sweat, and not from the heat and humidity.

The elevator opened to a rooftop deck. Bobbie's apartment at the crest of the hill above Georgetown provided a complete view of the city to RFK stadium and into Virginia and Maryland. Bobbie stood near a picnic table in light blue board shorts, a white polo, and gray thin jacket, with stark white tennies. He spoke with another man, who laughed. Bobbie smirked. He saw them and sauntered over, scowling.

"This is Carver Wright, my business partner."

Alice waited while the men shook hands.

"You can't manage twenty-five people by yourself?"

"Man, you'd pass up a view like this? Besides, this girl can't make a mixed drink to save her life." Carver winked at her and asked Bobbie where he wanted them to set up.

"Not a fan of the hard stuff?" Bobbie asked.

"I don't drink much," Alice said. "Where should we…"

"Don't drink?" He crossed his arms. "You religious, addicted, have a bad experience—what?"

Alice cocked her head. Did this arrogant ass expect people to be honest with his question dripped in judgment? She bit her tongue; Bobbie held a lot of sway with Delany.

"Where do we set up?" Carver asked again. Bobbie led the way, Alice pushing the insulated pan cart behind them. A grill sat in the corner, close to a small hut for them to work out of. Alice left Carver to unpack and went to get the rest of their stuff from the van in the alley. She lowered her head in the elevator. Just before the doors closed, a hand came between them, Bobbie getting on with her.

"I'm glad this worked out," he said as they rode down.

"Uh-huh." She tried to keep her tone neutral.

"Bulldog raves about your food, barely get him to talk about anything else."

"I'm sure you and Mr. Clare have plenty of other things to discuss."

"Still, be nice to see the new acquisition in action." Bobbie waited for her to get off the elevator first. Alice walked to the van, Bobbie staying with her. "I asked Katy to see the details, want to be sure Bulldog didn't give away the store. I mean if Delany wanted to take on a catering company there are others that are more established than yours."

"Did you come down for something?" Surely this wasn't all a veiled attempt to find out what she and Delany agreed to. So far, he seemed content to treat her as a vendor and recommend her to his network. Part of her wondered when the request was coming. He could not be doing all of this out of goodwill or because he loved her street tacos that much.

"Carver mentioned it might be a lot to carry. I'm here to help." He smiled wide. Alice did a once-over on him before she started unloading the van, able to feel Bobbie scrutinizing her form. She wore a looser tunic with muted flowers imprinted on it and black cropped leggings, not wanting to give Bobbie the wrong idea. She was not here for him to flirt with or make passes at. Isn't that why he had Carrie?

"I am going to park the van. If you can take this last load up." She finished loading the dolly.

"Don't think you have a shot with Bulldog." Bobbie said when she finished. Alice started to respond, but he talked over her. "You're the caterer. He's not here for you to get rich from. Don't forget—I'm watching." Bobbie said he'd see her at the top and walked away with the food. Alice got into the van and found a place not that far away to park. She took the back entrance and prayed for rain.

Carver was mostly set up when Alice got back, Bobbie talking to a smaller group of people. Harry's laugh filled the air. *Great.* Carrie came onto the roof with a few of her girlfriends. The patio filled with people, most of whom Alice had never met, Carrie's life since she left D.C. a mystery.

Alice was sixteen when Tabby bought her best friend from USC home for the summer. Two clichéd sorority girls: tanned, ideal form, perfect and beautiful. Tabby took Carrie to parties with children of senators and interns on The Hill. After Carrie graduated, she lived with the family until she got her footing. Alice went to her first wedding to a lawyer, the guy totally vanilla. Alice didn't know how he snagged Carrie in a city of more powerful men. They barely made it two years before Carrie left him for a surrealist artist whose 3D installations took the art world by storm. Alice lost track of her as they traveled the world, living the high life. By then she was working with Cornelia and lived in that basement apartment outside Georgetown she loved. Tabby gave her updates sometimes, but Alice always felt Carrie looked through her, humoring her as Tabby's naïve little sister.

"You're a sight for sore eyes." Harry came to the hut between courses.

"Do you need another drink?"

"Come on, Lil." He tilted his head. Alice took a deep breath. "What happened with your sister wasn't ideal, but we can still be friends."

"Who's the girl?" She motioned toward the stunning brunette talking to Carrie.

"Some friend of Carrie's. We should get dinner sometime."

Alice put her hand on the counter and leaned into it. "And what would we talk about?"

He came around the opening of the hut, Alice leaning on the counter. He put his arms around her.

"Right conditions…we wouldn't have to talk at all."

She felt his body heat, able to see his brown eyes through his sunglasses. His arm went around her back, Harry lining up for a kiss.

She laughed. "Do women fall for this?" She pushed back on his chest. "Still not interested."

He let her go. "One meal. Let me show you I'm not who you think."

She laughed. "You are exactly what I think. What did I tell you the last time we talked?" She crossed her arms and waited. Harry shook his head and looked at the horizon.

"What would you have me do now?" he asked.

"Care about someone else. Give your time and talents to something that matters. You are the sole heir to millions. Go play charity golf or build houses for those who can't afford them."

"I tried investing in a startup company of a woman who wants to change the world."

Alice groaned and shook her head. He just did not give up.

"Funny, you blow me off and yet take Delany Clare's money." He scowled. "I thought your morals wouldn't let you get into bed with the guy who screwed your sister. Or am I missing something?"

The air went out of her chest, all of Alice's arrogance gone. She leaned on the counter, having nothing to say in her defense.

"You're just like your sister," Harry added.

"I am nothing like Tabby." Alice told herself to calm down.

"No, you are. Judgmental. Self-righteous. Think you have it all figured out. How would Tabby react knowing you're working with Delany Clare? Are you all that different from me?"

"Can I get a bottle of white?" Carver asked. Alice leaned off the counter and moved to grab the wine. Carver uncorked the bottle and took it to the table. Harry went back to his place. Bobbie took a sip of his wine, looking between Alice and Harry.

# CHAPTER 18

HALF A DOZEN FOOD TRUCKS lined The Community Center's parking lot. Picnic tables and pop-up tents selling cotton candy and drinks filled the massive lawn. People filled the bleachers around the basketball courts. This was Delany's favorite day: the finals of a bracketed tournament with youth teams from all over the D.C. area. They held qualifying events at local high school gyms for the last few weeks, the final eight making it to today where they'd play with college and professional recruiters in the stands. For some of these boys, this was their chance.

Eddie found him and said hello. Eddie Hart ran Delany's nonprofit that worked to get food on the ground after a natural disaster. Comida worked in any kitchen available to start bringing meals (or comida) to people who lost everything. Delany got the idea while watching a hurricane devastate the Virgin Islands. His mother sat immobile as she watched the TV and wept. Delany used his connections to go help. While there, he talked to people who all complained about the inadequate food they received.

He met Eddie in 2000 at an NSO event. At the time Eddie did logistics for the Army. He told Delany what he wanted to do might be possible if they could get the supplies in before the storm. Then 9/11 happened, and Eddie got sent to Iraq. He lost his left leg in a bomb blast in 2005. Delany saw Eddie again and asked if he wanted to go on the next Comida trip with him. They ended up in Florida after a hurricane, Eddie in his element. Delany asked him to join Comida full-time. Eddie led their efforts all over the world, bringing good meals to people after the worst moments of their lives.

Delany walked with him toward Alice's food truck. The slight Caribbean vibe gone, the truck now reflecting her heart and how much she loved D.C., *Hasty Pudding* across the top. She was starting to take herself seriously. Today she served the street food that was slowly building her reputation. Carver sold his famous cakes and tarts in his van next to her.

But a younger woman was working Alice's window, and she wasn't at Carver's van either. He let Eddie order first and then went to the back doors of the truck where Alice worked at the grill in a red short jumpsuit, long orange apron, a wide blue wrap over her hair. Ne-Yo played on the radio, Alice singing along and bopping as she cooked. He laughed to himself, something simple and honest in the moment.

"You look good," Delany said. Alice jumped. She smiled at him, wiping her hands on her apron and handing two boxes of food to the woman working the front.

"How was the trip?"

"My daughter does not like nature that much after all." He crossed his arms loosely and looked at Eddie. "I took Helene to the Galápagos. She loved the water and some of the animals, but the bugs got to her. By the third day, she refused to go anywhere without my sun shirt. I tried to tell her to get one before, but she told me she wanted to get sun kissed. Now I'm burned."

Alice handed another box to the woman. "Is this your order of tacos?" She slipped some pork onto the grill.

"Why do you think that?" He smiled.

Alice shook her head. "The Valencia special. I can't guarantee it will be as good now."

"I trust your judgment." He talked to Eddie until Alice handed him their meals.

"So does this mean you need me to start dropping off meals again?" As part of their arrangement, Alice cooked meals for him over the week. He had someone who coordinated with the nutritionist on the team before he retired, so it wasn't anything new. Delany realized his daughter needed to be getting well-balanced meals somewhere.

"If you don't mind."

He found a place to sit with Eddie, who stopped talking and closed his eyes.

"That's heavenly," he said with the bite still in his mouth. "It just melts." He groaned. "Damn, that's good."

"Don't let Morse hear you say that." Delany took a bite, unsure how she did it. It was cumin and garlic, onion and citrus—maybe. Yet when she put it together the flavor came in waves. The meat melted on his tongue; the tortilla freshly made. Maybe she could make some of the food he liked in Ecuador.

"Might get him to step up his game." Eddie took another bite. "We need to pray for a slow rest of the season. Morse asked for some time, his wife got diagnosed with breast cancer. His attention was really divided."

Morse was the lead chef they took on the trips to coordinate the meals, a truly vital piece to what Comida strived to accomplish.

"Maybe the hurricanes are done for the year." Delany took another bite. Not what Valencia made, but close.

They finished their meals, Eddie walking back to his car. The announcer came on the speakers—the tournament would start in ten minutes. Things would be quieter then; he could ask Alice about the last few weeks. Only, he loved watching the guys play. It reminded him of when the game was fun, and he could just play with his friends after school. He sat with some of the recruiters as the first game started, Delany forgetting everything but what was happening on the court.

He congratulated the winners. The next teams coming out to play. Delany threw the ball for the tipoff and then went to stand beside the bleachers.

"So when do the girls get to play?" Alice asked behind him. Delany turned. Her hand rested on the railing, her apron gone, the blue wrap still in her hair. He reached to get a fleck of cilantro off her cheek. She thanked him and reached for it. Delany ran his fingers across her palm and between her fingers, hooking them together.

She pulled her hand back and cleared her throat before repeating her question.

"What do you mean?" He faced her. Even after working for hours in a hot truck, she was gorgeous. He'd thought about her a lot on the trip, wondered how things were going or what she was doing. It would have been inappropriate to call her. Alice made it clear from the start this was a business arrangement. Still, her pale green eyes drew him in. The muted pink lipstick he hadn't noticed before showed off her full lips.

"Well, you're doing all this work for the boys to get noticed, when do the girls get their shot?" she asked.

Delany looked over his shoulder. "Oh!"

"You own the Mystics, right? I'm sure some of them would appreciate the representation."

"I never thought…"

"Hard to know the score if you don't watch the game." Bobbie's hands were on his shoulders as he shook him, Alice taking a noticeable step back.

"Why are you here?" Delany shrugged him off and glanced at Alice as she walked back to her truck.

"You know how I love these charity events."

"You avoid them at all costs."

"It's our neighborhood, Bulldog." Bobbie hit him in the chest. "I realized maybe it's time I took more of an interest in our philanthropic endeavors. Make sure you're not giving away the store."

"Keep your head on acquisitions. I don't need you checking up on me."

Delany glanced toward Alice's truck, Bobbie following his gaze.

"Bulldog, don't trust the caterer. She's just after your money."

"Alice Gibson is not after my money." His heart sped up, his skin tingling.

"I'd be on my best behavior too if that much dough was making eyes at me. You can't trust outsiders." He crossed his arms.

"I'll keep that in mind." Delany turned to go back to the game.

"She's dating Harry Clarks."

"From TabiKat?" That didn't seem possible given her level of hesitation working with him. He could not see Alice dating the man who sold out her sister, plus she never mentioned Harry. Not that he'd guess that was her type.

"They were both at Carrie's birthday on Friday, basically making out in the cookout area. She's not who you think."

"Go home, Bobbie. We all know you hate where you came from." He turned to leave.

"This is why I told you to let me handle things." Bobbie's tone changed from playful to incensed.

"What?" He faced Bobbie again.

"I don't get why you hired me to run Macon if you were going to come in and step on my toes. Why don't you trust me anymore?"

Delany took a deep breath, Bobbie was having a harder time adjusting than Delany thought he would.

"I didn't hire you to run Macon. I hired you to identify acquisitions."

"I've run that company for the last two years."

"While I was still playing." He got closer, not needing there to be a scene. He relied on Bobbie more before he retired, and maybe a few lines got blurred. Bobbie lacked the people skills to lead a team, so Delany put him where he could flourish—finding companies and helping Macon grow. For some reason, that wasn't enough. It couldn't be the money, Bobbie made mid-six figures.

"Why are you shutting me out?" Bobbie asked.

"How am I—?"

"You're never in the office and yet took my power to run things. I never know where you are. You're taking meetings without me." Bobbie huffed. "I didn't need you to babysit me at the TabiKat acquisition."

"How did I babysit you?" Delany crossed his arms.

Bobbie stood taller. "Coming in at the eleventh hour to close the sale. I find companies and bring them on board and you..."

"I—what, Bobbie? Tell me what I am allowed to do at my own damn company."

"You haven't been there until now." His body was tense.

"You're right. I've been the silent head of Macon since we started. But I'm here now, so get used to my being at the acquisition meetings and reading over contracts and being more present because Macon is my company. You work for *me*, remember?"

A cheer erupted from the stands, Delany looking over his shoulder. This wasn't the place for this conversation. Bobbie said something under his breath and stalked away. Delany went to watch the game. He could get why being relegated down the hall, as Bobbie said, felt like a shift. But his best friend needed to realize he was another VP and get back in his lane. He was not the face, decision-maker, or brains behind Macon.

Most of the food trucks were gone when Delany checked before the championship game. He watched from beside the bleachers as Alice took a series of pans from her truck and put them in Carver's van, wanting to know what changed when Bobby came up. He'd seen Alice interact with dozens of people at the events and she'd never been so skittish. Katy told him Bobbie started sniffing around for a contract, asking if Macon planned to acquire Hasty Pudding. That man would not understand an altruistic action if his life depended on it. Delany had no desire to acquire Alice's company. This was trying to help someone get their dream off the ground. Besides, he did love her food.

His phone went off, Nadia inviting him to a movie night. *'Little Boo is asking for you.'* Not wanting to go back to his empty apartment, he made the drive to Baltimore. Nadia let him in, her T-shirt loose and low-cut, running shorts tight to her frame.

"Where's Helene?"

"She crashed. I thought we could hang out; you could tell me about your trip. I got some Hennessy." His favorite. She hated it. "You trusted me once, remember? I haven't always been the enemy."

He sighed and went to sit on the sofa in the backroom. She came back a minute later with two drinks, setting the bottle on the table. She asked about their time, seemed interested in what happened. Most times she found his forays around the world, as she called them, boring. She didn't get why he chose to go to smaller hotels and off-the-grid locations when luxury hotels waited with people ready to take care of his every whim. Sitting on the beach drinking mai tais sounded like a form of torture to him. She kept offering to book a family vacation, convinced she could help him appreciate the perks of being rich.

She refilled his drink before turning her body into his, her arm resting on the back of the couch.

"When's the last time you got any stress out?" She held his gaze, her fingers reaching for the buttons of his shirt.

"I thought you wanted to hear about the trip." He smirked. "Nod." It's what he called her since high school. Her hand lingered after she got his shirt undone.

"Come on, Bulldog. We had fun once. Kept each other company."

"In high school."

"First love." She moved to sit on his lap, her knees beside his hips. "All those other women leave, but I'm still here and don't ask anything from you. You think some bimbo Bobbie finds will get where you came from?"

She did have a point. But this was playing with fire. He was exhausted from the trip, wanting to sleep. There was a mountain of things he needed to do before work in the morning. His first day back was always chaotic.

"I should go."

"Three glasses of Hennessy, you're not fit to drive."

Her hand slid over him as she kissed his neck. It did feel good. He sat up more and looked at her. She waited for him to lean in and kiss her before she wrapped her arms around his neck, grinding against him.

They had sex every place they could in high school. His mother told him to be careful, unwanted kids could derail everything. He took the lesson to heart, had always been careful. Nadia knew how to turn heads. He asked why no one in her life seemed to stay. She bemoaned how men refused to step up. Who besides him was worthy of her little girl?

She laid back on the couch. Delany moved over her, his hand sliding under her shirt. At their age, it was a nice release sometimes. It didn't mean anything; they both knew it. Someday, one of them would meet someone.

"Mommy!" Helene called down from the stairs. "I can't sleep."

"I told you to go to bed!" Nadia shouted back.

"I'm not tired."

"I thought she crashed," Delany whispered.

"This girl's sleep cycle is all off thanks to your little trip. Helene Goin, go to sleep!" She watched the entryway, both of them waiting. Delany looked at what was happening, pulling back. They'd only slept together a handful of times since Helene was born. Nadia always seemed to call right after a breakup, a solid reminder of why he shouldn't trust outsiders. Women all pretended to be okay with Helene and Nadia's place in his life, but something always came up and they left.

"I'm going to go." He stood, Nadia shifting to the couch.

"Come back, Boo." She waved her fingers in his direction. "I can do what you love."

"I'm good." He crept to the front door, casting one last look toward Helene's room, unsure why he ever agreed to come up that late.

# CHAPTER 19

THE ALARM WENT OFF far too early the next morning, Alice praying for five more minutes. Her body ached from being on her feet all the time. Her hands were calloused and dry. If she never did another dish as long as she lived... Carver was right—they didn't need to stay at the event until the end, but Alice got lost in watching the guys play. Something about the joy of the moment, the community.

Delany's hand in hers made her knees weak. He rarely touched her, minus the occasional hand on her back when he introduced her or touching her arm to point something out. Every time her heart raced, and she could barely think. She missed him while he was gone, thinking of a dozen things she wanted to tell him. They talked sometimes while she cooked at his place, Alice loving his opinion and view of the world. She told herself to be okay being just his friend. Only they weren't friends—she was an employee, a vendor. She had to keep things casual.

For the first time since before Cornelia died, Alice enjoyed what she was doing. She never thought she would like a food truck, always saw catering as a second-class choice. Something about the lack of snobbery, the community, the variety she loved. What if she didn't need her own brick-and-mortar restaurant to be happy?

While the water heated for her shower, she picked up after the twins, putting the toothpaste cap back on, collecting the dirty clothes into the laundry bin, and rehanging the towels. It was good to not be alone, even if she rarely saw the family anymore.

Tabby called hello as Alice walked into the kitchen. Annie slid out of her chair, coming to hug Alice good morning.

"Come with us to the zoo."

"I can't, sweetheart. I have to work."

Tabby told Annie to finish her breakfast. Alice glanced through the open paper on the counter, stopping on the update on the Old Post Office renovation. The developer planned to turn it into The Cora, a five-star hotel and apartment space. It would be a complete interior renovation while retaining the distinct charm of the D.C. landmark. The flagship restaurant was rumored to be a restaurant by Jonas.

She read the line again. Jonas was getting a restaurant in her building! The building she'd set her sights on as the pinnacle of her career. The one place in D.C. she wanted to go. Her blood felt like it was on fire; the hair on her arms bristled. She read the line again to be sure.

Tabby said her name, and Alice looked up.

"What's wrong?" Tabby asked. Alice studied the photo. The chances of someone buying the building and not tearing it down were slim and she would probably never get a restaurant there. But Jonas! Didn't anyone care he had no idea what he was doing? His food tasted like it came out of an easy-bake oven. How did he keep getting everything she wanted?

"Nothing." Alice closed the paper, ready to move on. Tabby told the twins to go brush their teeth, Alice kneeling to intercept Annie.

"I'm sorry I'm working so much."

"I never see you. I'm starting school next week. I want to hang out."

Alice's heart hurt. "I will be here tomorrow night, okay?" She hugged her niece and watched her walk away, taking a moment before she stood.

"What time did you get home last night?" Tabby asked from the sink.

"One. The event went later than I thought. I didn't wake you, did I?"

"No, I was up. Not sleeping much anymore."

Alice heard her sister's steps in the hallway, the TV on in the living room.

"Why aren't you sleeping?"

Tabby sighed. "What do I do now, Lil? Paul tells me to dream big, but all I can see is another version of TabiKat…"

"And the intellectual property…"

"It's gone. Whatever I created for the company stays with the company. I might not have been so forthcoming with my ideas if I'd known."

"You couldn't have seen this coming." She watched her. "Have you heard from anyone?"

"Carrie messaged me. I told her to go screw herself. I've blocked all of them on social media. What could they possibly say that I'd care to hear?"

Alice hugged Tabby from the side. Her sister put her hand over her arms.

"Can you watch the kids Thursday? It's back to school night. If you say no, maybe I can send Paul by himself."

"I will be here. I need to see them."

Paul came out of the bedroom, asking if Alice was ready to go. She went to get her messenger bag. They listened to sports radio on the way in. Alice studied the river, thinking about The Cora. It was a building for goodness' sake. Probably whatever developer bought it was going to turn it into a gaudy monstrosity she would never want to set foot in. That building needed to be cared for. Appreciated. There was so much history to it. The inside needed a lot of work, but the heart of that place was gold. Was. Because after Jonas got through putting in his poor excuse for a restaurant, nothing good could come out of it. No one with any taste Alice could respect would let Jonas into that space.

Cornelia told her she'd be an executive chef someday, promised to buy her first embroidered coat. But what if he'd been the one who couldn't see what was real? What if what was around her—a cute food truck and catering company tied to one person's generosity—was all she was going to get? The happiness she thought she found washed away under the reality of how far she stood from what she wanted.

\#

DELANY STEPPED INTO CARVER'S BAKERY, filled with people enjoying a late lunch. He called Carver about an idea after he got to work Monday and Katy handed him his mail from while he'd been gone. Carver told him to come by the bakery. Not seeing him, Delany asked for Alice who came out of the kitchen a moment later.

"He's on a call. Can I get you a coffee or…"

"I can wait with you." He held back his smile. She led him into the kitchen. People in white coats or aprons worked on cakes and other desserts, some pulled food from the ovens, others worked at a stove. She stopped at a gray table in the center with two younger chefs on the other side.

"So?" She crossed her arms. They looked at each other. "There's no wrong answer here. Which one do you prefer?"

Two mini pizzas sat on the table, one topped with a lavender, the other an orange flower he didn't know. The first chef glanced at the other, as if waiting for them to speak.

"Delany." Alice faced him. "Which do you prefer?"

The second chef cut him a thin slice of each. The first was salmon and rosemary, the lavender subtler than he expected. The second had a pesto base with tomatoes and a white cheese.

"What's the flower?" he asked.

"Nasturtiums. So?" She tilted her head. It was a side of her he'd never seen, a peek behind the culinary curtain. It was a bit intimidating to be asked his opinion and he wasn't expected to know tastes and flavors like the young kids next to him.

"I would never have thought of putting lavender on a pizza, but it's nice once you get it."

"Do you think people will leave the flower on?" the first chef asked. The second lowered his gaze.

"They might not if it's not a group that knows to trust your tastes." He caught Alice's gaze, who blushed.

"Fine!" Alice threw up her hands playfully. "We can chop up some of the lavender and make people wonder what it is. It's okay to state your opinion. I ask because I want to know."

Carver came out of the office, asking Delany how he was. Delany reached for the rest of the lavender pizza and followed Carver into his office. He came to ask Carver about speaking at a luncheon at Howard later in the month for an incubator program trying to raise funds to invest in minority-owned businesses. Macon donated three million in seed money to get the fund going. He hoped Carver would come speak about his experience as a business owner.

Alice came in with a stack of checks she needed Carver's signature on. He started to sign, Alice asking what Delany wanted.

He repeated his request. She sat on the edge of the desk. Her purple apron protected her dark slacks from the mess of flour and other ingredients on the front. He loved the wrap in her hair the more times he saw it. This was her element, her court, where she did what she loved. He always loved practice more than the games when it was just the guys. Maybe she preferred days like this to events. It's where she could play and do what she loved.

"Do they need a caterer?" she asked.

"Unfortunately, I think they already hired someone else."

"Yeah, well their loss." Alice took the signed checks and walked out. When he looked back, Carver smirked. Busted.

"I'll send you the details." Delany slipped out of the chair. Alice folded checks at a thinner table between the office and what appeared to be a pantry.

"You're coming over later, right?" he asked.

She nodded. "I need to make a stop first."

"Can I tag along?" He told Katy he would be working at home the rest of the afternoon, wanting to be there when Alice came over.

"Sure." She reached for her apron, leaning in the office to tell Carver she was leaving.

"Have fun, you two."

"Don't start with me. Ready?" The blue T-shirt hit her frame just right. She pulled her messenger bag over it, directing him toward the back door.

"What were you doing back there?" He asked as they walked toward The Mall.

"The tasting? I want to help our staff understand flavors better and be willing to risk new things. We did these test meals when I worked for Cornelia where we'd present our ideas and get critiqued. It lets us play and try new things. It also taught us how to give and receive feedback. A lot of chefs have their R&D teams but don't realize a lot of ideas exist in the heads of their lower-level chefs. I would rather have a chef try and fail then keep their ideas to themselves because of some instilled hierarchy."

Katy texted to ask if she could bring over a box of merch a company Macon owned in Chicago needed signed for a fundraiser. Delany told her no problem and moved to catch up with Alice, who was already crossing the street.

"Everything okay?"

He glanced at her. "Work stuff."

"You didn't have to come with me, Delany." She touched his arm to indicate they were going left.

"I wanted to. It's good to get out of the office. I'm still not used to four walls and meetings all day."

"Do you miss it?"

They paused at the red light, Delany taking a second.

"Yes and no. When I tore my ACL last fall, I really thought I'd come back. I'd done it before, knew the drill. Then I got into rehab and started to question what I was doing. I took Helene to Europe for Christmas and ate anything I wanted." He smiled when Alice laughed. "I drank whatever and slept in and thought, 'Why am I doing this again?' I guess that's how I knew it was time. I miss the game. I don't miss the schedule and the workouts and being away from my little girl all the time."

"She matters a lot to you." They crossed the street.

"She's the most important thing I'll ever do."

"We're here." She stopped outside an apartment building near the National Archives. She went inside, the guard greeting her by name. Delany followed her into the elevator. Alice pushed the button for the top floor.

"This your place?" Delany asked. Alice set her hands on the back of her hips and watched the numbers.

"My apartment is on the 7th floor. I need to check on my dad's garden, make sure it's okay."

Bobbie texted asking where he was. They had been avoiding

each other all week. He didn't know what else to say, Bobbie's job was what it was. He sensed Bobbie's mood wasn't about the shift of things at Macon. Better to let him sulk for a few days.

At least Bobbie didn't know he was with Alice. Any mention of her name sent him over the edge. Bobbie kept saying Delany didn't need to go to pre-meetings for events. The CEO's admins could easily work out a menu with the caterer. That's what he called Alice: *the caterer.* Delany asked what his issue was, but Bobbie kept saying Alice was trying to get with him. If only that were true.

The elevator opened to a rooftop terrace with a few older outdoor tables and a grill. He followed her around the corner, a massive greenhouse taking up much of the back side. The glass panels were down, a myriad of tomato plants, peppers, and leaves of various plants filling the space.

"Your dad planted this?"

"Yeah, we do it together every spring. When my parents moved in, he convinced the HOA to let him build one. He checks it when he's in town, but they're in Toronto for the week so he asked if I could come by." She handed him the collection of vegetables and motioned to the crate by the door. "Can you get the peas?" She pointed him to the multiple vines growing up both sides of a lattice in the center.

"What do you do with all this?"

"Take it to Tabby's house sometimes, or my dad's old admin from his other work loves fresh veggies."

"What's your dad's other work?" He collected peas off the vine.

"He works to preserve natural spaces around D.C. Right now, it's the Anacostia River. He realized those who live there are isolated from the food resources they need. A lot of lower income families can't eat as healthy as they should, either because there's no access to supermarkets in the area, or their budget doesn't allow it. He's big into foraging and helping people recognize the food around them. He works to plant community gardens and get people eating what they can grow."

Delany knew that reality. Too many meals of mac and cheese and ramen noodles growing up. Powdered milk because of how much he consumed. His mother called it a food apartheid, restricted access to grocery stores and healthier foods in lower income areas.

"People think you need all this space to grow food." Alice went on from across the greenhouse as she worked. "But you can do it on a balcony or a small patio area if you know what to do. My dad believes food should be accessible." She appeared beside him and handed him a cherry tomato.

"That's good. Juicier than what you get at the store."

"That's what happens when you eat it off the vine and it's not mass-produced and shipped halfway across the country. If people learned to eat with the seasons, we'd all be better off."

"You're really passionate about this."

She shrugged and walked past him to the crate of food. He collected the peas and added them.

"If I had my way, Hasty Pudding would only use locally grown ingredients. We try to partner locally as much as we can, go with minority-owned farms." She grabbed the crate. Delany took it from her while she closed the greenhouse. They got off the elevator, Alice reaching for her phone. "Hey, Tabby." She scrunched her nose. "Mom and Dad are coming? Okay, well, I have work tonight....I get that, but my job isn't 9 to 5." She rolled her eyes. "Really, Tabby? I'm going now." She hung up her phone. "Sorry."

"Everything okay?"

"My sister. She can be unreasonable, shall we say, when she's mad. Like, I get it, I do. I just—how long can she carry this torch?" Alice shook her head. He put his hand on the front door but didn't open it.

"I never meant…"

She put both her hands around his arm, seeming to force a smile.

"I don't want to talk about my sister or TabiKat or work, okay?"

"Deal." He took his hand off the door to shake her hand. She chuckled. They started to walk to his apartment. Turned out, they lived less than a mile apart.

"Having you cook for Helene and me has been a game changer, Alice, really." He said when they got onto his elevator.

"Yeah, your cupboards are a bit pathetic. How do you not know how to cook?"

"My mom cooked growing up. I had the athlete cafeteria at UMD. Then, I don't know, between going to my mom's and my sister and the chef I used to have, I never learned."

"Well, if you keep showing up when I'm here, at least we'll get you to know the basics."

Alice opened the door with the key he gave her. She held it for him before going to the panel of windows.

"I love your view."

"Isn't your place this good?" He set the crate in the kitchen before going to stand beside her.

"I look over the FBI building toward the White House. That is not this."

He studied her, smiling to himself. She saw wonder in the world, beauty. Helene was like that, everything on the Galápagos new to her. It helped him see the world differently. Helene lived in possibility and wonder. Alice did too with her flavors and the way she interacted with others.

"What?" She studied him.

He shook his head. "How can I help?"

"Well, we're going to make a pot pie." She tilted her head. "Do you know how to turn on the oven?"

He pushed her shoulder slightly and walked to the kitchen. Alice opened the drawers, gathering what she needed.

"I still can't believe you trust me in your apartment alone."

He trusted her with everything he had. He leaned his hip into the island close to her, lightly crossing his arms. "I have no secrets from you."

She looked at him with those intoxicating green eyes. He shifted closer and Alice backed against the counter, his hands running along the granite as he leaned in only wanting to kiss her pale lips. She lifted her face towards his and closed her eyes.

"Delany?" Katy's voice rang out. Alice scooted away from him, going to the pantry. Katy came into the kitchen. "Hey, boss, I have that box for you. How are you, Alice?"

"Uh-huh," she said from the pantry. Katy scowled and looked at Delany, who couldn't quite find a way to be casual. A playful smile filled her face, Delany glaring slightly.

"You should stay for dinner." Alice came back with some flour and spices.

"I came by to drop off that merch I need signed. I'm hoping to get it out by the weekend."

"Of course. Stay, the more the merrier. Do you want red or white wine?" he asked Alice.

"Have you had the zinfandel from the vineyard Delany owns?" Katy set her purse on a chair and went toward the wine fridge in the corner. Alice glanced his way before turning back toward the counter. "What is all of this?" Katy came back with the wine. Delany reached to get glasses from the cabinet.

"It's from my dad's greenhouse. We went there before this." Alice started to pull veggies from the crate. Katy smiled at Delany and raised her eyebrows.

"I can fire you," he whispered.

"Oh, but you won't." Katy fished the corkscrew out of the drawer.

"Can you chop those?" Alice motioned toward the stack of vegetables beside his sink. Delany opened his mouth to make an excuse. Alice leaned on the edge of the counter and crossed her arms.

"Please tell me you know how to dice vegetables, Mr. Clare."

Katy snickered; oh, she was enjoying this. Not wanting to let her down, Delany went to try. Katy put a glass near Alice then him. Delany kept himself from drinking half or, better yet, reaching for the bottle.

"Can I go look in the second bedroom for some stuff for your office?" Katy asked.

"You're actually going to ask?" Delany tried to keep his tone light. Katy glared and took her glass of wine to the bedroom.

"What's going on?" Alice asked.

"She wants to decorate my office. Calls it bare and ridiculous. I don't care about it, but she says it would be a good idea."

"I see." She went back to her dough. A moment later the oven door opened, Alice sliding something inside. Katy called his name, Delany going to see what she wanted.

"Is it okay if I take this?" Two boxes held a collection of game balls and trophies, some mementos from his work with Comida. "Just tell me yes and I will get out of your hair."

"It's fine." He glanced over his shoulder. "Take whatever. It doesn't matter to me."

"Says the guy with three gold medals!" She put a lid on the second box and stood. Delany scowled; Katy never cared about his career before. "People care about this stuff, use it to your advantage." She picked up the box. "So, you and Alice."

"Don't go starting anything."

She opened her mouth, taking a moment. "Delany, I value your privacy, you know that. It's nice to know why you're suddenly working at home twice a week."

She went to tell Alice she was leaving.

"You can stay," Alice said. Delany set the second box on the counter beside Katy.

"I have a mountain of things to do. Can you bring that box into work tomorrow?"

"What if I bring both of these and the merch you need me to sign. Not that I don't trust the Metro."

"No, I get it. Have a good night, Alice."

"Bye," Alice said hesitantly before turning back to the pan on the stove. Delany reached for his wine.

"What are you doing now?" He leaned on the counter close to her, Alice unable to hold his gaze.

"Getting the vegetables soft. I'm going to teach you to make a roux." She motioned for him to take her place before setting an open bag of flour beside him.

"I don't want to mess it up."

"That's why I'm here. Up to half a cup of flour and coat the veggies well." He did as she said. She gave him a box of chicken stock to pour in slowly. Alice found her glass of wine, taking small sips. The timer went off. Delany backed up, Alice pulling a pie dish with dried beans in the center. She lifted the bowl made from butcher paper, a golden pie crust underneath.

"It's called blind baking. It keeps the bottom from getting soggy. Do you mind grabbing the pan?" She handed him an oven mitt. He poured the thickened mix in. She covered the pie and pinched it closed before adding three slices in the top and covering it in beaten egg. He slid the pie back into the oven.

"Now we wait."

"Grab your wine." He refilled his and led her to the guest room. They avoided the boxes Katy just went through. He opened the door to the side balcony. She stepped out, taking in the view of Chinatown. He started to point out the Old Post Office Pavilion, wanting to tell her about his plans to renovate it.

"How did you find this place?" she asked.

He leaned onto the railing next to her. "Luck. I wanted to be near the arena. As I got older and started making more, I could afford to move up. I told the owner if this place ever came open to call me. I love it. Thanks for the cooking lesson."

"Not as though you did much." She scowled. He laughed. Her face got serious. "Can I ask you something, what do you see coming from all this? I mean—we've never talked about what you expect to get out of this. I need to know you're not going to push me out or…"

"Do what I did to Tabby?"

Alice dropped her gaze. He sighed, still not understanding how Bobbie read the situation so wrong.

"I never meant to hurt your sister. I thought she knew." He paused. "I don't want your company. I'm not asking for shares. And I won't take what you're building here."

"So why help me? Why do any of this?"

The answer must not be as transparent as he feared.

"Because this is what you want to do. It's your thing, Alice. It's what you love. If I can book some events with you and tell my friends what an amazing woman you are—what do I have to lose?" He realized what he said. "Chef. You're an amazing chef."

"This is more than a couple events, Delany."

He wanted to lean down and kiss her. To be this close and yet know nothing could happen. He never desired to just be with someone else. He wanted her opinion on things and loved how she interacted with Helene. If she'd trust him with whatever happened to make her so guarded and cynical, he'd never give her a reason to doubt him. Realizing he had to say something he told himself to focus on what they were discussing.

"I don't see you as my employee, Alice. You can stop taking my events at any time and that's okay. This is me helping a friend."

She nodded and smiled hesitantly, looking at the view. He made himself face forward, taking a longer sip of his wine. A friend. What if that was all she ever was to him?

# CHAPTER 20

TABBY WALKED THROUGH the halls of the twins' school wishing they put her kids in the same classroom. She'd lost Rock-Paper-Scissors to Paul who got to go to Mac's classroom with the fun teacher who was young and loved to snowboard and would integrate pop culture into his lesson plans. Annie, and thereby Tabby, got stuck with Mrs. Prim and Proper. She was probably older than the school. Never smiled. Kids had it too easy, she said once at a PTA meeting; it was her job to make sure they took their education seriously. Not that Tabby minded. Annie needed to be challenged, and Mrs. Proper would do that.

She skimmed the pathetic collection of snacks in the back of the room. For what they paid in tuition, the school could hire Alice to cater the event. Maybe she should take the open spot on the PTA, at least then they'd have something good to eat.

It was the first time she'd seen many of the parents since losing her company. They all knew, of course, and gossiped about her. Well, look who was back with nothing to do, the stay-at-home moms would say. Then there were men she'd chided, saying a woman could make it in a male-dominated industry. Only, who lost her company to a man with no tech experience? But her mother taught her how to hold her head high. She refused to indulge their false pity masked as curiosity. Let them talk; she'd find her footing again.

She sat at one of the desks and pretended to pick at the meager offerings she collected from the buffet. She dragged her feet, so they got to the open house right as the sessions started. Surely Mrs. Proper could not be happy to be running so late.

"Can I sit here?" a woman asked. Tabby had never seen her before. Loosely curled chestnut hair, matching oval eyes. Heart-shaped face, natural makeup, toothy smile. She wore a gray dress with a bunched collar and a dark blue cardigan. "I'm Cyndi. We're new here." She sat at the desk next to Tabby and slipped a cracker into her mouth.

"Tabby Black." She put out her hand. Cyndi smiled and shook it. "Where did you move here from?"

"Japan. My husband works at Andrews Air Force Base. Our son is in this class, and we have a little girl in third grade."

"My twins are in fifth, too. How did you get in?" Some people put their newborns on the list just to be sure they got a spot. For the higher grades, the wait could be years long.

Cyndi bobbed her head as she finished her bite of cheese. "The head of my husband's unit made some calls. I guess he knows the PTA president or something."

"Interesting." Tabby bit into a flavorless cracker. Mrs. Proper came to the front of the room. Tabby sat up more and got ready to count the cement blocks in the wall behind her head.

Cyndi reached for Tabby's plate after the presentation finished. Tabby thanked her, saying she could have gotten it.

"Would you want to get breakfast sometime? It would be nice to talk to a local about what there is to do."

"Are you free tomorrow?" Tabby dug in her purse. Finding an old card for TabiKat, she crossed out the front and wrote her cell on the back. Paul poked his head in and pointed to his watch. Tabby told Cyndi to call her and hustled to the door.

They compared notes on the drive home. As she suspected, Mac was going to have a lot of fun with someone who could somehow make the X *Games* relevant to the classroom, and yet probably wouldn't push his students beyond the given criteria, while Annie would have more work and yet leave fifth grade fully prepared for middle school. Maybe it was better that she wasn't working. Annie had basketball practice several nights a week, and this way she could keep Mac from playing his console all the time.

She checked her phone, surprised not to see any updates from Alice. Usually, Alice flooded her phone with images of the twins making a mess while they baked or built a couch fort in the living room. Once they tried to give Taco a bath. Tabby swore she still saw water marks on the ceiling. She was tempted to call and check in.

"How goes the job hunt?" Paul reached for her hand. Tabby pushed her cell into her purse. It was the only time they'd been able to talk because of his stupid case.

"Three more resumes off today." The darkness kept him from seeing her eye roll, but she failed to keep the bite out of her tone.

"Any more thoughts on consulting?"

"Who's going to hire me to consult on anything? Tips on how not to get your company stolen? Why you don't trust your best friends with money?"

"Mac's teacher said they might need a programming teacher."

Tabby crossed her arms and glared.

"What?" He slunk away. Tabby sighed and shook her head. "It might be a way to get out there," Paul added. Tabby watched the scenery outside. She didn't want to get back out there; she wanted her company back.

Taco bounded down the hallway when Paul opened the door. The twins' playful yells came out of the living room. Alice sat on the couch while Mac and Annie ran around with Nerf guns.

"You okay?" Tabby touched her shoulder.

Alice jumped. "How was the meeting?" She cleared her throat. Tabby repeated her question. "Just tired." Alice stood. "Hey guys, we have to finish defending the planet tomorrow."

Paul took the Nerf guns and sent the kids to brush their teeth. Alice started to wipe down the counters, distracted. Tabby stopped at the island to sort the mail. When Paul stepped into the twins' bathroom, Tabby went to lean on the counter beside the sink and waited for Alice to acknowledge her.

"We need to find you a man, Lil." She knew that would get a rise of Alice.

"What?" Alice dropped the glass in her hand. "I don't have time."

"When was the last time you looked at a man?"

"I notice men." She rinsed the glass.

Tabby cocked her head. "Who?"

Alice put the glass into the side sink. "You had your chance at matchmaker. I am not letting you set me up with Paul's coworker again."

"Rupert was a poor choice. Maybe…"

"No, okay. I barely have time to shower and see you all as it is. I don't need to date. They all cheat or leave anyway."

"That was one guy."

Alice finished the last dish and put it in the side sink. "I'm not going to be your fall project." Alice kissed her cheek and walked out. Tabby leaned on the counter. Something was going on with her sweet little sister. Normally, Alice would spar more, bring up Tabby's disastrous dating history, maybe even mention

Harry as a defense against single men in their thirties. This was more than being busy. She'd been off since they got back from Europe. She went from telling the family everything about her day to being almost cryptic.

Maybe she should get more involved with Tasty Pudding. She could help Alice schedule events, do the back end. Then Alice could be around more, and it would give Tabby something to do. Tabby leaned off the counter and went to help Paul put the kids to bed with an idea swirling in her head.

#

ALICE SAID GOOD MORNING on her way to the coffeepot the next morning. She needed to get her head out of the clouds. Dinner with Delany was lovely, and just what she needed after finding out about The Cora. But she had to get her emotions under control. She could not date him. Tabby would lose it if she found out.

Tabby called her over to where she sat at the end of the island, turning her laptop for Alice to see the starting of a website for Tasty Pudding.

"It's Hasty," Alice said. "What is this?"

"Your website. You need a digital presence. This way people can see an assortment of what you've done before, contact you. You should be able to take payments on the website too."

"How long have you been working on this?"

"Since last night. Sit, sit." She pat the seat next to her. Alice drank her coffee while Tabby walked her through the drop-down menus, telling her all the places she needed photos.

"You have some on your laptop, right?" Tabby asked.

"Um, let me send you some. They're mostly on Carver's computer." She set her mug on the island. Tabby eyed her. Alice had never been overly private, but the last thing she needed was Tabby to find a photo with Delany in it.

Annie hugged Alice from the side and rested her head on her. Alice kissed into her hair. They talked about her game the previous night, Annie getting a copy of *Sleeping Beauty* from the library to use as her template as she worked on her storyboard. She showed Alice her list of characters and ideas, and was studying the games she loved to figure out what she wanted to have happen. It was after eleven when Alice told her to go to bed, promising to help her more over the weekend.

"Mom, can I stay with Aunt A?"

"No, sweetie," Tabby said. "We are meeting Cyndi and her kids. I want you to know them, so they have friends when school starts."

"When are you meeting your friend?" Alice asked.

"Ten near the Torpedo Factory."

"You might want to get going then."

Tabby looked at the clock and jumped. She told Annie to get dressed and called for Mac to come eat. Alice promised Annie they'd hang out soon and sent her off to change. Tabby found milk and cereal from the cupboard.

"Why do I need this?" Alice slid the laptop over and started looking at the website.

"How do you get customers now?" Tabby set a bowl of cereal onto the counter.

"Word of mouth. Facebook. Twitter."

"Well, this is a digital word of mouth for adults. You'll thank me later. Come on, kids!" She shouted before leaving to change. Alice laughed and reached for her coffee.


\#

TABBY LIFTED HER HAND at Cyndi and told the twins to come on. They made their way through the park to where Cyndi sat on a bench by herself. Before Tabby could tell the twins to be careful, they ran toward the playground. She forgot how long it took to feed the twins and focus them enough to get them to brush their teeth and find their shoes. Annie pleaded to stay with Alice; Tabby was not in the mood for her daughter's theatrics. Things had gotten too relaxed since their trip. Before the twins understood that when Tabby asked them to do something, she meant it. She got that it was summer, and once school started their free time all but disappeared, but they needed to stop pushing her boundaries. They were only acting this way because Paul was gone all the time.

She got sidetracked, working on Alice's website, and forgot about the list of things she planned for the morning. Hopefully the kids could entertain themselves after they got home so she could make some follow up calls on some resumes she sent out.

Cyndi went to help her youngest on the swing. Tabby reached for her notepad, calling a potential lead for a job. She'd met the man while working on WlkmNt. He was starting a tech company in D.C., seemed impressed with her work. She read in the paper he was hiring a new manager to oversee his programming unit. Tabby waved to Mac at the top of the slide. The man picked up the phone.

"Hello, Mr. Keiths, this is Tabby Black. We met last year at…"

"I remember you. How are you, Tabby?"

"Doing okay. I am calling about your open position. I was hoping we could get lunch; I'd love to hear more about what you're doing."

He sighed. Tabby held up her hand to keep Mac from running up to the bench to tell her about whatever just happened.

"I would love to, but we are working a deal with Macon, and Mr. Dunn's made it clear we can't work with you."

"Did Mr. Dunn give you a reason why?" She tried to keep her tone light.

"Something about a noncompete agreement. Once this deal goes through, I'd love to talk to you. It might not be until the start of next year." The silence hung on the line. Tabby sucked her lips, that lying rascal. There was no such agreement.

"I understand. Have a good day, Mr. Keiths."

"You too, Tabby." He hung up the phone. Tabby lowered hers and closed her eyes, taking several deep breaths.

"Mom, Mom? Are you okay?" Mac leaned on the bench close to her. Cyndi stood with her two kids and Annie a few yards back.

"I'm good. Where do you want to go for lunch?" She put on a smile and walked with everyone back to their cars. She waited while the twins got into their car seats. If Bobbie Dunn planned to lie to block her out of the industry, maybe it was time for Tabby to settle in and adjust to life at home.

# CHAPTER 21

DELANY WAITED IN LINE at Carver's bakery, checking emails on his BlackBerry. Nadia offered to bring Helene to the apartment, but Delany wanted to keep things in the open. Since whatever started at her house, she'd been texting him, the messages flirty and suggestive. She was back to calling him "Boo" and tried to get him to stay whenever he was there. She even offered to bring Helene down the night before saying it had been too long since she enjoyed a night in D.C.

He ordered a London Fog and two chocolate croissants before going to find a table. He hoped mentioning his mother was on her way would keep Nadia from staying. He glanced toward the bar again, looking for Alice.

The server put his items down at the same time Helene yelled, "Daddy!" He stood, wanting to catch her before she hit the table and spilled his drink. Nadia followed close behind, a fake smile on her face at the happy family reunion. He hung Helene's backpack on his chair and told her to eat her croissant.

"I was thinking I could take the day, and maybe we could go to the Natural History Museum."

"My mom's on her way. I think they're going to Air and Space."

Nadia's smile tightened. "Michelle offered to watch her on Friday if you want to get dinner. Come over after." She reached to adjust his tie, Delany catching her arm.

"Stay here, Bear. Okay?"

She nodded. Delany pointed toward the door, Nadia going with a huff.

"What are you doing?" he asked after they got outside.

"Boo, when are we going to admit…"

"Listen, before was a mistake. We aren't back together. I'm not your boo."

"Come on, Delany. Just give us a chance." She pressed her body closer, her gaze on his. "I know what you like."

"Nod, we're not doing this. Stop, okay. No." He went back into the bakery, running his hand over his head. He sat at the table and asked about Helene's week. His mother texted to say she was running late. He got Helene reading a book before pulling out his portfolio. His mother wanted to talk about doing a garden at his new charter school in Anacostia. He loved the idea, but had no clue where to begin.

"Hey, pretty girl." Alice's voice caused him to look. Helene ran at her in a full run, Alice putting her hand on the chair next to her to keep from falling over. "How are you?"

"I'm going to the Air and Space Museum!"

"With your dad?"

"No, my grandma!"

"I love that place!" She stood and looked at Delany. "You okay?"

He nodded, not wanting to get into it.

She tilted her head, looking at the page on the table. "What is that?"

"We're doing a community garden, and I don't know what I'm doing."

"Where?" She sat at the table and pulled the drawing her way. Helene climbed into her lap, Alice putting her free arm around her. He told her what they wanted to do.

"It's doable. Two horseshoe beds would give the greatest number of kids access. Maybe five feet across. You might be able to make some removable covers so they could still plant in the spring. What would you think they should plant?" she asked Helene.

"Can we do apple trees?"

"They could try."

"Maybe strawberries."

"If they clear some other space, it might work."

"I'm sorry I'm late." His mother came toward them. Delany stood while Alice looked up.

"Alice, this is my mother, Coretta Clare."

Alice stood and put Helene where she had been. "Ma'am." She shook her hand.

"My son has told me all about you."

He groaned, Alice glancing at him.

"I can assure you whatever he said is exaggerated."

"Grandma, come see my drawing!" Helene called from the table. His mother moved to say hello, Alice hitting him lightly with the back of her hand.

"What do you tell people about me?" she whispered.

"The truth."

She glared. "It was nice meeting you, Mrs. Clare."

"You as well, Alice." She pulled a third chair up to the table. Delany asked what she wanted, going to get her cappuccino. When he got back, Helene was reading.

"Your daughter tells me Alice is going to help with the garden. Since when do you care about horticulture?"

"You're the one who says our area is a food desert."

She smirked. "I've been saying that since you were a child. Why are you listening now?"

"You always said I was thickheaded."

"And transparent." Coretta sat back while the server put her drink down, taking the dirty plates with him.

"I think you might know her father, James Gibson." Delany said the name slowly, hoping that was right.

"Dr. Gibson? That man is a saint."

"How do you know him?"

"I met him through some mutual friends from that welfare rights group I was with. He works to preserve the River." She paused. "If Alice is anything like her dad, you'd be lucky. Better than the women you usually date." She took another sip. Delany glanced toward the kitchen, if only Alice would give him a chance.

# CHAPTER 22

**D**ELANY WALKED INTO HIS OFFICE the next morning and raised his hand hello to Katy, who was talking on the phone. He reached to start his computer. The short bookshelves across from the couch were filled with what Katy took from his apartment. She had done a masterful job at combining books with items from his playing days and small touches from Comida, highlighting his various accomplishments and what he held important.

"Good morning." Katy came in with a cup of coffee and a stack of papers. "The head of the construction company is awaiting your call."

"Did you figure out who talked to *The Post*?"

Katy sighed and looked down. "Yeah, it was Bobbie. I asked him about it, and he told me to get back in my lane."

"I'm sure that is not what he said." Delany laughed.

"Okay." She walked out of the office. Delany called and left a message for the foreman, still unable to believe they got the Old

Post Office Pavilion. He hired the best design team to return the space to its glory days. The designer did her homework, bringing him images and ideas that harkened back to the 1920s, when it was D.C.'s premiere hotel.

He saw it walking around one night after practice, the tower catching his attention. Inside was nothing but a sad food court and some offices on the floors above. The main hall opened to the skylights ten stories above, flooding the space in natural light. It's what got him interested in venture capitalism. He financed other hotels, done other remodels. It was all leading to this. He planned to live in the penthouse suite. The idea of it being so close made him giddy.

"Are you free for lunch?" Bobbie came into his office. "I want you to meet the chef I hired for The Cora."

Delany stood and reached for his jacket off the chair beside his desk.

"I'm not ready to make a final decision on the chef yet, regardless of what you tell *The Post*."

Bobbie laughed him off. "Trust me, Bulldog. This man will have the restaurant booked solid before we open."

They got into a cab and rode into The District. Delany watched the city outside. He wanted to keep Bobbie out of the renovation, but then Bobbie showed up at meetings and acted like Delany was going to hand it off like any other project. Bobbie tried to hire the construction company, then tried to bypass him to approve the plans. His latest stunt involved telling *The Post* Jonas was going into the space. Delany wanted to make him clear out. The Cora was his shot to take, but he did not want to deal with another one of Bobbie's tantrums.

They stopped outside of Marigolds, the restaurant Alice cut her teeth at. He ate there a lot when Cornelia ran it. At the time, it looked like a Parisian café. Now there was boring off-white paint, all the chairs gray and totalitarian. Where was the art? The color?

The host led them to a table by the windows. Delany sat and looked at the menu. After eating Alice's food, it all sounded plain and predictable. He told Bobbie to hold off asking for the chef, wanting to try the food without the man knowing they were there. Bobbie sat back and looked over the space. The server came to greet them. The special was the Weeknight Cioppino, made with a white wine base, featuring shrimp and tilapia. Delany asked for that. Bobbie, never one to try something new, got a hamburger.

"Cioppino?" Bobbie asked. "When did you get so fancy?"

He reached for his water. Alice said once that chefs try to get rid of their excess via specials. They would give it a special name, but really, it was what they couldn't sell over the weekend. Seeing what this man could do with the leftovers in his fridge would give Delany a glimpse into his creativity.

The server brought their beers and a calamari appetizer. The breading looked wet. Delany sniffed one before dipping it into the red sauce.

"Are you coming to the fundraiser tonight?"

Bobbie laughed and took a long drink of his beer. "You know my heart is far too small to pretend to care."

"It's for the Eubie."

"You know my opinion—bulldoze it and let something else come in."

"I own part of that theater."

"Yes, but you often get hooked on lost causes. Besides, I got a hot date with my girl tonight."

"How is that going?" Delany sat back. He didn't care, but it was a safe topic. What did they talk about before he retired? His game, who Bobbie just met, some girl Bobbie thought he should notice, highlights from Macon. Only now Delany knew about work and the list of interesting people around had dwindled. He wasn't going to ask Bobbie about horse racing or whatever game he just bet on and lost.

"She's great. Nice rack. Great in bed."

"Perhaps the next Mrs. Dunn."

Bobbie laughed. "I learned my lesson. Three is enough."

The server put their meals down, Bobbie asking if Jonas was there. Maybe he'd gotten spoiled by Alice who seemed to care about how every dish looked. Her dishes felt like masterpieces, collections of color and texture carefully plated. This felt dull and routine, broth with bits of shrimp in it. But maybe the taste made up for it. He ran his spoon through the soup and took a bite before reaching for the salt.

"Bobbie!" An overweight man in a white chef's coat walked toward them. *Jonas Executive Chef* embroidered on the left chest. Bobbie stood and shook his hand. Delany forced the bite down with a gulp of water and stood.

"Delany Clare, I've heard a lot about you." Jonas shook his hand. Bored brown eyes and a salesman smile that reminded him of the men who came to his house to be his agent. Quick talking, full of promises, and made of nothing but bravado. "How is the food?"

"Fantastic!" Bobbie jumped in. "I wanted to give Delany a sample of what you can do for the hotel."

"I wish I'd known. The soup is just a clearing of what we had in the back. I can get you something else." He started for the plate. Delany moved his hand toward it.

"Nonsense. I wanted to see what you do with your leftovers." He held his gaze. Jonas forced a smile and leaned back.

"The designer came by yesterday." Jonas looked at Bobbie. "I was wondering how much control I have over aesthetics. Cute '20s style isn't my bag."

Delany saw the plans for the restaurant, and that wasn't how he'd describe it.

"She's open to ideas," Bobbie said.

"I wanted to talk about doing a bar on the top floor. I think that would help us move our vision for this place forward."

"And what would that be?" Delany said. The men looked at him. Bobbie closed his mouth and buttoned his jacket.

Jonas chuckled. "Sorry, I've gotten used to dealing with Bobbie on things."

"What would you do with the restaurant?" Delany's body tensed.

"Something more modern, more like this place." Jonas motioned behind him. Cement flower boxes, boring black chandeliers. Totalitarian was not an aesthetic Delany appreciated.

"I'm hoping to put my sous chef over there. He's talented…"

"So you wouldn't even be there?" Delany asked.

Jonas studied him. "I heard you're working with Alice Gibson. How is that going?" He smiled. Delany shifted his weight. Alice would never serve the bland slop he just ate. Her food truck held more sophistication and culture than this bleak excuse for a restaurant.

"You get what you pay for." Bobbie rolled his eyes.

Jonas laughed and tilted his head. "Alice can be cute to look at, but lacks the talent I expect from my staff. I tried my best."

"We should get back." Delany reached to finish his water.

"If you want me to cater your events—I can do better than that Cuban drivel. We'd provide more than cheese boards and frozen yogurt bars. Believe me."

"I'll let you know." Delany buttoned his jacket and let Bobbie pay for the meal. The less time he spent in this desolate place the better.

The drive home was quiet. Bobbie got on his phone, singing along with the radio in the cab. Delany left Bobbie at the elevators, walking to the head lawyer's office. The man motioned him in while he talked on the phone. Delany paced the back of the space. No way that chef was going to anchor his hotel. He was not going to settle for boring, overpriced cliche hotel food when he tasted better food on Alice's off days.

"Everything okay?" the lawyer asked when he hung up his call.

"How far are we on the Jonas deal?"

"I am working on a contract…"

"Why?" He shifted his weight and crossed his arms.

"Mr. Dunn said he's the choice."

"I'll tell you who I want for The Cora. Mr. Dunn doesn't speak for me."

The man paused. "But he has for the last two years, Mr. Clare. Mr. Dunn claims he is your voice in the company."

"Well, I'm here now. If it's a decision you need my approval on, get my approval on it."

"Of course." The man smiled politely.

Delany started for the door. He paused, debating whether to ask if there were other things he should know about. But he had to trust Bobbie. It was one impetuous choice.

# CHAPTER 23

DELANY CALLED THE DESIGNER on his way to the Metro to tell her Bobbie did not get to decide anything related to The Cora. Apparently, Bobbie called to say he was now the primary on the project.

"Yeah, Mr. Dunn can be a bit domineering." He tried to keep his tone light. "I'm still the one making the decisions. We're going to go with the aesthetic we talked about. Keep the plans I approved, please."

"Will do. Thank you for clarifying."

He started down the long staircase at the Rosslyn Metro, ready for the day to be over. He needed to stop by his apartment to get his car and the tie Elle gave him. On the Metro, he leaned into his knees and pushed his thumbs into his eyes, unsure what to do with Bobbie. He was tired of the guilt trips and the temper tantrums.

He opened the door to his place, music coming from the kitchen. Alice worked at the island with her head down. Sliced tomatoes rested on a baking sheet next to her.

"Why are you here?" he asked.

She looked up and smiled. "We have events tomorrow, so I needed to come tonight. I thought you had something to be at."

"I forgot the tie Elle sent me. Never mind." He went toward his bedroom. If Elle would not kill him, he'd stay home with Alice. He needed her uncluttered way of seeing the world, her joy. Someone knocked at his door. "I got it." He called and went down the hallway on the other side of the kitchen wall. Nadia turned when he opened the door. "Hey, Nod. What are you doing here?"

"We need to talk." She walked into his apartment and set her purse on the couch before crossing her arms. Delany glanced toward the kitchen. "For some reason Helene thinks she's going to your little charter school next year." Nadia flexed her taut body toward him.

He sighed. "She's been asking to go there. I thought maybe…"

She stepped toward him, her first finger up. "Listen, you're the sperm donor, okay. Where my daughter goes to school is up to me."

"The amount I send you monthly implies otherwise." He met her gaze, tired of her acting like he only existed to send money. "She doesn't like where she is, why not let her go where it's the best of everything?"

"I did not work my ass off to get out of there for you to pull my daughter back."

The oven went off. Delany looked over his shoulder. Nadia scoffed and walked around him, ignoring his telling her to come back.

"Who the hell are you?" She stood in the entryway with her stance wide, hands on her hips. Delany reached for her forearm.

"I'm sorry, Alice." He pulled her back into the living room, unwilling to let his ex invade his personal life.

"That's the caterer?"

"Listen, Helene shouldn't be stuck in public school because it's convenient for you."

"Convenient?" She rocked her head. "I'm with that girl 24-7, how convenient do you think that is?"

"Hey, Delany, I'm going to get something from the store. If the timer goes off..." Alice pointed toward the kitchen.

He nodded, waiting for the front door to close. "Who has Bear?" he asked before Nadia could get going again.

"My mom. You act like I'd leave her to fend for herself." She leaned back and crossed her arms.

"I tried to Skype her today."

"I took her computer time. She was being belligerent."

"She's six." He put his hands on his hips.

"She's always an angel for you, but trust me, that girl can be a stubborn ass."

*Like you*, he wanted to say, but thought better of it. He took a deep breath and unflexed his jaw.

"I think we should go away for Thanksgiving." Nadia pulled her gaze off the front door.

"What?"

Nadia waited; she was serious. "I think we should be a family." She pressed closer to him, her hands on his sides.

"We have never been a family." He tried to step back, but she held on.

"Helene would do better with both her parents close. I think that's why she acts up so much."

"I thought I was the sperm donor." He reached for her wrists and stepped back.

"I shouldn't have said that. It's hard to compete sometimes. If you think your school is best, I could drive Helene over on my way to work."

"Wait, now you're moving in?" He laughed.

"We've been doing this since we were teens. When do we stop and admit what's been there all along? You're it for me."

Her big eyes looked up at him. How many nights those eyes got him to forget all the reasons they would never work.

"We're not a family, Nod."

"We never had issues getting things going." She held his gaze. Sexual release and true attraction were not the same thing. The timer sounded, Delany going to get whatever Alice left in the oven. He set the tray of tomatoes on the stove, leaving the oven mitt next to it. Nadia sat on the couch when he came back, her legs tucked up under her.

"You need to go. You can't barge into my house, claws out, and then think being cute will make up for it. I have somewhere to be tonight." He went to the door and opened it, praying she got the hint. Nadia tilted her head and stood, sauntering toward him.

"I'll find some locations for November." She gave him a light kiss and strutted toward the elevator. Delany closed the door and looked at the time before going to find the tie Elle gave him.

The front door opened again, the blender starting a moment later. He went to the kitchen.

"I didn't know if you were still here." Alice poured the tomato mix into a to-go container.

"I'm sorry you had to hear that." Delany sat at the island.

"I'm sorry for invading your privacy." She paused. "I can come back, if you want to be alone."

He reached for her wrist. "No, please stay. I can order dinner."

"What about your event?"

He shook his head. "Not in the chatty mood anymore." He left to find his phone and call Elle, promising to make it up to her. He changed into gym shorts and a Wizards shirt. Alice cooked at the stove, two glasses beside a bottle of wine.

"I might need something stronger," he said.

"Just not a sidecar, please?"

He laughed and went to make two old fashioneds. He came

back to find Alice cutting up the last of the vegetables from the crate. He sat at the island and took a long drink.

"Do you want to talk about it?" she asked.

He shook his head. Alice came around the island and opened her arms. He set his drink down and hugged her. The emotion hit him, the frustration at Nadia's games, the inability to do right by Helene, the pain of being a single dad. He held her tighter as tears overwhelmed him. His body shook.

"It's okay." Her gentle voice filled his ear. How had she become the one he relied on the most? Alice made him feel moored to something. In her arms, he could rest. He'd been on edge since tearing his ACL, his life a series of plays he never expected. With her, the world made sense again.

He looked up, and Alice wiped the tears off his cheeks. He held her gaze, hating the questions and how she held herself back. This couldn't all be one-sided, the safety, the connection, the ability to fully be who he was. She looked down and exhaled.

"I have to go."

"Please stay." He wanted to return to moments before, but she was already retreating.

"There are veggies if you want to sauté them and pasta in the cupboard. You can add olive oil, or I made fresh sauce, which I need to put away." She slouched, defeated.

"I can get it."

She reached for her bag and started to leave before turning back. "I'm sorry."

The front door closed a moment later. Delany rested his head in his hand, unsure what to do with everything going on.

# CHAPTER 24

ALICE LET OUT HER BREATH, the floors ticking away on the elevator to Macon's offices. She spent all weekend thinking about the night in Delany's apartment and how good it felt to hold him. When he looked up at her and she brushed the tears off his cheek, it took everything in her to not just kiss him. Katy's interruption earlier in the week should have been enough for Alice to admit she was too involved. Instead she let herself comfort him and pretend they could be together. Then the alarms went off. She had too much on the line to give in to her heart. It was time to do what she should have done in June and get Delany out of her life. She and Carver were getting ready to hire a backup who could take the existing Macon events until they could be phased out. It was playing with fire, and thus far she hadn't been burned, but it was time to walk away.

It had been building since the basketball fundraiser. Before Bobbie showed up, she found herself leaning toward him. Her heart rushed when his hand brushed her palm and he interlaced their fingers, Alice holding her breath. She loved that he was always at his apartment, that he stayed to talk to her. It wasn't until the moment when he told her he had no secrets from her and then got close that she knew what she'd had been denying for months. Before that, she told herself it was all in her head. Why couldn't it just be in her head?

Katy's desk was empty. Delany stood just inside his office, his gaze on a TV screen. The afternoon news played on low, a fire raging somewhere.

"What happened?" Alice asked.

Delany looked at her, his eyes heavy. "There's a massive fire in New Mexico."

"Do you know someone there?"

Something in his gaze made it feel personal.

He shook his head. "I just hope we're able to do something."

Katy came into the room. She smiled when she saw Alice, hugging her from the side.

"Eddie called. Morse can't go," Katy said to Delany.

"Does he see…"

"Yeah, he does. He told Eddie he was done for the year. The cancer's pretty aggressive, Delany."

He ran his hand over his head.

"What's wrong?" Alice asked Katy, who looked at Delany.

"The chef who normally goes with Comida backed out."

Alice shook her head, having no idea what that sentence meant.

"Delany has a nonprofit that brings meals to emergency areas. Normally, Eddie and his team, a chef included, would leave from D.C. tonight to start cooking. There's a team there already working to get things set up. The fire has already taken out 20,000 acres and a hundred homes. People are living in shelters and need to get fed."

"I can go," she said before she realized what she was saying. Delany looked at her, a lightbulb going off for him. *Of course.*

"It could be a while before you're back," he said.

"What about your events?" Katy asked. Alice closed her eyes and slid her hands into her back pockets.

"Let me talk to Carver. We should be able to shift things around. Please, let me do this after what you've done for me." She looked at Delany. What happened did not negate that he had given her everything. She could do this, and then they'd be even. Alice could walk away not feeling like she owed him a thing.

"We leave from DCA at 8:30." Delany said.

"I'll be there."

#

TABBY WAITED AT THE CAFÉ for Cyndi who had been cryptic on the phone, saying she had a project she needed Tabby's help on. Cyndi came in with two women their age. One was heavier-set with curly red hair and blue eyes. The other was tall and lanky, brown hair in a bob cut. Her gray T-shirt tucked into raspberry-colored shorts.

"Tabby, this is Martha and Joanie." Cyndi made the introductions before they sat. "This is the woman I was telling you about," Cyndi said to her friends. "She used to run her own business, started it from nothing. I think she'd be the perfect speaker."

"Speaker for what?" Tabby asked, the other women nodding.

"We run a chapter of a group dedicated to helping businesses owned by military spouses," Joanie, the taller one, said.

"With moving every few years it's hard to get a good following," Martha said. "Some of us have brilliant ideas, but don't know how to write a business plan or get funding."

"We're hosting a workshop in September," Joanie added. "We have panels and people coming to help with business plans. Someone is coming to talk about how to use social media to promote your products."

"And we want you to be the lunchtime speaker." Cyndi almost interrupted Joanie.

"Me?"

"Come on, Tabby. You're perfect. You grew that company to what it was."

Tabby waited while the server came to get their orders. Maybe she could do this.

"Where is it?" An event center on the water in Alexandria. "Do you have a caterer?"

"Not yet. I have some places to call," Martha said.

"Let me save you the trouble. I know another female-owned business you all can support."

They spent the rest of the morning talking like old friends. Martha hand-painted wooden signs in her home using song lyrics or movie quotes. Joanie did group fitness out of her garage, but she wanted to expand into marathon training too.

Over Cyndi's shoulder Tabby saw a man who offered her funding for TabiKat when she was just getting going. He later partnered with some guys in their twenties to develop iPhone apps, the process taking longer than it should. She knew what to do from WlkmNt. Tabby swallowed her pride and told the ladies she'd be back, making her way to where he stood talking to another man at the front of the restaurant.

He saw her and raised his head. He remembered her. She waited for him to finish his conversation before going to say hello.

"I didn't expect to see you here. Still enjoying days off, I presume." The man offered her money for her company in the same breath as trying to get into her pants. If those twenty-somethings could figure out what they were doing, their apps could be top grossers. She might have lost her ideas, but that didn't mean she could not work on something similar.

"I was wondering if that drink was still available."

He chuckled and smirked. "I heard about TabiKat. You

didn't want to talk before, don't come groveling now that you got tossed out."

"You told me I was a woman of vision."

"You told me I was a man without any." He raised his hand to someone standing behind Tabby. "A word of advice, Mrs. Black. No one in the tech industry is going to hire you. Macon might have been kind toward you in their PR, but Bobbie Dunn made sure we all know what a diva you are. Your ship has sailed. Have a good day." He walked past her. Tabby flexed her jaw, her pulse racing. She went back to her table, Cyndi telling her friends about her kids' first day of school.

She told the twins to start their homework before going to the fridge. White wine was not going to cut it. She poured a double of Paul's whiskey and sipped while the kids did their homework, replaying the encounter. Just what had Bobbie been telling people—that she dared stand up to the great Delany Clare, that she didn't grovel and demanded better for herself.

Paul called hello from the front door, the kids barely answering back from their video game. Tabby left her glass by the sink and followed Paul into the bedroom, where he rambled about his day and the case she long stopped giving two hoots about. She leaned in the doorway to the closet.

"You okay?" he asked. She kissed him, Paul moaning. She reached for his T-shirt. "What got into you?"

"I think we should have another kid." If she was going to be stuck at home, it would give her something to focus on for a bit.

"What?" He stepped back and met her gaze. She said it again. "Why would we do that? We're halfway to freedom, Tabs. Why would we start over?"

"If I'm going to be your little housewife, it would make sense, right?"

"What happened to trying to get back out there?"

Tabby stepped back and crossed her arms. "I am trying, but it's not easy with a man hellbent on destroying me."

"What happened?" He touched her forearm. Tabby pulled it back and went to make dinner. She didn't want another child, but it was something to fill her day. She couldn't sit around the apartment. What was she supposed to do—get a job at the local coffeehouse? Go back to retail? She was thirty-five and created the biggest launch in stock market history and had nothing to show for it.

"Does anyone know where your aunt is?" They were not Alice's private hotel. It would be polite of her sister to tell them if she planned to be there, help Tabby to know how much to cook. Tabby found her cell phone and called, but it went to voicemail. She thought about calling back.

Paul heard from the kids about their days before asking what he could do to help. He eyed the glass by the sink, looking at her curiously.

"Don't judge me."

"Is this why you're on edge?" He leaned into his arm on the counter. Tabby studied the TV. "Tabby."

"You think it's easy being stuck at home all day?"

"I know it's not, which is why I thought you were going to get another job."

"You make it sound so simple. I'm trying!"

"I know you are…"

"It's not as easy as you think. Both you and Alice bailed on me and expect me to do all of this myself."

He leaned on the counter and crossed his arms. "We didn't bail on you. We're working. Alice's job is not 8-5, and neither is mine right now…"

"Oh, right, I forgot—your big case." She set her arm on the counter, the other on the back of her hip. Paul studied her, Tabby breathing deep.

"What is going on?" he asked calmly. Tabby shook her head. "We can get someone to clean the apartment or take the kids to school. Your mom might be able to help…"

"I am not going to call my mom to come sit with my kids."

Paul paused. "I was going to say she might have a lead on a job."

"I don't just want a job, Paul. I want something I'm good at. Something I enjoy. You walked into your ideal job after law school. I had what I wanted and…" She stopped, tears building. Paul moved off the counter and tried to touch her. Tabby recoiled. "Don't pity me. And don't act like I am doing nothing right now. You try staying home with nothing useful to do. It's not as easy as you think."

She left the room. Next time she saw her sister, she'd remind her about common courtesy when living with other people.


#

ALICE UNDID HER BIKE from the rack outside Macon, unsure how to explain her decision to Carver. She thought she was going to tell him she'd walked away from Macon, instead she needed to explain she was leaving for an indefinite amount of time. But she couldn't *not* go. Let her use her cooking for something positive. Let her do more than stand behind a buffet line at an event.

Carver was far more understanding than she expected. They called Rita, the woman they wanted to hire, who agreed to come in that afternoon. Alice talked her through the events on the schedule for September, hoping to be back before her birthday in October. But Carver was good, and with Rita ready to go. The staff would help where needed. It would be okay.

Telling her sister was another matter. Alice played over what to say. She collapsed her bike at the apartment and slipped it into its place. One more deep breath. Tabby worked on dinner, the kids watching TV in the living room. Paul said hello from further down the island where he sat working on his laptop.

"Did you get my message?" Tabby asked, her tone impatient.

"I'm going out of town." Alice leaned into the island for support. Tabby turned from the stove. "A nonprofit in town got my name. They help with food after a natural disaster. They asked me to go with them to New Mexico."

"Where that big wildfire is?" Tabby crossed her arms, her body taut.

"Their usual chef can't go, so they asked me. We're leaving tonight."

"You're intentionally going into the path of a wildfire?" Tabby said with more emphasis. Alice could only nod. "And you really think…"

"When do you leave?" Paul cut her off.

"In two hours. I need to pack." Alice pushed off from the island. Tabby started to say more, but Alice kept walking. She dug her backpack out from under her bed. Take her good tennis shoes and a couple jumpsuits, underwear. Hopefully there might be a way to wash her clothes. Annie knocked on her door, her body slumped. Alice sat on the bed and hugged her close.

"I'll miss you." Alice kissed by her ear. Annie handed her the stuffed panda Alice gave her to take to summer camp the year before. For luck and bravery, Alice told her. Alice thanked her and slipped the bear into the pocket of her short blue jumpsuit.

"I'll be home before you know I'm gone."

Delany stood with the man from the basketball fundraiser, dressed down in zip away cargo pants, a longer sleeved, button-down hiking shirt open over his gray T-shirt. He said her name. The second man turned and reintroduced himself.

"Thank you for agreeing to come," Eddie said. He had a T-shaped frame, tanned skin, and a balding head. Alice tried not to focus on his prosthetic leg, or the scar on his long face. His kind eyes reminded her of the Potomac at night. Eddie's easy smile helped calm Alice's fear she was making a terrible mistake.

They boarded together. Eddie sat in the aisle seat, Delany by the window, Alice in the aisle across from them. Eddie told her about their teams already on the ground and what would happen once they got there. She was supposed to help in this chaos by making sandwiches?

"I brought you this." Eddie handed her a notebook. "It's our training manual, so you have some idea what people usually know. You can toss it in a crate once we get there."

"Thanks, Eddie." Alice turned on her light and started to read. Delany and Eddie talked for the rest of the flight, Alice desperate to silence the dread that she was in over her head.

# CHAPTER 25

SLITHERING RED LINES BROKE into the pure black, the earth seemingly tearing itself open. The sear seemed to go on forever. Alice leaned back from looking out the window and reached for Annie's panda, praying for those affected, those trying to defeat something so overpowering.

A member of the team waited at the airport and talked as he drove, updating Eddie on where things were. Delany sat beside Alice in the back. She had started to jot down some ideas in the manual now on her lap. The materials said they started with simple meals: PB+Js, fruit, water. Would people who just lost everything care about the equivalent of a kid's school lunch? It was a three-hour drive to the fire. She studied the darkness, slowly falling asleep.

Delany touched her leg, waking her.

"Are we here?" she asked.

"Yeah. You okay?" He tilted his head. Alice swallowed and nodded, determined to not let him see just how terrified she felt.

He opened his door. Alice checked the time, close to one a.m. Eddie gave her a hotel room key, their first meeting would be at five. Alice shouldered her pack and took the elevator to her room.

THE NEXT MORNING, she followed Delany and Eddie into a smaller ballroom in the hotel. Papers covered a series of round tables, with several maps hanging on the wall. On another section a large pad of paper listed the food and quantities available. Delany went with another man to see the damage and get an idea of what Comida was already doing. Eddie called her name. He stood with Samson, the man who got them at the airport, he was about her age, bald head, with simple framed glasses over almond-shaped blue eyes. He wore a blue polo with the Comida logo and cargo pants.

"Samson is going to take you to find a kitchen."

"I thought you had one identified?" Alice asked.

"We did. Winds shifted and the fire jumped the boundary," Samson said.

"We need to start cooking for the firefighters and first responders," Eddie said.

"Sounds like we'll be busy." Alice tried to keep the apprehension off her face.

Volunteers loaded crates of meals into the back of a white 4Runner. Samson told her about the situation as they drove. The area around them was full of ridges and valleys, making it harder for the firefighters to establish fire lines. With things being so dry, the winds kept kicking up, carrying embers and starting new fires. As of that morning, the fire had moved closer to the Colorado border and was still largely uncontained. It was September, meaning people were tired, and resources depleted. A dozen other fires raged in the region, some in more densely populated areas. This area consisted of smaller towns with populations under

10,000. The bigger fire companies were trying to work with mostly volunteer units who may or may not have any training in fighting wildfires.

Everyone worked overtime. Comida would be there making meals as long as needed. So far, the main shelters run by national entities were accepting Comida's help as it allowed them to divert funding and people to other fires. They were also taking meals to smaller, local shelters and those in communities the fire ravaged earlier.

They went to a primary shelter in the center of the burn area. Alice helped unload the boxes and boxes of meals. A bigger van pulled up, filled with volunteers and more food. Samson told her to get into the 4Runner; he heard of a kitchen they might be able to use.

"Don't we need to stay?" Alice asked.

"There are people who cook. People who serve. People who distribute. People who move stuff. We all do our part. We need to get you a kitchen."

Everywhere they went looked like a sea of black, charred earth with the burned remains of buildings and communities. They drove down a street, nothing but the skeletons of cars and an occasional staircase leading nowhere. They took meals to firefighters, people guarding ravaged communities, and a few national guard troops before Samson pulled into an older restaurant, the only structure still standing on what was once a main thoroughfare. An older man came out to meet them with receding white hair, chapped skin. He wore stained overalls and an undershirt full of holes.

"Thank you for letting us see your space," Samson shook the man's hand.

"We won't be needing it now." His voice was raspy. Alice introduced herself and shook his hand.

Inside the stench of smoke hung in the air. Ash covered every surface. It felt like walking into something that had been undisturbed for decades, though according to the owner, people ate there earlier in the week. The man turned on the power, the lights flickering. The kitchen was in the same state as the front. The lights tremored again. Alice wanted to ask how she could cook with the fluctuating energy, and what if the state decided to shut off the power.

"Might not get stable power. They could be diverting it since there's nothing left." Samson seemed to read her mind.

"Are there any food trucks around here?" she asked.

The man thought about it. "I think one or two might work in Bay Vista."

"If we could get them to come, maybe they could help cook and distribute." Alice looked at Samson.

"Let me call Eddie." Samson got on the phone. Alice glanced at the space around her. Who was she to complain about not having enough of a kitchen when so many families just lost everything? Most restaurateurs here would kill for the space she shared with Carver.

"What were your most popular dishes?" Alice asked. There were only so many days people could eat sandwiches, and she sensed the prescribed meals in the manual might not be what people around here would choose to eat.

The man scratched his chin and widened his stance. "Can't say as I reckon. You should ask my daughter; she's the chef."

"If she's open to talking to me."

Samson came back and thanked the man for his time, they'd be in touch. Alice found an order pad and wrote down her number for the man's daughter.

They ended up at the high school in the next town over where things were still green. The smell of smoke reminded Alice the fire was not that far away. A sea of one-man tents lined the football field, the school the base of operations for the firefighters. It felt like the safest place to be. The principal met them outside and showed them to the kitchen, which consisted of a small range top and a couple of tables. They wouldn't be able to do much. But there was electricity. It was clean and centrally located. Samson declared it perfect and got on the phone.

"So now what do we do?" Alice asked when he got back.

"The truck is on its way with food. You tell us—what do you need?"

"What did Morse do?"

"Chili and mashed potatoes, grilled cheese sandwiches."

"Is that what they eat here?"

Samson cocked his head. Alice's phone rang, the woman from the restaurant on the line. Alice went to talk outside. She explained who she was and what she hoped the woman could do. The woman sniffed and said she'd be at the high school in twenty minutes.

A food truck pulled up, and a younger couple got out both dressed in sweats and T-shirts, the woman's hair pulled into a messy bun. Alice wanted to ask when they last slept, but they were there and eager to help.

"You the woman my dad talked to?" the woman asked. Alice introduced herself. She didn't realize the man's daughter was the one with the food truck.

"My mom runs the restaurant while I do this. Call it creative differences. I want to make what people around here are used to, not boring diner food."

"We have food coming to start feeding people, but I was wondering, well, two things. Can you teach us what to make, and do you have any other food truck friends who might help us?"

The woman smiled wide. She could help with both of those things.

By the time the van of food arrived, the woman and Alice planned out three days of meals based on the guidelines Eddie gave her. The meals would be things the locals loved, something consistent in the loss of everything around them. The woman's husband worked the phones, four more food trucks agreeing to help.

A sea of volunteers started to empty the van of food into the fridges. Eddie came in, Samson telling him how they wanted to make the space better, part of what Comida aimed for. It didn't do any good if all the resources got pulled after they left. They aimed to enable people to keep cooking after they finished their part of things.

Alice carried in box after box of vegetables, fresh meat, and spices. Crates and crates of corn and wild rice. It felt like a Costco unloaded the essentials in the kitchen by the time it was all said and done. Alice introduced the woman to Delany before they got to work. The woman taught some of the volunteers how to make fry bread and homemade corn tortillas. Alice cooked chicken for tacos while another woman worked on pinto beans. A volunteer set to work on a three sisters stew made with beans, corn, and squash. Once the items were cooked, another set of volunteers worked to make to-go boxes. Others packed the to-go boxes into crates, another set loaded them into SUVs that would deliver them. Everyone had their part, and because of it, things ran efficiently.

Delany came to see how she was doing.

"We'll have four more food trucks here tomorrow. Samson is going to give them some food so they can cook for the outlying communities. I am going to switch gears and go cook for the firefighters."

"What are they getting?"

"Fried chicken, potato salad, and biscuits."

"They'll be thrilled."

Eddie asked Delany if he wanted to help him deliver food. He squeezed Alice's arm on the way out of the door. Alice looked around at everything that was being accomplished. Pretty remarkable.

# CHAPTER 26

TABBY WATCHED THE TV at her parents' house, grateful for somewhere to take the kids. Being stuck at home over Labor Day weekend might have driven them all crazy. Paul was putting the kids to bed, her mother on a call with someone back in D.C. Her father tinkered in the greenhouse. Alice's website waited on her laptop on her lap. Tabby wanted it ready to go whenever her sister got back, but still needed photos. She was tempted to dig through Alice's bedroom to find her laptop or maybe ask Carver for some. How hard was it to give someone what they asked for? Didn't Alice appreciate what she was doing for her?

The news started covering the various fires happening in the West. It showed footage from the one where Alice was, nothing but forests of red and destroyed homes. It looked like something after an apocalypse, scorched, and otherworldly. Families sifted through the rubble. Somewhere in all that carnage, all that darkness, all that chaos, her sister was cooking for people. Annie asked when Aunt A was coming home. With the fire barely contained not for a while, or maybe Alice would regain her senses and come back.

Her father sat on the couch and took a drink of his beer, dirt under his fingernails. His hair looked like it hadn't been brushed in days. At least it wasn't lost under a sweat-stained Wizards baseball hat.

"Have you heard from her? Does this make sense to you?" she asked.

"She said it was a good opportunity. Who am I to tell your sister what to do."

"You could have told her going into a disaster area was a stupid idea."

Her father cocked his head, his brow drawn tight. "It's not like she ran in with a flashlight and a backpack. She went with a group that knows what it's doing. She's safe. It's okay."

"How do you know she's safe?"

"She called the other day. We couldn't talk for long, but she sounded good."

Tabby scoffed. "Nice of her to contact me."

"She figured I would tell you." He studied her. "Do you need to talk about what happened?"

"What do you mean—what happened?" Tabby caught her tone. If her mother heard her, she'd get yelled at for sure.

"Getting bought out. It obviously still bothers you."

"That's not what bothers me." She shifted in her seat and put her laptop on the table. "What bothers me is my sister being allowed to run off into an area the military has to keep secured, and you, as her father, thinking that's okay."

Her father shook his head and looked at the TV again. Paul called her name from the doorway. They had a long-standing tradition of trying to have sex on Friday nights. The kids had gone down easy. Her parents would do nothing but watch TV until they went to bed. It was late enough they wouldn't question them turning in for the night. They had done it at her parents' house hundreds of times. But his reaction to her asking about another baby still stung. Plus, he'd been lost all week on this endless case and didn't appreciate what she did to keep things running. He motioned his head toward the stairs and smiled.

"Not tonight." She looked at the TV again.

"I haven't seen you all week."

"Whose fault is that?"

Paul sighed and went to the bedroom anyway. Tabby set her gaze on the TV. Her mother came and sat between her and her dad on the couch. Before she could speak, Delany Clare's face filled the screen. Tabby reached for the remote and turned up the volume.

"Retired basketball star and business mogul Delany Clare is in New Mexico helping to feed those affected by the fires. Clare's nonprofit, Comida, has groups working across the West, feeding 40,000 daily." While the man spoke, images of Delany flashed across the screen. One showed him crouched down, a wide smile on his face, children clustered around him. "Clare has been critical of the government's emergency procedures, asking why providing quality food to those who just lost everything is not higher on FEMA's list."

"That man just can't resist the spotlight," Tabby said. "What right does he have to be in places the locals can't even get into?"

"You do know that is who Alice is with," her mother asked. Tabby pinched her brow and looked at her mother, her heart racing. Her dad focused on the TV. "Comida is Delany Clare's nonprofit. Their last CEO spoke to my committee about shifting how we do food delivery after a disaster. It's remarkable what they're able to do."

No wonder Alice was so elusive about what she was doing. A pain radiated in her jaw. Tabby wanted to call her sister and demand she tell her what the hell was going on. How did she know the scoundrel?

"How did he get her name?" Tabby asked. Her mom paused, her father squeezing his wife's knee.

"It's a small world, Kitty Cat," her mother said. "I'm sure someone at one of her events knows Mr. Clare. Don't forget, your sister can cook."

"Premier chef in the city, so *The Post* said." Her father added. Tabby scoffed and went to refill her water. Her chest tightened, a pounding built in her ears. She looked at the website. All this work to get her sister's company noticed and she ran off with the man who orchestrated the coup of her company. How could Alice work with him?

# CHAPTER 27

DELANY SHIFTED HIS BACK, looking over the parking lot of the hotel. He sipped his coffee and checked the time on his phone. Helene should be up. He called Nadia's house and took another drink. A door closed somewhere down the hall. People were awake on what promised to be another long day.

They had been on the ground for a week. Firefighters were starting to get a handle on things, the fire now mostly in the national forest. People still needed clothing, shelter, and basic supplies. But that was not their game plan—they distributed food. It felt like a drop against what people needed, but it was something. Something. Helene's voice came on the phone asking when he was coming home.

"Hopefully soon. How is school?"

He let her ramble on, an edge to her voice. He couldn't pry too hard, needing to focus where he was. They talked for a moment before Eddie knocked on the door and called his name. Delany opened the hotel door and told Helene he had to go.

They chatted while he finished getting dressed. He slept in the bed furthest from the window, not that the extra twenty feet made any different for the noise. Eddie reached for the book he was reading off the other bed. The spare bed helped organize his life on the field with binders with information, the few shirts he brought, pants neatly folded beside them. There were notepads with notes from meetings and daily totals of how much food they served, communities they reached. A picture of him and Helene from Halloween a few years before sat on the table between the beds. It helped to see her first thing.

They drove to the kitchen at the high school only a few blocks away having moved hotels after getting the kitchen established. Alice had already been there for hours, hundreds of meals waiting. Before Delany could say hello, Eddie pulled him into a string of interviews. Once the press found out he was there, he was bound to become part of the story. He tried to keep it off him and on the people of northern New Mexico and what they needed.

He walked toward the kitchen, ready to do something productive. Alice came out of the door, waiting while he got closer. They chatted for a minute, Alice trying to check her watch again. "Are you late for something?"

Her eyes went wide. "No, I just don't want people to think I ran off."

He crossed his arms. Samson mentioned how much she'd been working, how he had no idea when she slept, and how it felt like she was always at the school.

"When was the last time you were out of this kitchen?"

"Does the hotel count?" Alice chuckled.

"Have you seen the area at all?" He rocked back. She shook her head. "Come on."

"I need to be here." She pointed toward the kitchen.

Delany reached for her wrist. "I think you need to see what you're making possible."

"Delany." Eddie appeared at the end of the hall. "FEMA wants a word."

He lowered his head, failing to keep back his annoyance. Alice slipped her arm back and walked toward the kitchen.

Delany found her later on the football field, working to serve the firefighters from a food truck. She started it the weekend before, wanting to provide fresh meals around the clock for the men and women fighting the fires as they got off their shifts. She did a variety of meals, breakfast bowls or pancakes in the morning, hamburgers and fries for lunch, meatloaf for dinner.

He stepped through the back door of the food truck. Alice set some fried chicken on top of the French fries and coleslaw with corn, black beans, and peppers. He'd tried some in the kitchen before coming out, the lime adding an unexpected tang.

"Are you here to help?" Alice asked.

"No. FEMA cleared a way for us to reach some places near the Colorado border that have been cut off because of the fire. We need to take some food to them. Come with me."

She hesitated, looking out the window. "I should stay." Her tone betrayed her. She asked the firefighter outside what he wanted. Delany filled the to-go box and handed it to him, the man thanking them.

"Come with me." He put his hand on her back. "Eddie can get someone to cover."

She nodded. He left to find a volunteer. They were almost done loading the cargo van when she came out of the school, drinking a bottle of water. It had been full sun since they arrived, yet she was still pale. Her hair hadn't been washed in a few days. She walked a bit slower, her eyes heavy.

"Are you sleeping?" he asked when she got closer.

"I'm fine."

Samson called they were ready to go. Alice walked to the

passenger seat of the full van. Delany got an apple from the crate before closing the side door. She was texting someone when he hopped into the driver's seat.

"For you." He held out the apple.

She pressed her lips, not taking it. "Mr. Clare…"

"Stop with the Mr. Clare, okay? After all this. You need to take care of yourself, Alice."

She reached for it and turned in her seat, dropping it back in the bin. He started to call her out when she leaned further back and got two bananas, handing him one. He slid it into the cup holder and started the van.

"We were about to have a conversation," he said.

"I get it. I know." She started to eat. They fell into a caravan of medical people and FEMA staff. The truck ahead carried a tank of fresh water for the community. The back of their van held enough food for a few days along with crates of Alice's fresh cooked chili, her wild rice, and cranberry salad. At one point he looked over and found Alice asleep, her head against her fist by the window. He reached to turn on the radio. Someday he'd ask how many hours she worked.

They drove on, the sun setting lower on the horizon. It was a slow drive, the road gone in some places. They waited as the forest service cut through fallen trees to make a way. The forest around them was nothing but black trees and ash. Alice looked around her, her hands under her legs.

"Pretty crazy, huh?" he said.

"How do you recover from this?"

"It takes time, but people are resilient. How are you doing?"

Alice gathered her thoughts before she glanced at him.

"This is amazing, Delany. What you've started, what you all do…" She shook her head. "Thank you for the opportunity." She held his gaze.

"Thank you for coming." He glanced at her, getting up his nerve. "Can I ask you something, did Jonas train you?"

Alice closed her eyes and laughed. She apologized, the chuckle still running through her.

"That hack? He wouldn't know cinnamon from cardamom if his life depended on it. He better be grateful Cornelia died or he'd still be peddling his garbage back in L.A. No. I was the sous chef under Cornelia. After he died, Jonas got hired and told me I'd be going back to sauce prep unless I 'earned my keep.' I told him to stick his sausage in some béchamel and walked out. That man has been denigrating me to whoever will listen ever since." She shook her head. "That's why I'm here. He's made me a pariah, implying I only got to where I was with Cornelia because I slept with him. He acts like I offered, and he turned me down. There isn't a woman alive Jonas would not sleep with."

"I see." Now it made more sense, Jonas' tone toward Alice, their different cooking styles and preferences.

She went back to watching the scenery. It was the first time they were alone together since leaving D.C. He wanted to talk about things, ask why she refused to give him a shot. After she left with Katy he wondered if she came to quit, the idea making his heart ache. He'd reset whatever boundaries she wanted, *just don't leave.* Since meeting her, he wanted to do more than go through the motions. He knew the difference now between existing and living.

"You okay over there?" Alice asked. Delany smiled, unsure what to say. Katy mentioned something when they talked earlier about an invoice for Carrie's birthday Bobbie refused to pay. Bobbie told Katy to include it with the other invoices for what *the caterer* did for Macon. But it was a private event. Delany paid Alice for cooking for him at the house, Bobbie needed to pay for that meal himself.

"Bobbie's been calling all day. It's nothing."

"Why do you keep him around? If I can ask."

"We go way back…"

"I know that. It seems sometimes he's against everything you stand for. Would he get what's happening here?" She closed her eyes. "I'm sorry. Not my place. I'm exhausted. Forget I asked."

"It's okay. He's like a brother. We grew up together." He met her gaze for a moment, Alice saying a quiet okay before looking out the window. Things went silent again.

"When I was in seventh grade some guys at the high school thought it might be a good idea to put me back in my place. They planned to grab me after one of our home games and beat the crap out of me. Bobbie overheard them talking about it at the local convenience store and told his dad. His dad came to the game, made sure I got home safe, and then got some of his friends together to find this group and let them know if anything happened to me, they'd be back. His dad served in Vietnam, was this big broad man." Delany puffed his arms out. "My mom knew who he was, Bobbie's mom her hairdresser at the time. His parents were oil and water. They'd be in love, and then fight down the block. My mom told Bobbie he could be at our house. He was there all the time. He's been at every birthday and major life event since I was thirteen." He rested his head on his fist against the window. "He's one of the few people who was there before I became this basketball prodigy that had to make it for an entire community. I don't have to pretend with him."

"I see. Where does Bulldog come from?"

He snorted. "I hate that nickname. Can't get rid of it." He took a deep breath. "I don't know who my dad is. Well, I do. But he left my mom and didn't give two shits until I made it big. My mom raised me. She's why I am here. That man's fifteen-second contribution doesn't make him my father." He ran his hand over his head. "The one time I saw my dad growing up, he brought me a stuffed animal of Georgetown's mascot. He said it was his dream school growing up."

"A bulldog."

Delany nodded. "Even then, I knew it was all BS and threw it away. Bobbie saw it. My sister told him what happened. He thought it would be funny to call me that and, well, the name stuck."

"Did you ever tell him to quit?"

"Yeah, but we were, what, fourteen at the time? No one listens, and once it got around…"

"I get back then, but he still calls you it now. Why not tell him to cool it?"

Delany shrugged; it was a battle he would not win.

"I get that Bobbie is brash and loud. But to me, he's just trying to live up to his dad who was larger-than-life. Bobbie doesn't get that people respected his dad because of how he treated them. His dad bought me my first suit, taught me how to do a tie. He taught me how to approach women and to help those around me. Bobbie is all bluster, but below that, he's a decent guy." Or at least he used to be.

They pulled into the community after dark. Everyone waited for the caravan inside the one building with lights. Medical personnel went in a side entrance to set up a clinic. Delany carried another crate of food into the building. Alice worked to distribute hot meals, a firefighter giving out bags of food. People sat in clusters, blankets over their shoulders, shellshocked. Kids sat quieter than they should be. After the line went down, Alice thanked the man for helping. He had come to check for hot spots, but there was nothing for the fire to burn.

Alice set a stack of empty trays in the insulated crate. Her chin shook and she tried to take deep breaths. Delany cupped her arm and pulled her out the side door. She leaned into him and wept. He hugged her close, Alice's arms slowly going around him. The things a person saw, the magnitude of the devastation. It weighed on them. It was okay to cry, meant they were human.

"I'm sorry." She brushed at the tears on his shirt.

"It's okay." He could barely find his breath, having her that close.

She touched his cheek, Delany leaning into her hand. Her gaze stayed on his as she leaned up and kissed him. She wrapped her arms around his neck when he dared pull her closer. He ran his hand into her hair, meshing itself under the wrap. A faint moan escaped her.

A voice called into the dark, Alice turning to face the woods. A man stepped closer toward them with two beers in his hand that he offered to Delany before going back inside.

"Do you want one?" He wasn't sure what else to say, still coming off the kiss. She turned back toward him, unable to hold his gaze.

"Can we do this?" She took the beer he'd opened, Delany working on the second one.

"You have to rest sometime. You're not good to these people if you don't take care of yourself."

She sat on the back of the water truck. They watched the scene inside the building. He wanted to reach for her hand, to kiss her again, but sensed she was struggling. He didn't want to ask if the kiss was how she felt or the emotion of the moment. The leader of the caravan came out. The medical people were going to be longer than anticipated and the truck of water needed to stay until the morning. The woman asked if Delany and Alice could take the firefighters down with them. He let them ride in the front, Alice asleep with her head on his leg in the back. He rested his hand on her side, her question lingering. Bobbie was his oldest friend, but lately, it started to feel like a scheme that might not work anymore. Instead of being someone he could pass the ball to, it felt like his best friend tried to block him. He'd heard things while he played, people making comments about Bobbie. He always wrote it off as people who didn't know who Bobbie was. But he started to wonder if maybe he didn't know his best friend like he thought.

# CHAPTER 28

TABBY SIPPED HER WINE, her gaze on the muted morning show. It felt like she was coming undone, one good spark from blowing apart. She snapped at the twins the night before, tired of their incessant need to be entertained and the never-ending questions about when Alice was coming home. She didn't know or care. Let her sister stay in New Mexico until Tabby could find a way to move her back to her apartment. She was over being Alice's free hotel room when her sister didn't understand the meaning of the word loyalty.

Her mother called midmorning, and Tabby let it go to voicemail. When she called back, Tabby realized she wasn't going away and answered the phone.

"I have a luncheon at one. You will be there."

"Mom…"

"No daughter of mine is going to sit at home feeling this sorry for herself." Tabby rolled her eyes. "Don't roll your eyes like you're a moody teenager. You need to do more than wallow at home all day. I will see you at 12:50 sharp!" She hung up. Tabby knew all about this luncheon, a bunch of socialite women with nothing better to do than get together, gossip and donate money.

She put on a cream-colored suit with a purple blouse and her favorite dark blue heels. It felt good to dress like an adult, even if it was to mingle with a bunch of rich White women and pretend to care about the latest gossip. She rode the Metro in and walked toward the hotel.

The smaller ballroom was a sea of color, women with straightened hair, big jewelry, steeped in power. Maybe she could get some business for her sister, surely some of these women needed a cutesy food truck for a child's birthday or backyard event.

Her mother smiled when she saw her, inviting Tabby into the circle of women around her. She made introductions. Several were married to men who worked on The Hill, another's husband ran the hotel they were in. One ran her mother's favorite florist shop; another wrote the society column for *The Washington Times*. Tabby's husband worked at the EPA, and she had two adorable ten-year-olds. Tabby twitched her mouth into a smile. Her identity was back to being wrapped up in her relationship to other people.

Across the room, Carrie stood talking to an older woman whose diamond earrings kept catching the light. She wore a pale-yellow dress, her hair pulled into a higher ponytail. Tabby didn't even recognize her anymore. Where was the girl who felt like a sister, who always told Tabby to hold her own, and at one time seemed so fearless?

Tabby sat by her mother and listened to the presentation. Maybe there was something to her mother's champagne lunches. Paul made enough. She could be generous. Get on some boards, come to things like this. If she let her mother control her calendar, she could be out of the house every day. She tried to buck the system and failed. Even in 2009, women couldn't have it all.

Her mother told the other women at the table she'd see them next month. Tabby checked her phone, nothing

"See, that wasn't so bad."

"Mom, can I ask you something?"

Her mother reached for her wine and waited.

"Most of the women here, you identified them by who their husbands are."

"I guess so. But what else would you identify them by? They are only able to attend something like this because of what their husbands do all day."

"What about who they are?"

Her mother put her glass down and turned to face Tabby more. "What am I supposed to say? Mary has two kids and loves British baking shows. Amina just got over cancer and hopes to be a writer someday. Elizabeth worked at The Newseum until she got pregnant, only to lose the baby, and she still hasn't found her footing again."

"I just…" She took a moment. "What if I always introduced you as the wife of horticulturalist Dr. James Gibson?"

Her mother smiled. "There would be worse things to be identified by."

Tabby groaned and put her napkin on the table.

"I hear what you're saying, Kitty Cat. I do. There are seventy-two women in the House this term. Seventy-two out of 435 seats. That is abhorrent, and yet, for the," she did the math in her head, "roughly 350 women here because of their husbands, this is what they can do. I agree with you that too often we get labeled by our husband's achievements. But what I want you to see is that just because you don't run a company anymore does not mean you still do not have something to give." She took Tabby's chin in her hand like she did when the girls were little. "You have tremendous power, Tabatha Black. Whether you run your own company or raise those twins well. You have privilege and power and means. Do something positive with it." She raised her eyebrows.

"Yes, ma'am." She said what she had to.

Her mother released her and set her napkin on the table. "I need to make a stop by the boutique on my way out, do you want to come?"

Tabby shook her head. Her mother stood and reached for her purse.

"The longer you deny your anger, the harder this transition is going to be. I love you." She kissed Tabby's cheek and headed for the door. Tabby thought about texting Paul, offering to take him coffee. But what was the point? She sighed and grabbed her purse.

"Tabby," Carrie said as soon as she stepped out of the room.

"What could you possibly have to say to me?"

"I know, I'm a horrible person who did an unforgivable thing. But how can you still be so mad at me with what's going on with Alice?"

"What do you mean, what does Alice have to do with anything?"

Carrie stepped toward her; Tabby unsure she'd ever seen Carrie so unsure. There were bags under her eyes; she was thinner than she should be.

"She's working for Macon, catering almost all their events. She's Delany's personal chef, at his place a few times a week cooking meals."

"Since when?" Heat rushed her body, Tabby pulling at the collar of her blouse.

"July. Listen, Tabs, I know what I did was repugnant, but I miss my best friend."

Tabby laughed, bending forward slightly. It broke the charge that had been building since she found out who Alice went to New Mexico with, Tabby needing the release.

"This isn't like stealing my sweater or sleeping with Ricky in college. You sold my company to your bedmate and screwed me out of my life's work. Miss me all you want; I don't give a damn about you anymore." She walked away, her skin on fire. In a disaster zone or not, her sister had some explaining to do.

#

ALICE HANDED THE FIREFIGHTER her sloppy joe and potato fries with fresh aioli. The woman thanked her before going to get a soda from the ice chest at the far end of the food truck. Alice looked at the space around her, wondering why Val never thought about doing shelves along the ceiling. A breeze came in the back doors, taking the smell of smoke further away from them. She'd found a rhythm between making meals, serving meals, coordinating dozens of volunteers, and keeping track of what food they had on hand. Delany hinted they might be close to leaving, resources already being diverted elsewhere. Samson left the day before to be on site of a fire in northern California. Eddie asked if Alice wanted to go too, but when she left New Mexico, she was going home.

Delany came in the back with a pan of sloppy joes and more buns. Alice thanked him and slid them into the warming tray before turning to take the fries out of the fryer. He talked to those who came to the window, Alice getting their meals. Several called hello to Alice, who leaned over to wave. With Delany there to help serve, she could work on dinner, shredding lettuce and dicing tomatoes for taco salads.

"What time did you start today?" Delany leaned on the front counter and crossed his arms. Alice got a bin of lettuce hearts from the fridge and pulled more to chop.

"Listen, you didn't care what time I started for two weeks. Don't go asking questions now."

He lifted his arms and turned to help the person outside. He leaned toward the window more to talk to them, the truck almost too short for him to be in without having to stoop. Alice sucked her lips. She came on the trip prepared to quit. Make amends, even the score and get out. But after feeling the strength in his arms as she cried, the way it felt to kiss him, Alice questioned if she had the strength. Her head told her to walk away. Everything would change when they got back to D.C. But she had never wanted to be in the trench with someone, to figure out life and face things together like she did with him. Feeling Delany's heart break after the fight with Nadia, Alice wanted to speak to him as someone engaged with his life, someone there for the long haul. Delany was the first man she ever saw a future with that did not require her to deny or give up any part of herself. Watching him laugh with whoever stood outside the window, Alice admitted she might be in love with him.

Her cell rang, Alice touching Delany's shoulder.

"I'm going to take this." Alice slipped out of the food truck. "Hey, Tabby."

"How is Mr. Clare doing?"

"He's fine." She plugged her ear to hear Tabby better, the connection not the best. "Why do you care…"

"Mom told me who you're traipsing through the desert with. But I guess it's not a random nonprofit, since you've been Delany's personal chef since the summer."

Alice swallowed, sound seeming to fade. "How did you…"

"That's your response? I find out you've been lying to me for months, that your rise came by aligning with the man who stole everything from me, and you ask who spilled the beans? Why didn't you tell me?"

"Do you care, or do you already have it all figured out?" Alice drew in her breath. Delany stood in the back door of the truck, Alice shaking her head. "I was going to tell you…" She turned away, her heart racing.

"When? I've been home since August and you've been scurrying out of here at all hours like we're your private hotel, lying to my face. If you wanted to tell me, Alice, you would have."

She hung up. Alice lowered her head and focused on breathing.

"What's wrong?" Delany put a hand on her back.

"Tabby knows."

# CHAPTER 29

ALICE WORKED TO SHUT DOWN the kitchen for the final time. With the fire almost contained and the community relying on other support, Comida's piece of the puzzle was done. Alice went with Delany and Eddie to ensure the kitchens and food trucks were good to keep going, dispersing their remaining food and supplies. She hugged those she met, the chefs in the communities teaching her so much. In only a few weeks, they'd given her a masterclass in southwest and indigenous cooking. She was excited to incorporate what they taught her. How had the culinary world overlooked indigenous chefs for so long?

She sat at the airport with Eddie, Delany getting them coffee. Give her a proper shower and fresh clothes and let her eat something she did not cook. When Eddie got off his call to his family, she asked how he got to Comida. He told her about his time in the military, organizing supplies in and out of Iraq, how he loved doing community projects, trying to help people in small ways. He didn't know what to do after he got injured, was in a dark place when he ran into Delany again. The work was a lifeline, helping bring purpose and focus back into his life.

"You see yourself staying with Comida for a while?"

"I can't imagine doing anything else. Before this," he hit his prosthetic, "I planned to cycle from Joburg to London. Doesn't seem possible now."

Delany came back with their coffees. Alice thanked him and took a sip. It wasn't hotel or mass-produced coffee, it was incredible.

"And what do you want?" Eddie asked.

Alice shrugged. "What I have right now is pretty nice."

"No, come on. I told you my dream was never going to happen. Let's hear it. I know there's something."

Alice took a long drink of her coffee. What did she have to lose?

"When I was little my dad used to love this curry kitchen in the food court of the Old Post Office building. I always thought it would be cool if someone bought it and restored it. I was going to run the restaurant in it." She shook her head and took a drink.

"It just sold, right?" Eddie said. Delany took a drink of his coffee.

"To some stupid conglomerate that's going to come in and ruin it."

"That's pretty cynical." Delany laughed.

Alice looked at him, her chest constricting. "Forgive me, but I don't have a lot of hope given they just hired the worst overinflated chef to put his bland as dirt food in there. I just—" She stopped. No use getting worked up over what she could not change. "It's hard to see it sit for so long, then have it sell to someone who does not even care to give it to a local chef, much less a decent one."

They boarded their flight, somehow Alice ending up with a window seat. She thought about reading or taking a nap, but her mind wouldn't settle. Delany sat next to her in the aisle, reading a book a volunteer gave him. His beard had filled out since they left. He'd smiled more the last few weeks, an ease to him she never encountered in D.C.

No way someone like Bobbie or Jonas could have done what Delany did. He was in the trenches, working hard, helping people, not caring about the credit. The only time he complained was with the press making him the story. What they saw all day was challenging, yet he treated everyone around him with care and dignity. He saw people. They weren't charity cases or numbers. He took the time to talk to people, know their names, and remember things about them.

After working together for so long, she believed he was being honest about how things went down with Tabby. Bobbie's need to control with Carrie and Harry's desire to sell, no wonder they didn't give her sister any warning. And that wasn't Delany's fault. It was wrong for Tabby to blame him for Bobbie's decisions. Delany was a kind man who tried to do right by people.

Her head told her to walk away. Her heart wanted to lean in, to scoot closer and kiss him, to stop pretending she did not care about him. She had no idea what was going to happen with Tabby. It was wrong not to tell her, but Alice stood by the choice. She hoped her sister would give her the chance to explain, and maybe Alice could help Tabby see who Delany was.

# CHAPTER 30

ALICE TRIED TO PUT TOGETHER a cohesive rundown of the trip for Carver the next day at the bakery. It was busy for a Wednesday, but Carver seemed ready to block it all out. Alice needed to process what she'd seen, what she had been a part of. It felt weird to be back in a place with such abundance. People went about their days with no consideration for those who were suffering in other places. The uneaten croissant on Carver's napkin would be well-appreciated where she'd been. How did she let the staff throw away as much food as they did? Surely there was something better to be done with it.

She went with Rita to their usual setup on K Street. She didn't need to do it anymore, except the local crowd appreciated they were there. Needing to not think, she let Rita oversee the front. There was something simple and uncluttered about the food truck. To go back to May with Valencia there. Only she wouldn't give up anything she was doing now. Comida felt like an unexpected gift, helping to realign Alice to what mattered.

Delany showed up after the lunch rush ended. Alice introduced him to Rita. They chatted while Alice made his lunch. He appeared at the back doors just as it was ready. Alice told Rita she'd be back and stepped onto the street. They found a park bench to sit on. Alice drank her water while Delany leaned into his knees and took a few bites. She studied the line of his chin, his broad shoulders. He was back to wearing his usual tailored slacks and blazer, his trilby hat.

"How is the office?" She broke the silence.

He looked over his shoulder and shrugged. "Still there. Katy's good. She could run that place."

"And Bobbie?"

He laughed. "Sometimes I think half her job is keeping Bobbie from running away with things." He finished his meal and set the box on the bench beside him before he wiped his hands and sat back. "Nothing can get done without my okay. How are you?"

She shrugged one shoulder. "A little overwhelmed to be honest."

"Yeah, it can be like that. We come back to all this, knowing what we left." He faced her on the bench, his arm behind her. "I'm here if you want to talk. I know Eddie is available too."

"Do you want to get dinner tonight?" It flew out of her mouth before she could stop it. He smiled wide, Alice's heart racing.

"That would be lovely." He touched her cheek.

Alice studied his eyes. Rita called her name, a line waiting at the food truck.

"I have to go." She stood.

"I can pick you up at seven if that works."

"Let me meet you there." Easier than trying to think of something to tell her sister. "If that's okay."

"That's fine. I was thinking Emre."

"I will see you tonight."

She texted her sister to say she was working late. Annie clued Alice into Tabby's reaction to what was going on, who thought Alice went with a credible organization, not some rogue cowboy. Annie mocked her sister's tone in the car, Paul laughing too hard to scold her. Apparently, Tabby ranted about things to Cyndi, a new regular in her mother's life. It sounded like Tabby had a captive new audience for the drama of her takeover, the family starting to be less supportive of her decision to seethe.

It would be best to lay low for a few days. Not hard considering all the work piled up for the back end of Hasty Pudding on top of prepping for their upcoming events. It might be time for her to move back to her place. She'd be closer to the bakery, and it would give her a bit of privacy.

She went to the clothing stores around Carver's bakery and found an off-the-shoulder, dark-blue, straight cocktail dress that fell to her knee. She bought some new heels and prayed she could walk in them. Carver gave her his fob for the gym down the street so she could shower. They had done it before when she came in covered in sweat from the ride in or needed to shower before an evening event. She changed into shorts and a T-shirt she kept in a bag in Carver's office. He motioned to the dress on the back of the door.

"That's not for an event, Lil."

"I have a date tonight."

"With whom?" He looked up from his work and smiled.

"Don't think I'm a sellout."

He stood and tossed his pen onto the checkbook. "Are you giving Delany Clare a shot?" He came around the desk.

"We're going to Emre."

"Damn. Not that I'd expect any less. I want a full rundown in the morning." He sat on the back of his desk and crossed his arms. "My, my. We should have sent you all away sooner."

"Because a disaster zone is where you find love." She rolled her eyes. He laughed. "This is okay, right? I mean, after what…"

"His company did to your sister? His second-in-command did to your sister? This is a good thing. You deserve to be happy. I don't know if I have ever seen you smile like that."

Carver got a photo of her all dolled up. She promised to email it to Valencia, who kept sending playful Skype messages from Spain. Things were going well with her mother. Valencia loved getting to know her siblings, but sounded restless. Alice kept herself from asking Val to come home. She wanted her friend there, able to see a host of things they could do together with Hasty Pudding so well-established.

Alice let out her breath and walked to Emre. She'd been on dates since her ex left. Bad setups, or men who seemed charming at first, but only wanted one thing. It had been a while since she'd been attracted to someone, and she had forgotten these fun emotions. Her stomach was in knots, and she felt above her body and happy. Hopefully those were good signs.

Delany stood outside the restaurant with a small bouquet of white peonies. He had changed into a blue suit, no tie, the first two buttons open. His brown hat brought out his eyes, and he'd trimmed his beard back to only accenting his chin. *Holy cheese puffs.*

He saw her and smiled, doing a once-over on her.

"You look incredible," he said when she got close. He reached for her hand and gave her the bouquet of her favorite flower.

"How did you know?"

"You mentioned it once. Have a tattoo on your thigh, right?"

He held the door for her, the host leading them to a table in the back. When the server came, Delany ordered a bottle of red wine.

"I have to admit, it's pretty intimidating taking a chef on a date. I mean, what if you hate the food?"

"This is one of my favorites. I know Garrett."

They ordered their meals, and then there was nothing to

distract her from the person she'd been trying to convince herself not to care about for the last three months and a mountain of emotions she was not expecting. She asked about Samson in northern California. Delany reached for her hand, telling her they didn't have to talk about work.

"Have you ever been to Spain?" Delany asked. She shook her head. "Europe?"

"Tabby and I went for a few months after I graduated high school."

"Did you all stay in hostels?"

"Have you met my sister?" Alice asked. He leaned into the table and laughed, Alice smiling too. "Yeah, no. Besides, my mother would never have let us stay in one. She'd be too scared of us getting hurt or contracting a disease or getting robbed." She reached for her wine. The server came with their first set of tapas. Alice slipped a slice of rolled ham into her mouth, wanting to know how they got it so flavorful. It sat on her tongue, Alice closing her eyes and trying to pick out the spices they used. The menu said it was cured for twenty months. It must start with the pig—something local, humanely raised, no additives in the diet. She could eat the whole plate if Delany wasn't there.

She forced herself to chew and swallow. "What?"

"Just enjoying watching the master appreciate food. I don't know if I've ever seen you leave the room like that."

Her face warmed. They ate, talking like old friends. He told her why he chose to retire, sharing fears Alice wondered if he ever told another person. A new side opened to her, someone well-read and observant, who thought a lot about the world around him and his place in it.

The executive chef came to the table after Delany ordered dessert and another bottle of wine. It was obvious Garrett knew Delany, that he came to Emre a lot. Garrett asked Alice how she was. They talked before he went back to his kitchen.

"Can I ask you something," Delany said when Garrett left. Alice took a bite of her dessert and waited. "Every time we see another chef, they are nice to you. I get Jonas did you wrong, but why not just work in another kitchen?"

Alice sighed. "In Cornelia's kitchen I was second chef, so when he was away, I ran that place. We worked on menus together. I got a say in who we hired. He started talking about my taking over when they found their next location. And then he died." She sat back. "I could work in another kitchen. I could work for Garrett. But it would be as a station chef or as the meat chef. And that's where I'd stay. There would always be an excuse why I was overlooked, a reason why some man with half my experience got promoted over me. There is a ceiling in this industry. There is rampant sexism. I worked too hard to be making sauces forever or prepping vegetables. I am a good chef with creative ideas and the only way I can cook what I want is to do it this way. So I went to Carver and am taking a less traditional route that lets me cook the food I want, my way."

"Do you want your own restaurant?"

She thought about it. "If you asked me a year ago, hell yeah. But that's capital I don't have. Now, this, what we're doing, I'm kind of enjoying it."

They walked toward The Washington Monument, lit up for the night. Delany undid his jacket and put it over her shoulders, Alice thanking him. He took her hand, Alice floating. If she met Delany under any other circumstance, she'd fallen over herself to get another date. Maybe things had to come slowly so she trusted him. He was nothing like her ex, unlike anyone she'd ever met.

"Helene's birthday is this weekend. I know she'd love to see you."

"Do you want me to cook for it?"

"You can just come." He chuckled and smiled.

"I know, but I'd love to make something fun and special for her. See if I can stump that incredible palate of hers."

He laughed. "Let me call Nadia."

They stopped walking. She faced him, the look in his eyes humbling, full of respect and care.

"I had a good time tonight, Alice."

"I did too."

He kissed her, Alice moaning. She opened to him, her knees threatening to give out. His hand on her cheek, the strength of his arms. The earth tones of his cologne. It had been so long since she'd been kissed in a way that made her heart race. She only wanted to stay on that patch of grass with the lights on the monument, the trees around them changing colors for the fall.

She tried to catch her breath when he left her, her eyes still closed. His thumb stroked her cheek. It wasn't just the emotion of New Mexico; she was falling fast and hard.

He kissed her again in the cab outside Tabby's building. Alice kept herself from asking to go back to his place; it was too soon for that.

"I can come by the bakery after work tomorrow."

"I'll see you then." Alice made herself get out of the cab. In the lobby she realized she still wore his jacket, the cab gone. She took the elevator to Tabby's floor. *Please let them be asleep.* She needed to stop smiling. The second she tried the beam overtook her face again. She shook her head, still unable to believe what changed in just a few short days.

# CHAPTER 31

ALICE CAME OUT OF HER BEDROOM the next morning still on cloud nine. The twins ate breakfast in the kitchen. Alice kissed Annie on the head before going to get a cup of coffee. For the first time in six years, Alice was with someone who cared about her. She told herself she'd never meet a man not like her ex. But Paul was right—if she never trusted someone, she would never know what was possible. It was wrong to let one person taint her view of every other man. Not that her ex was close to the kind of man Delany was and what he did for her. She always felt like her ex settled to be with her, nothing she did was enough, who she was was not enough. Delany made her feel like an equal, called her out of her shell and to take up space as herself.

Tabby leaned on the counter and crossed her arms. "What event did you have last night?" She was fishing. Alice understood her sister felt betrayed, but nothing would spoil her mood.

"I stayed to catch-up on office work. It's impossible to get anything done with Carver there."

"Interesting. When are you going to tell me why you've lied to me for the last six weeks?"

Paul came into the room and poured himself a cup of coffee. He stayed facing the pot, but looked toward Alice and shook his head, seemingly as over the conversation as Alice was.

"Five minutes," he said before leaving them alone.

"Delany asked me to go with his nonprofit. It was a once-in-a-lifetime opportunity. I know TabiKat was your dream, but you still have a roof over your head and a place to sleep. Your kids are safe. You have running water. Stop using Delany as a scapegoat, bitterness doesn't look good on anyone." She went to get her messenger bag, sliding Delany's suit jacket just under the flap. Paul held the front door open, telling Tabby to have a good day. Alice asked Annie about basketball, ready to think about something else. In the garage, Paul unlocked his BMW X5, the twins running to their doors.

"I think what you did is remarkable," he said.

"Most people would agree." Alice got into the passenger seat. They pulled out of the apartment, taking the twins to school before joining the slog into D.C. The metro passed them as they waited to get onto I-395. Alice set her head on her fist. She refused to play her sister's cat-and-mouse-game. Normally, she'd beg and justify and apologize to no avail because once Tabby set her mind about something, it became like dried gum paste. It was easier to salvage a broken roux than to get her sister to reconsider her opinion. She'd all but written Carrie out of her life, calling her nothing but a backstabbing gold digger—and that was her best friend of fifteen years! Their time at USC and since meant nothing because she betrayed Tabby. Mo Mo practically lived at the apartment for over a year as he and Tabby worked to code WlkmNt. He brought her food and water, was there for her to bounce ideas off of, became her sounding board. He did as much work for the website as she did but to hear her tell it, she did it all by herself.

Tabby decided Delany was nothing but a scoundrel and nothing Alice said could change that. All his good work, how he treated others, how he treated her, would get lost in the fact he bought out Tabby's company. It was a fight Alice couldn't win. If Tabby would let go of her anger and give Alice a chance, she would love to apologize and explain. But she refused to do it with that smug superiority in her sister's gaze, Tabby not actually listening but just waiting to tell Alice what a horrible person she was and how she would never have done the same thing. As if her sister hadn't done things other people would consider horrible or unforgivable.

Paul dropped her off at the bakery. Alice walked inside calling hello to those working in the front before going to the office and hanging Delany's coat on the hanger on the back side. She reached for an extra white coat to cover up with, the A/C chilling her to the bone.

Carver stood beside the pastry case in the front.

"And?" He smiled at her.

"We had a lovely time." Alice took a muffin and went to try and warm up in the office.

Rita arrived midmorning. She was in her mid-fifties, slender frame with flecks of gray in her auburn hair. Her close-set black eyes helped call out her narrow features. Her fingers looked like they should be flying over the piano, not marred by the spices they used in hand tossing their meats.

Delany emailed ideas for Helene's birthday that weekend, Alice ready to see what she could pull together. She worked on the back end of things for a bit, Carver doing almost nothing while she was gone. She sat through meetings for upcoming events, trying to get back into a rhythm. Things felt different now. After seeing what people faced in New Mexico, the loss of everything, the way a simple meal could affect their day, petty trivialities didn't appeal. Maybe that was why she had no time for Tabby's theatrics.

Yes, she shouldn't have lied, but she was over the torch Tabby cultivated to keep from having to try again. Pre-acquisition Tabby would never let Bobbie keep her out of the industry. She would have figured out a way to start over, yes, without the funding from The Stooges, but she knew more now than she did before. Tabby acted like her only ideas were the ones Array now held. Delany was an excuse, and Alice would not indulge her sister's need to keep being the victim. Alice picked herself up after Jonas pushed her out of Cornelia's kitchen and the industry. Tabby could get over what happened with Macon and move on.

# 

DELANY SANG ALONG WITH BEYONCÉ while the elevator got to his floor. He smiled wide, not caring who saw. He was crazy in love. Alice Gibson held his heart, and he only wanted to see her again. Hollywood couldn't have written a better first date. They were in the zone, where the magic happened. Throwing the game winning three at the Final Four was nothing compared to how it felt when Alice moaned as he kissed her and pressed closer. It took all his restraint not to ask her to stay the night. But he cared about her and wanted to show he was there for the long haul. After three weeks together things felt off without her close. Just let him whisk her away to somewhere warm and private but he had to work. The day was going to be alright because she waited at the end of it.

The elevator opened on his floor. He walked toward his office, Katy leaving his paper and coffee on his desk.

"You're happy today," she said. Delany smiled and set his hat onto the edge of his desk. "Date went well?"

"I'm the luckiest man in D.C! Send some flowers to the bakery, something with peonies and maybe a hibiscus in it."

"I'm on it. Moe is here to see you." Katy walked out. He

logged into his computer and beat his fingers on his desk like a drum until Mr. Manuel came in. Delany stood and shook his hand, asking how everything was going. One thing he appreciated about Mr. Manuel was he knew he was getting the truth. When he said things were going well and the employees were finding a rhythm, the cultures of the previous companies almost opposite in tone, Delany knew he wasn't just trying to appease the boss.

"What's going on?" Delany asked after Mr. Manuel gave him the update.

"We're having some issues with BackDoor. We're working on the feature that integrates the data into a snapshot, enabling systems to be pulled up almost as a desktop versus individual files. Tabby started to program it before everything happened." He chose his words carefully. Delany leaned into his desk, starting to ask Moe about the sale from his perspective. "Unfortunately, no one in the office knows app coding as well as she did it. We decided to start a new file to see if we could figure it out, but now the app overrides the backups."

This wasn't the time to dredge up what happened over the summer. The timetable for BackDoor was quick, but they wanted to get a second app out before the press died down.

"What do you suggest?" A coach told him once to ask those around him for solutions. If he wanted Macon to be able to run while he was gone, he needed to empower those he hired to do their jobs. He never wanted a funnel like Bobbie cultivated.

"I'd like to call Tabby, if I may."

"Do you think Mrs. Black would be open to helping us?"

Moe bobbed his head. "I think Tabby sees these apps as an extension of herself. If I can approach things from that angle, she just might be willing to help."

He sat back. "Offer her whatever you think is reasonable. I'd love for Mrs. Black to hate us a little less." It might be a step toward maybe getting her back in the building, and it might help Alice too. They never spoke about the phone call she got in New Mexico, Alice seemingly unwilling to talk to him about it.

"I'll call her." They both stood. Delany shook his hand again before Moe walked out the door, saying hello to Bobbie who came into the office with his brow pinched.

"What did Mo Mo want?" Bobbie pointed toward him. "Do I need to take care of something?"

"Mr. Manuel was giving me an update." He sat and looked at his emails, nothing he particularly wanted to take on. His cell phone sat just off to the side. He debated texting Alice good morning. Might be a bit bold, but this girl made him want to be upfront. There was no pretense with her, only raw honesty. All the pressure and pretense of the life around him fell away with her. Delany knew he could be himself, really himself, letting her into the thoughts and ideas that never got shared. He'd never met another person he connected to like that. Maybe this was how it was supposed to be, finding someone to be real and unfiltered with.

Bobbie said his name. Delany looked up; he'd missed something. Bobbie sat in the chair across from him, his left foot on his right knee, a game ball under his hand.

"What's going on with the Jonas deal? Legal won't give me a contract. I tried to get it done while you were gone but they kept dragging their heels." He tossed the game ball from Delany's first championship. Delany told him before not to do it. His best friend was uncoordinated, and there were things around them that couldn't be replaced. Alice would have to wait.

"We're not hiring Jonas." After tasting his food and hearing what he did to Alice, Delany would not support or associate with a chef like that. Even without Alice in the picture, better chefs lived in D.C. Delany hired Derek Collins as The Cora's general manager. He had overseen successful hotels in Miami and New York City and got the vision of what Delany wanted. Delany planned to get his unbiased opinion on what chef to hire. Bobbie caught the ball again.

"Bulldog, I've vetted the viable chefs in D.C. Jonas will bring in the clientele. His reputation is impeccable."

"His food sucked. I'm going to talk to Collins about hiring Alice."

"The caterer?" Bobbie set his hand over the ball on his leg. "I know you're sweet on her, but she's a bad omen. No one wants that girl. Why do you think she runs a food truck?" He shifted the ball to throw it again. Delany stood and caught it midair and put it back on its holder on the bookshelf before leaning next to it.

"This is my dream project, Bobbie. I don't want Jonas involved."

Bobbie put his foot down and leaned into his knees. "That's a mistake. Jonas is looking at new locations. If we miss this chance to get him, it might not come again. Trust me on this, Bulldog. The hotel will be better for it."

Maybe he was exhausted coming back from New Mexico, but Delany thought he was being clear he didn't want Jonas. In fact, he never asked Bobbie to find a chef or be involved in The Cora at all.

"I'll call Jonas and get him to do another meal. He was having an off day."

Delany stood, his heart beating faster. "Listen, The Cora is my project." He talked over Bobbie. "We are not hiring Jonas. Do me a favor and go do the job I hired you for and pretend my hotel does not exist. You have no say in anything that happens within the specs of that building. Got it?"

Bobbie sat there with his mouth ajar, paled if possible. "Yeah, Bulldog. Of course."

Delany started to tell him to stop calling him that but swallowed back his frustration. It went down bitterly.

"Go do your job, Bobbie. There are plenty of other things you should be focused on." Delany walked out of the office, needing to clear his head and not be near his best friend.

#

TABBY TOOK ANOTHER DRINK of her wine, a morning show on the TV. After all she had done—putting her neck out there, starting that stupid company, leveraging her family's savings, her marriage, time with her kids—her little sister chose to repay her by gallivanting with the scoundrel. She would still be wallowing on K Street in that little food truck if not for her! Instead of showing any appreciation, Alice acted like Tabby did nothing at all. As if letting her live rent free for a year while she pushed Alice to do more than wallow was a given. Paul told her to see the bigger picture. She did see it—her little sister thought she could have her tasty pudding and eat it too.

The cleaning lady called into the apartment. Tabby turned off the TV. She didn't like to be there while the woman cleaned, it made her feel pretentious. She stood and put her wineglass in the sink, steading herself on the counter. She was in no position to drive. Fortunately, there were a dozen coffee shops and cafes within a mile. A walk might do her good. She grabbed her purse and told the woman to have a lovely day.

The September humidity weighed her down. Within a few blocks, she shed her lightweight pullover and slipped her hair into a messy ponytail. A few people jogged past her on the path that ran alongside the river. Her cell phone rang. Tabby scoffed. What in the world could Mo Mo want?

"Hello." She found a bench in the shade and sat.

"Hey, Tabby, do you have a minute?"

"I have all the time in the world for you." She didn't care about her tone.

"Thank you for making time," he said. Tabby rolled her eyes. Get a backbone for once and tell her what a jerk she was being. How did she lose her company to this worm? "We need your help."

Tabby laughed. "That's rich, Mo Mo." She waited for him to speak again. "You're serious."

"It's for BackDoor. We need help getting the backups to not save as individual files."

"And what do you expect me to do about that? I don't work there anymore, remember?"

"I do." He paused. "I was hoping maybe you'd help us. I can pay you as a consultant."

"You want me to work as a consultant?" Her voice rose at the end. A jogger looked at her as he went by. Tabby closed her eyes and told herself to breathe.

"Can I meet you at The Willard and show you what's going on?"

Choosing her favorite spot in D.C., nice touch. At least he had the decency to not ask her to meet at Array's offices.

"Would this afternoon work?" Tabby asked, unsure why she agreed to help. Only, BackDoor was her baby and she wanted it to succeed even if that scoundrel got all the credit. She would always know who coded it and he would know it only worked because she stepped in to save things.

Tabby walked through the bar at The Willard. Mo Mo stood from the table. Pressed shirt, gray slacks, purple-striped bowtie. Maybe running things forced him to grow up.

"Thank you for meeting me," he said.

"What is the app doing?" Tabby reached for his laptop. One of her kids was sick and she needed to make it work. Tabby half-listened as Moe explained the problem. She got into the coding and scoffed. They let total amateurs touch her work, no wonder nothing worked. A server came to the table, Moe ordering her a cucumber mojito.

She put her head down and started to troubleshoot. It required her to remove entire parts of the code, but she could rewrite it in her sleep. The app store was still an anomaly for most people. Someday it wouldn't be such a dismal place. Tabby was ahead of the curve with no way of getting her talents out there. This was the one favor she'd give Mo Mo and that ridiculous Delany Clare.

Cyndi texted when she got the twins from school. Tabby looked at the time, unsure where the afternoon went. She asked Moe to run the update on his BlackBerry waiting for it to come up on the laptop. She turned it to face him, the data showing as one cohesive screen.

"Thank you, Tabby."

She shook her head and stood, shoving her phone back into her purse.

"I have some contacts if you're still looking."

She paused and looked at him. "Your boss has told every tech firm in a fifty-mile radius not to touch me."

"That's all Bobbie. Listen, have them call me. I'll tell them Delany offers nothing but a glowing recommendation…"

"Would he?" Her chest tightened. That scoundrel would not assuage his guilt by helping her land on her feet.

"Yes. Listen, I'm sorry for how things went down. I am. I was going to sell you my shares, then Carrie took me to meet with Bobbie. He told me a verbal agreement was as binding as a real one and since I already said I'd be willing to sell to Macon…"

"That's not true, Mo Mo. You had control of your shares until you signed them away." She looked over the restaurant not seeing it, her purse weighing a ton. She could still have her company. "If you just talked to me, told me what was going on, I could have helped. Paul could have done something. It didn't have to end like this." Emotion rose in her throat, Tabby tamping it down. Tears were for weaklings and fools.

"I should have. But it was the three of them against me. Harry told me to stay quiet. Bobbie was threatening me. I was scared, Tabby."

She scoffed. "Yeah, you're a scared little shit that cost me everything."

"And I can't undo that. But I know Delany would support you getting a job anywhere you wanted one."

The only job Tabby wanted Mo Mo currently held. Even if she'd stayed, she wouldn't be leading things. Mo Mo sold her out to become top dog. Tabby built TabiKat without his help; she would not rely on the traitor now.

"I am not going to take career help from a man who couldn't find the gumption to do the right thing." She reached for her purse and walked out.

# CHAPTER 32

**A**LICE DROVE THE CATERING VAN behind the minivan full of servers through Naylor Gardens. Rolling green mounds, manicured lawns, kids playing soccer. A lovely Saturday morning, idyllic almost, except for the fact Alice was not ready to officially meet Delany's ex. The encounter in the apartment lingered, her anger, her presence.

She searched Nadia's name online finding images of her and Delany from when they dated. Delany always made it sound like a casual hookup, but they were together for almost two years, ending with a well-crafted press release saying they remained committed to parenting their daughter as friends. It almost sounded like a divorce instead of a breakup. Everything he said made things sound contentious, and the fight at his apartment confirmed it. It was obvious Nadia knew who she was and that she was a woman used to getting what she wanted.

While they worked to unload the van into the dark stone gazebo they were using as the staging area, the manicured lawn with established dogwoods and a cornucopia of wildflowers blooming between the trees became a Kentucky Derby-themed tea party with pink streamers and balloons, fine china on the tables. Maybe Helene hit a princess phase while they were in New Mexico.

Some of the servers worked on a popcorn stand for the kids with caramel, cheese, and rainbow flavors. Alice grabbed a tray and carried it to one of the kids' tables, setting down three teapots filled with lemonade in various flavors. Tiered trays contained a mix of PB+Js, ham and cheese sandwiches, and various desserts, including macarons and mini cupcakes. Another buffet closer to the gazebo held hot food options and a fruit salad in a horseshoe-shaped bowl. The drink menu featured Derby themed cocktails: mint juleps, old fashioneds, and bee's knees.

Young girls' giggles filled the air. They posed on the red carpet by the parking lot, two photographers snapping photos and telling them to smile. Little girls waited in line in fun dresses and big hats, the boys in colored suit jackets and maybe a hat. The parents dressed for the theme too. Nadia butted her way to the front and walked with Helene, who was dressed in a multi-layered teal halter dress. Nadia wore a hot pink dress that hugged her curves and a matching wide-brimmed hat. They got through before Nadia released Helene's wrist, telling her to have fun and stay clean. Alice dipped back into the gazebo, hoping to go unnoticed.

"So, you're the caterer," Nadia's voice filled the space. Alice swallowed before she turned to face her. Highlighted dark hair framed her square face. Perfect eye makeup caused her big brown eyes to pop. She had a fuller nose and plump lips. Alice ran her hands over her backside, feeling dowdy and unworthy.

"I've heard about you; heard you're trying to get Delany into bed in hopes of getting at his money."

She never would have guessed Bobbie and Nadia were so close. "It's lovely to meet you. Helene talks about you sometimes."

"Don't say my daughter's name to me. Don't act like we're friends or that whatever you think you have with my boo is going to last more than a month. I've done this merry-go-round before. Don't forget that whatever else he tells you, there's a real woman waiting for him in Baltimore." She walked out. Alice felt like someone hit her in the stomach, it took a moment for her to get her breath back.

"You okay, chef?" A younger server came into the gazebo. Alice nodded and turned to find something to do, determined to stay in the background. She could make Helene's day great from afar and give Delany the fun flavored macarons she made for them to try.

"Hi, Alice." Helene stood in the entrance to the gazebo.

"Hey, birthday girl! Are you having a good day?" She knelt and gave her a hug.

Helene sighed. "I look like a cupcake!" She huffed. Alice dropped her head and tried to stifle her laugh. She took both of Helene's hands in hers and met her gaze.

"You are getting a ton of daughter points, believe me." She knew the feeling, having been dragged out to campaign events since before she could walk. Alice chose to forget the outfits her mother made her wear in middle school.

"Why are you hiding out? Are you mad at me?"

"Not at all. I want to make sure you have the best 7th birthday ever." She touched her cheek.

"My dad's going to take me to the Liberty game in New York next weekend. Will you come?"

"I'd love to go." She hoped her smile was convincing.

Delany stepped behind his daughter. "See, I told you she was here."

"Can we get a picture?" Helene looked up at him.

"Here?" Alice started to reach for her camera she took to events.

"No. The red carpet." Helene pointed toward it. Alice looked at Delany, who gave her a hopeful smile.

"Anything for you." Alice stood and took off her purple apron. She felt silly in her strapless off-white dress with its lace cutout overlay and fringe at the bottom. It was all she had in her closet that might work for the day.

"Sweet Jesus," Delany breathed.

Helene laughed. "Daddy."

"Sorry, Bear. Miss Alice looks incredible, doesn't she?"

"Take your time, chef." One of the servers put her hand out for the apron. "We got this."

Delany reached for her hand and kissed the back. He wore a light brown suit with a teal tie that matched Helene's dress, a Gatsby hat.

"You look amazing," he said.

"You look pretty swell yourself."

Helene giggled. Alice remembered she was there and took her hand, letting Helene lead her to the red carpet. She knelt beside her and got some photos before she stood and tried to leave. Delany told her to hold on. He picked up Helene and stood beside Alice, his arm around her. Her heart raced, the thump drowning out the other noise. Delany put Helene down and told Alice to trust him. Before she could understand, he dipped her down. She let out a surprise yelp, then started to laugh. He brought her up and kissed her.

"Thank you for being here." He held her gaze. Alice could only nod. "I want a copy of those." He gave one of the photographers his card before redoing his jacket button. Helene ran to play with her friends. Alice tried to retreat to the gazebo, but Delany caught her wrist.

"Hang out for a bit." Over his shoulder, Nadia huffed, standing beside an older woman with the same square face and dark eyes. Part of her understood that Nadia, like Bobbie, got by on bluster, but did she want to get on the radar of someone who moved through the world so aggressively?

"It's been a while since I've had someone I wanted to be with at one of these things," Delany added.

"Your daughter's birthdays hard social events for you?" Alice looked for Bobbie or Carrie. The last thing she needed was someone telling Tabby she was now dating Delany Clare. This was a mistake.

He chuckled and shook his head, sliding his arm around her. "What's going on?"

"This is just so not my world, Delany." She felt like everyone was whispering about her, asking who she was. Wasn't she the caterer? Yes, she was just the caterer. Here was a man who dated supermodels and actresses and women who looked better when they woke up than Alice did even if she tried. Nadia looked like she came from a *Vogue* shoot. Alice could feel the flour on her fingers.

"This is too soon, isn't it?" he asked. No, that wasn't it at all. She wanted to believe what he told her and the feeling his touch sent through her. But she was back to being in Chase's apartment after the woman dropped her bombshell, questioning everything.

"I forgot, given how much Helene loves you, that this just started."

"Your daughter does not…"

"She does, Alice. You see her. I can't say her mother does." Delany motioned with his head to what was around them. Alice smiled. "Come to the game with us. Please."

Alice couldn't stop the beam that took over her face. Delany kissed her, asking if she minded meeting his sister. Olive stood when they got close, in a black-and-white dress that looked like it belonged in the thirties. Alice stuck out her hand, but Olive bypassed it and hugged her.

"I never got to thank you for my wedding."

The wedding felt like a hundred years ago before Valencia left, and she believed in herself enough to give Hasty Pudding a real chance.

"My brother told me to trust him. I'm glad I did."

They talked about her time in New Mexico, and what Olive loved to do. Alice forgot to be nervous and enjoyed getting to talk with someone so close to Delany. He always spoke about his sister with respect. Delany put his hand on Alice's back and pressed a kiss in her hair.

"You're going to be an uncle." Olive put her hands on her stomach and tilted her head. Delany took a half-step back before he hugged her.

"When are you due?" he asked.

"Hello, Alice." Coretta touched Alice's arm. "Delany said you made today's meal."

"Yes, ma'am. I wanted to make Helene's birthday memorable."

Coretta smiled and leaned in. "You make my son very happy. It's lovely for a mother to see."

"Thank you, ma'am. The feeling is mutual." Alice sucked her lips and tried to hold back her emotion. Delany was bringing her into the lives of those who mattered most, talking about her to them. It overwhelmed her but showed where she stood. She wanted to return the gesture, if only she could.

"How is your father?"

"You know my dad?"

"Yes, we've worked together since the '70s…"

"Miss Alice." Helene reached for her wrist. "Are there any edibles here?"

"What, pretty girl?" Alice put her hand on Helene's head as she repeated her question. They went to the edge of the garden where there was chickweed and spicebush. Helene ate some, smacking her tongue to get the full taste. She did have an incredible palate. Alice ate a sour clover, more in her hand for Helene to try. The chaos of the party faded, Alice enjoying Helene's joy.

"What are you doing?" Nadia's voice broke the moment.

Helene held up what was in her hands for her mother to see. "Why is my daughter eating leaves off a bush?"

"They're edibles," Helene said. "Miss Alice said…"

"Miss Alice needs to remember her place and go refill the buffet. I didn't pay good money for my girl to scrounge in the woods like a savage."

Alice flexed her jaw, debating what to do. The sadness that overwhelmed Helene told Alice the best thing to do was walk away. Remove what only provoked her mother and maybe they could all go back to having a nice afternoon. This was not the time for Alice to assert herself.

"I'll see you later, 'kay, sweetheart." Alice hugged Helene goodbye and started for the gazebo, her hands fisted. She refused to run. Instead, she held her head high, feeling lightheaded and like her skin was on fire. Inside the gazebo, she reached for the disposable platters they used when they planned to slip out early and gave them to the servers, telling them to break down the lines before she started to clean up what was around her.

"That is one pissed off woman," one of the servers said. Alice looked over her shoulder. Nadia stood close to Delany who held Helene, her head on his shoulder. Nadia's finger went from being in his face to the corner she found them in. Alice wanted to climb in a hole. She should have stayed in the gazebo. Nothing was worth the ire of that woman. Hopefully Helene was with her father that night.

"I think we're all set." Rita came back. "I told the grandmother we were leaving. She said she'd pass the news along."

Alice found her purse and reached for the keys for the van. She would talk to Delany about Nadia later. It didn't matter who she was, Alice would not be belittled and humiliated by some jealous ex who refused to accept that Delany moved on. She had been another woman's punching bag before. Alice refused to be treated that way again.

# CHAPTER 33

**D**ELANY DIDN'T EVEN KNOW what happened. One minute he was talking to Olive about the baby, Alice laughing with his mother. The next Olive gripped his arm and motioned behind him. Nadia towered over Alice, who hugged Helene and walked back to the gazebo, her body taut. Then Nadia grabbed Helene's wrist and started to rebuke her. He walked toward them, Helene on the ground, crying. She ran over when she saw him, burying her head in his shoulder.

"What happened?" Before Helene could tell him, Nadia let him know his girlfriend thought it was a good idea to let Helene eat dirt. "They were having fun. It's harmless."

"Harmless?" Nadia snort-laughed. "My daughter being taught to eat grass and any old berry off a bush is harmless? There could be bugs, snakes, poison ivy. It could kill her—harmless." She put her hands on the back of her hips. She wasn't mad about the foraging. She was upset because all day she schemed to make them appear like a happy family, butting into conversations, trying to be on his arm, even suggesting they take family photos on the way in. Delany pulled her aside and reiterated what he said at his apartment, Nadia telling him he was delaying the inevitable and to wake up.

"We can talk about this later," he said.

"We'll talk about it now!" Nadia was ready for the fight. Delany looked from his little girl to the scene of her broken birthday. Activity had stopped; people watched. Before he could speak, Nadia launched into a tirade about her plight as a single mother and everything he did not do. Chasing a skirt and leaving her alone to raise their daughter. Making out with the help at their daughter's birthday. She questioned who he let into Helene's life, threatened to maybe not let her come to D.C. anymore. With him gone all the time, she was a single mother. She even planned the entire party herself.

Only bits and pieces of Nadia's pity rant made it to his brain as the rest of him focused on just how terrified Helene was. He knew Nadia yelled. At times, their personalities could be like opposing styles on the court. Her mother wanted a doll to dress-up and dictate, whereas Helene was becoming an outdoorsy girl who just wanted to run free and see the world.

"Give me my daughter." Nadia tried to take Helene off him, but she held on tighter and begged to stay with him.

"Don't make a scene," Delany said through clenched teeth. "She's with me all week. Take a breath, Nod. You're embarrassing yourself." He turned his shoulder protectively against her. Nadia stepped back, silenced. He walked toward his family, telling Helene she did nothing wrong. The gazebo was empty, compost trays on the tables. Alice was gone.

The litany of things Nadia screamed at him were unacceptable. If Delany's blood had not been to the point of threatening to outdo his heart, if his little girl hadn't been shaking as she clung to him, he might have let out everything he wanted to say to that woman since deciding to be in Helene's life. But it wouldn't do any good and only give her something to use against him later. Something needed to change.

He wanted to see Alice but needed to make sure Helene was okay. They got her favorite take out Saturday night. Sunday, he took her kayaking on the Potomac and to his mother's for dinner. Something in his stance kept her from asking about things. When he went to tuck Helene in Sunday night, she asked if what happened was her fault.

"No, Bear. Your mother overreacted. You were just having fun."

She rubbed her wrist where Nadia grabbed it.

"Everyone saw her yell at me. They're going to tease me."

His heart broke. "Try to get some sleep, okay? You're with me all week." He kissed her head and waited while she snuggled in. He turned off the light in her room and walked to the living room, unsure what to do.

HE DROPPED HER OFF at school Monday and then drove back to D.C., stopping by Carver's bakery. Carver saw Delany and raised his head.

"She's not here. She's setting up for a Mystics event later today."

"How did she seem this morning?" He was delaying going into the office. Bobbie probably told everyone who would listen about the blowup Saturday. Discretion had never been his strong suit.

Carver shrugged. "Quieter than usual. She said she didn't sleep well. I didn't ask. Why?"

Delany shook his head. If Alice didn't say anything he wasn't going to gossip about it.

"Maybe I'll stop by after work."

"I think she has a family thing tonight. You okay?"

Delany half-nodded and went back to his car. The drive to Rosslyn was easy. He pulled into his spot and took the elevator to the office. Katy stood when she saw him, biting her bottom lip.

"How's Helene?" She followed him into his office.

"Not good. What did Bobbie say?"

"Just that Alice overstepped her place and is lucky all Nadia did was yell."

Delany sat. He didn't see what happened but couldn't imagine what Alice could have done to deserve that level of anger. No one deserved to be treated like that.

"Collins will be here at two…"

"Ask if he can meet me at RFK. I want to talk to him without Bobbie."

Katy left. Delany put his head down and worked until Katy told him it was time to leave for the meeting with Collins. Bobbie called his name as he walked to the elevator.

"Where are you off to?" Bobbie asked.

"Mystics event at RFK."

"Want company?"

"Did you pay Alice for Carrie's birthday yet?" He waited as Bobbie stumbled over a response. "What is so hard about this? You get a check, pay Alice for what she did, and stop being an ass to her." He stepped onto the elevator and pushed the button. "I don't know what your issue is with her, man, but get over it." The elevator doors closed. Delany leaned on the wall. Yelling at Bobbie did nothing, he was only a surrogate for who he wanted to let loose on.

He pulled into a parking lot close to the decaying stadium. His uncle used to bring him to RFK when the Redskins were something to be feared. They'd sit in the top section and cheer for the home team. The stadium sat largely unused since the team moved to Maryland. The space around it had become a community space with soccer fields and open space and finally the

Anacostia River. Food trucks lined the back end of a parking lot by a series of basketball courts.

Collins called his name. The man was shorter than him with full black hair and square-framed sunglasses. He wore a tan, cotton suit with a blue button-up underneath, the top two buttons undone.

"Thanks for meeting me here." Delany shook his hand.

"I hate being in an office. You'll never find me in it once we open, hope that's okay."

"I've stayed in your hotels. Get this one on par with those and I will never second-guess you."

Collins smiled. "I heard the Jonas deal might be on hold."

"I don't know what Bobbie said, but I want the right chef in this location. We went to Jonas' flagship restaurant, pretty underwhelming. If he's your first choice…" He couldn't even finish the sentence before Collins shook his head. "Are you hungry?" He led Collins to Alice's truck. She leaned by the tailgate, talking to the center for the Mystics.

"Hello, Mr. Clare," the center said. Alice stood fully, a hesitant smile on her face. Delany made introductions, noting Alice ran the best food truck and catering company in D.C.

"Mr. Clare might be biased." Alice shook Collins' hand. "What can I get you?"

"You should try the Valencia special. It's not on the menu, but it should be." Delany smiled at her, Alice shifting her gaze.

"Sold," Collins said.

"Can I get in on that?" The center asked. Alice rolled her eyes playfully and disappeared into the food truck. Delany went to the front. A younger guy punched in the order and took Delany's card.

"You were at the basketball event," Delany said. The boy nodded.

"I talked to Ms. Gibson after we lost. She's going to teach me how to cook."

Delany took his card back and went to talk to Collins until

the food was ready. They sat at a picnic table and looked over the city while Delany gave him an update on The Cora.

"This is amazing." Collins took another bite. "I wish I knew more chefs in D.C. If you want to relocate someone, I have some names…"

"I want someone with local ties. It's important to me. Go around town, try some places, see who you like."

"Is she available?" Collins motioned to the food truck. "This rivals what I get in Miami. It's a fun menu, and might tie into the eclectic D.C. vibe we're going for."

Delany smiled. "If you try other places and if Alice is still who you want, we can talk to her. I know it would mean a lot."

He stayed after Collins left. The manager of Mystics thanked him for being there. Delany was happy to be present, he owned the team, after all. He stayed close while the team played basketball with local kids and gave them tips on the fundamentals. Most of the kids were connected to local nonprofits that worked with at-risk youth or those who needed adult figures in their lives. Halfway through, more press vans showed up. The manager must have tweeted he was there. It helped get the word out about the team. He stood and redid his jacket button, telling the team's captains to stay close. The press were not going to make the event all about him. He'd answer a few questions, but they needed to interview the players.

His sister texted after she got Helene from school. They were going to their mother's house. He'd go by after the event. Once things started to wind down, he wandered toward Alice's truck where she worked to put leftovers away. She saw him in the doorway and said a tentative hello.

"Do you have a minute?" he asked. Alice told the guy inside to wipe down the counters and keep covering what was in the prep table. She ran her hands over her arms when she got outside, dressed only in a short orange jumpsuit. He started to take off his jacket, but she told him to keep it.

"I can't acquire a collection of your jackets in Carver's office." She slid her hands into the back pockets.

"I just wanted to check in, see how you were."

"Got yelled at pretty good Saturday for no reason. Is Helene okay?"

"I think so. What happened?"

"I have no idea. I went with Helene to look at what was around the garden and next thing I know I am being called the help and told to get back to my place." She crossed her arms. "Is this what I can expect? Being degraded and belittled by your ex?" Her eyes were hard, mouth pinched.

"She overreacted. She didn't know what was going on…"

"And she couldn't ask? She came over ready for a fight, Delany." She studied him. "I have met this woman twice and both times she's come at me like I'm beneath her. She didn't care what was going on. She didn't care that Helene was happy. She hates me because I'm with you."

That was Nadia's way, dramatic and fired up. She'd always been the largest presence in the room. The day probably put a lot of pressure on her and maybe seeing her daughter eating leaves did look weird. He sighed.

"I'll talk to her." He had no idea what to say. "Do you want to come with me to get Helene and we can get dinner?"

She flexed her jaw. "I can't. I need to get the truck back and clean up." She turned to go.

"Are we still good for the game this weekend?" It was only Monday but, for some reason, he wanted to make sure. "I was thinking we could fly up, get dinner, go to the game." She looked beyond him, seeming to debate herself.

"Let me check the calendar, make sure we're not booked. I need to get this done."

He let her go. He turned back to his car and cursed to himself, unsure why it felt like things were shifting out of control.

# CHAPTER 34

**T**ABBY INVITED CYNDI INSIDE. They sat at the island in the kitchen, going over the details for the military wives' event at the end of the week. Tabby started her speech over the weekend, a warning on the need to keep your business in house and not to trust those around you. She tried to think about what she wished someone told her when she started TabiKat. *Don't hold things too tightly. It can all be taken away. Trust no one.*

"We asked for submissions from those coming who need a small business loan. Do you mind reading over what they wrote?" Cyndi asked.

"I could do that," Tabby said hesitantly.

"Great! Here are the applications." Cyndi pulled a stack out of her bag. "We are going to announce the winners at the luncheon. Is it okay if we say they can meet with you to go over their business plans?"

"I'm sure there's someone more qualified." She scanned the applications.

Cyndi tilted her head, her face sad. "I really wish you could understand what a powerhouse you are, Tabby. These women would love a role model like you. I'm sorry it ended badly, and your friends betrayed you. I can't imagine that loss. But women need to see a strong woman in the tech space. A strong woman in business. Whether it's a greeting card company or stamps or baby bibs—these women need to see someone passionate about their dreams, taking it seriously. That's you."

"Thanks, I guess."

"I don't know your sister, but I imagine some of your tenacity rubbed off on her if she's doing this well."

"I don't know about that." Tabby laughed slightly. She could give these women a fire for what they loved. She got it from seeing her mother take control of the House, maybe she could pass that on.

Cyndi left after lunch. Tabby turned off the TV and sat at the island in her kitchen, reading over the applications, unsure how much feedback the women wanted. There were some strong ideas. Others were barely hobbies. If she had to move every three years, risk Paul being deployed, maybe ending up in Japan or Germany, she never would have gotten WlkmNt done. While the odds might be stacked against these women, with a bit of determination, they could flourish. Her mother had the world stacked against her. People told Tabby she lacked experience and women had no place in programming. A vindictive ass tried to run her sister out of the culinary world. Still, they pressed on. Women were remarkable at overcoming challenges.

She left the applications behind and went to get her laptop. Opening it, she deleted her speech before letting out her breath and starting again.

*'Back in 1973, my mother had a vision.'* A woman with no advantages managed to finish her bachelor's while her first

husband drank and beat her. She left him, finished her degree, and went to work at the local rep's office, who moved her to D.C. There she gained the respect of her party who pushed her to run at only twenty-seven. She rose to prominence in the House, becoming one of the most powerful people in the country. That tenacity ran through her blood and Alice's too. Her mother reminded her girls anything was possible. For the first time since Tabby lost her company, things started looking a little bit brighter.

Alice got home after dinner. She set her bag by the door, slipping her feet out of her tennis shoes before she pulled the wrap off her head. There was something slow to her movements, sad almost. Over the weekend Tabby and Paul took the twins out on the trail beside the water. Paul asked if she'd tried to see things from Alice's perspective. Delany had his hand in dozens of companies across the area, the chance for Alice to partner with him opened doors that could have taken her years to reach. He told Tabby to separate the two, to see how Alice was getting what she wanted. Logically Tabby got it and wanted to be happy for her sister. But the betrayal lingered. To not say anything, to act like she was booked because of her hard work and not because of the scoundrel. It seemed like Alice had said all she was going to, now expecting Tabby to get over things. But she didn't want to; she wanted to hold her sister to account. Paul asked what her relationship with Alice was worth, Tabby still unsure of the answer.

"Hey." Alice washed her hands at the sink. "What are you working on?"

"My speech for the military luncheon on Friday. There're leftovers in the fridge if you want them. Where were you?"

"An event with the Mystics at RFK, then I stayed to work in the office for a bit." She pulled some leftovers and then started for her room.

Tabby called after her. "Cyndi said she emailed you about the event." She didn't know how to come back after a fight. In hindsight, after her anger dulled, her actions often embarrassed her, but she had never been good at apologizing. It became easier to say things and then cut the person out, acting like it didn't matter anymore.

Alice came back to the island. "Do you really want to know?"

"Yeah." To prove her point, she got up and reached for another wine glass. Alice sat on the stool next to her, describing what Cyndi and the others were thinking for food. Tabby poured her a glass, the menu sounding delicious. She debated bringing up what happened, but instead enjoyed being near her sister. They could talk about things later.

Alice reached into her pocket and pulled out a flash drive, hesitating.

"If you still want to help me with a website, it's some photos from the last few months."

"Of course." Tabby tried to give a reassuring smile. She loaded the photos while Alice took her bowl to the sink. Images of spreads of food, Alice and Carver at events, one or the other with various random people. One showed the food truck redone, Tabby telling Alice how good it looked.

"Thanks." Alice sat and took a drink of her water. Tabby scanned the action shots of staff refilling buffets or prepping food, images of full banquet halls. "Thank you," Alice said. Tabby looked at her. "For this and everything else, thank you. I don't tell you that enough. It's been a lifesaver living here."

Tabby debated biting her tongue. "If that's true, how could you get in business with Delany Clare?"

"It wasn't a conscious choice…" Alice lowered her gaze.

"Not a conscious choice? What does that even mean?"

Alice looked at her. "I met him before the TabiKat party. He called after the acquisition to ask if I was available for a company event. At the time, I didn't know he bought you out and after, well, I needed the booking. Everyone told me to separate what happened to you from what Delany was offering. Then we took off, and it felt good to have my dream, and I don't know, I kind of hoped you could just be happy for me."

"Happy for you? How am I supposed to be happy for you when you lied to me and…Don't you care about what he did to me?" People kept telling her she was licking her wounds but all she wanted was for someone to acknowledge her hurt.

"I think it was Bobbie. Delany said he thought you knew about the sale. I…"

Tabby clicked her tongue. "Isn't that sweet, covering his butt by blaming his best friend."

"You don't know him, Tabby. You've had one interaction with him. I've spent hours with this man since July; don't come at me like I'm naïve."

"Wouldn't be the first time some guy lied to you to get what he wanted." She closed her laptop. "Have you ever thought about what he wants out of this deal? What he expects? No one opens their Rolodex for nothing. Ever think he's doing this to get you into bed? What if he's not who you think, and you've banked your entire career on one person—again? God, if you'd listened to me about your ex, I tried to warn you that he was running around on you but no, you insisted on keeping me out. Left it all for me and Mom to clean up. And don't pretend like Delany is your only support. Tasty Pudding only exists because of my initiative. I don't think asking you to show a bit of loyalty is too much."

Alice studied her before she shook her head and walked to her bedroom. Tabby thought about calling after her. *Give it time.* Alice would find out what kind of man the scoundrel was, and when that time came Tabby would demand one hell of an apology.

# CHAPTER 35

**H**ER MOTHER STOOD TALKING to Carver when Alice got to the bakery the next day. She told her mother to give her a minute, going to put her stuff in the back office. It was time to move out. Hasty Pudding was viable enough and she long ago grew tired of the commute. Before she could chicken out, she sat at the computer and logged into WlkmNt taking her apartment down after the weekend. A few stragglers over the fall would have to find other places to stay. But if Moe kept the clause that they'd give them 15 percent off any rebooks, it should be okay.

"This is a surprise," she said. Her mother motioned to the chair across from her. Alice set her breakfast down and repeated her statement.

"We need to talk about your father's birthday," her mother said.

Alice closed her eyes. She forgot her mother asked her to cater it. Alice opened her calendar, it would take some shuffling, but Alice would make it work.

"It's the whole weekend at the house?"

"About forty people right now. We are having the big dinner that Saturday. The rest of the time it's going to be smaller meals. Nothing too fancy."

"I'll bring a crew up for the dinner. Maybe we can get by with pre-made sandwiches and buffet breakfasts for the rest."

"I trust your judgment. You all do full-bar service, right?"

"Let me see what Carver and I can come up with." She jotted down some ideas.

"Things look quiet here. Do you want to come to lunch with your sister and I?"

"Not particularly." She kept her focus on her notebook.

"Birdie, your sister is going through a hard time…"

"Mom, I see her enough at home. I am sick of her martyring herself and acting like I did something to cause what's going on."

"Have you talked to her about your decision to work with Macon?"

Alice rolled her eyes. Of course, her mother would take Tabby's side.

"I'm thinking we can do tenderloin for Dad's party." Maybe if she moved on her mother would too. They talked through the menu before Alice took a deep breath and got up her nerve. "I took my apartment off WlkmNt."

"Really?" Her mother tilted her head.

"It's time. Hasty Pudding is doing well. I'm tired of getting a cab at two a.m. if I could just walk five blocks. I want to talk to you and Dad about buying it."

Her mother set her coffee down. "Well, this is a change from July. We would love for you to take over the apartment, if it's where you want to be."

"It is."

"We were going to offer to fix it up for your birthday. New paint, new furniture, anything else you want to do. I can call Suzi and see when she's free to meet us."

"It's open starting Monday. Thank you, Mom."

"You're coming into your own, Birdie. It's quite lovely to see."

#

TABBY MET HER MOTHER at their favorite Mediterranean place, determined to get beyond the night. The level of her sister's ungratefulness. It felt good to give Alice a piece of her mind, remind her of all she'd lost chasing Alice's dream for her, until that is she went into the bedroom and saw Paul's face as he sat in bed reading. Unsure what to say, she went to get ready for bed. She got in, ready to defend herself, but the look on Paul's face said he already determined his verdict.

Her mother spoke on the phone when Tabby got there. She motioned that the host outside had their name. The September day was unusually un-muggy. Just let her sit in the sun and pretend the people in her life were on her side.

"Thank you, Suzi. I'll see you Monday. Ta." Her mother closed her phone.

"Are you and Dad redoing the house again?"

"No. Alice's apartment."

Tabby paused. "Why are you redoing the apartment?"

"So Alice can move home. Ah." She raised her hand, and the server led them to a table near the banister. The terrace sat raised from the street, her mother choosing the side that let her look at the Portrait Gallery.

"Alice is moving home?" Tabby set her purse down before snatching the menu from the host. *Just leave them alone.*

"She didn't tell you?" her mother said slowly.

"No." Tabby leaned back, wondering if it was because of what happened. Her mother started to look at the menu. Alice must not have told her about the fight. Tabby debated asking when her mother knew about Alice's little lie, but didn't want another lecture about moving on.

The server took their orders. Not wanting to think about the fight or her sister leaving, Tabby told her mother about the military wives' luncheon the next day and reading over the applications for the small business incubator. She thought about offering to do websites for the winners to help them get a solid online presence. It would give her something to do and help keep her skills fresh.

"It's good you got some of your spunk back." Her mother leaned back while the server put their first round of small plates on the table.

"I don't know if offering to do websites for women crocheting Star Wars characters is getting my spunk back."

"This is the first time I've seen you not raging about TabiKat since June. Maybe you can help women curate their dreams."

"How do I make money, Mother?"

"Why not give your talents for free?" She dabbed the side of her mouth with her napkin before reaching for her iced tea.

"Would you help women in politics for free?"

"What do you think I've been doing for twenty years? A rising tide helps all of us!"

Tabby laughed once and then took a drink of her water, ready to change subjects. "Did you get a menu figured out with Alice?"

"Tenderloin with a salad of fall edibles and a berry and cream dessert, your father's favorite. I do feel bad not doing anything for your sister's thirtieth birthday."

"She probably prefers it that way. Be glad she's cooking, or she might not even be there. I never see her anymore and she lives with me." For now. Tabby took a bite of her pita and hummus. Her mother shook her head and smiled sadly, taking her glass off the table. "What?" Tabby asked.

"You are so blinded by your anger you cannot be happy for

your sister. This is her dream. This catering company is her chance to put her name on something not attached to that bloodsucker, Jonas. And instead of being happy for her, instead of cheering her on, and maybe seeing if you can help her, you are finding any little reason to be mad and rain on her parade."

"Oh, so letting Alice live with me is not helping her?"

"Don't take that tone with me, Tabatha Gloria Black. You will not make me the brunt of your anger. Alice has lived with you for over a year. Your kids are better for it. Your marriage is better for it. *You* are better for it. It has helped your sister, and you know she is grateful." Her mother talked over her. "But you are jealous, and that is unbecoming on anyone."

Her mother waited for Tabby to react, who just shook her head.

"When's the last time you lost something you loved?"

Her mother's face fell. "I almost lost everything I love. Maybe you should remember why we're sitting here. Why I walked away from what I gave my life to."

Her mother reached for her iced tea and watched the road. Tabby let out her breath. No one wanted to think about Maryanne's heart attack in the middle of an impassioned speech on the House floor for the reauthorization of the Violence Against Women Act. Alice had been there with Annie, wanting her niece to see her grandmother fighting for a better future. They watched her fall to the floor, then chaos surround her. Tabby was at work when her sister called and told her their mother was in an ambulance on route to the hospital. The color drained from the room; Tabby unable to imagine a world without her mother in it.

"I'm sorry, Mom."

Her mother brought her gaze back. "My first husband tore me down every day of our marriage and I let him. He hated that I was getting an education, pursuing things that let me be independent of him. You were my reason for leaving, Kitty Cat. You got me out."

Tabby chose to forget that James was not her biological father. At eighteen, her mother married some loser from Pittsburgh who thought he found a woman to cook for him and raise lots of kids. But Maryanne watched her own mother live like that and refused to let the pattern continue. They moved to Cumberland, so he could work in the mines. Her mother got a job in an office and started to save money to go to school. She put herself through college, working two jobs, while her first husband did everything to derail her. Her mother left when Tabby was four months old. She had no memories of her life before her mother married James.

"I'm not downplaying what you went through, Tabby. I won't. I have watched things I fought hard for get swept away and torn apart. I know the feeling. But all we have is our response. And yours should be better than this."

#

ALICE OPENED THE DOOR to Delany's apartment, not hearing anything. She checked the time, needing to leave by four to make it to Annie's basketball game that night. Setting the bags of food on the counter, Alice unpacked before she pulled the pans she needed and slipped her earphones in. She worked without thinking, refusing to dwell on the fight with Tabby. Yes, she should have told her sister back in August, only she wanted to be close to Delany and knew Tabby would never understand. She tried to keep it casual, but New Mexico changed everything. And she got that losing TabiKat hurt. When Jonas forced her out of Marigolds, she thought she'd never be happy anywhere else. But now she was, and Delany was a part of that.

She sent Valencia a rambling email about everything going on. Maybe she was missing something or reading too much into things or letting her old fears hold her back. Val would be honest with her. Alice stopped herself from asking her to just come home. The undertones were there. Valencia enjoyed her mother, but was less thrilled with her half siblings and the lackadaisical culture the longer she stayed. She missed her life and friends back home.

A hand touched her back, making Alice jump. She pulled her earphones out. Delany stood there with Helene. "What are you doing here?" She put her hand on her heart. Helene hugged her leg hello, Alice kneeling to hug her back.

"She only had a half-day, and my mom has something going on tonight." Delany set some things in the fridge.

"What are you making?" Helene asked.

Alice stood and moved the vegetables off the burner, hoping they didn't get too soft. "This is for a lasagna, then there's vegetable stew in the fridge."

"How long have you been here?" Delany leaned on the island.

"An hour, maybe."

"Are you staying for dinner?" Helene asked.

Alice looked at her watch. "I probably need to go soon."

"We still have the mac-oons you made. Daddy said it's a guessing game."

Alice debated what to do. She'd missed Annie's games while she was in New Mexico and didn't want her niece to feel like Alice had abandoned her. But after the fight with Tabby, Alice wasn't ready to smile. Her sister needed to get over herself one of these days. The idea of not sitting in tension all night and doing something to make up for ruining Helene's birthday sounded ideal. She found her cell and texted Paul something came up at work.

After dinner, they sat around the small table in the kitchen. Delany made her a decaf latte, Helene sampling the mystery macarons Alice made. She got the cardamon one, and the lemon ginger, the Lady Grey stumping her. They hung out until Delany went to put Helene to bed, Alice moving to the large windows to take in the view.

Delany hugged her from behind. She ran her hand over his arm, his lips in her hair.

"This is not how I imagined you here this late."

She chuckled. "How did you see this moment?"

"Well, instead of taking you home after a date, we'd come here. Champagne. Turn on the fireplace." He kissed her neck. "I have to admit, I've always wanted to do it with the shades open, the city lights outside."

"If Helene wasn't here." She closed her eyes, his hand on her side bunching up her shirt. "What are you doing, Mr. Clare?"

"Is that okay?"

"What about your daughter?"

"We could host a party here and she'd sleep through it. She has a noise machine and an eye mask. It's a bit ridiculous."

She laughed as she faced him. He smiled at her, his knuckles on her cheek. This man changed her life in so many ways, made her feel safe and seen in a way she'd never experienced before. There were a thousand things going on outside his apartment, but for the moment, she chose to block it all out for the chance to feel what she did in New Mexico.

She kissed him, Delany's hand running into her hair. He led her to his room and laid her down on his bed, exploring her body with his lips. Alice let the emotion carry her, hoping this man was who he seemed.

# CHAPTER 36

SHE AWOKE IN THE guest room, Delany's voice filling the apartment. The smell of pancakes mixed with coffee. She thought about the night and beamed. It was everything she hoped—tender, attentive, and wow!—how he filled her. He told her to stay with him, but she did not want to risk Helene finding them together. She climbed into the guest bed after two and told herself to stop smiling. Their sweat and his kisses covered her skin. All she wanted was to crawl back into bed with Delany and spend the day with him. Instead, she saw the time and knew she needed to get going.

Helene called good morning. Alice kissed her head and asked how she slept before she went to get a cup of coffee. Delany kissed her good morning, the playfulness in his eyes making her face warm. She sat at the table, Delany setting down a plate of pancakes.

"It's from a box—don't judge me."

"Next time I'll cook." Alice took a drink of her coffee. "What are you doing today?"

"Going to see Grandma. Can I come to the bakery with you?"

"Maybe next time. I have an event over lunch." Alice pouted and Helene laughed.

"Do you need me to drive you to work?" Delany sat at the table with them.

Alice shook her head. "We're five blocks from the bakery. I can walk."

Delany reached for her fingers as they rode down the elevator together. She smiled and looked at him. He winked. She kissed his cheek and told him to have fun at work. The line at the bakery went out the door. Alice slipped in, raising a hand to Carver as she walked to the office. She sat at the desk and opened her email, one waiting from Valencia. It included a photo of her at an olive vineyard she went to with her stepbrother. She wore a wide brimmed hat and a wider smile. After filling Alice in on her latest fun she got to what Alice emailed her about after Helene's birthday. Nadia would do whatever necessary because she felt she deserved the life Delany's money and fame provided. *That girl will keep Delany single until he runs out of options and goes to her.* If she let Nadia push her away from Delany, then Nadia won. Instead, she could stay close and let Nadia see she wasn't easily intimidated. She never got to make a stand with her ex, not that Alice was sure she would have if given the chance. But with Delany she would not just walk away. It would be easy for her to get out of the basketball game, to let Nadia's attitude push her back. Not this time.

The cursor blinked on the reply email. Alice leaned in and typed the one thing she wanted to say since Val left in July. '*When are you coming home? Things are picking up w/ HP and I could use my best friend.*' She hit send and looked at the time. *Cheese puffs!* It was too late to call Paul and ask him to bring her a change of clothes. She could swing by the apartment on the way to the military wives' luncheon and deal with her sister later. If she found a way to keep making a name for herself in the face of a man who only wanted to destroy her, Tabby could get over how things ended with TabiKat. It was time for her sister to do more than wallow.

She pulled the van into the circle in front of the apartment building, telling Rita she'd be back. Hopefully Tabby was already at the venue, not that she wouldn't rip into Alice there. Was it better to have the conversation in public or private? Tabby wasn't that different from Nadia—both women needing to take someone down to feel better about themselves. Alice unlocked the door to the apartment and went to her room, starting to change. She thought through what she needed for the day. Part of her hoped for a repeat of the previous night, waking up with Delany a welcome reprieve to things, but she had to face her sister sometime. Get through their tiff and tell Tabby she was leaving. She headed toward the front door.

"I thought I heard the door." Tabby leaned against the wall to the dining room. "Sneaking in and out now, are we?"

"Don't have much to say."

"I would have thought 'I'm sorry' might be on that list."

Alice paused at her purse. "What do I have to apologize for? You're the one who freaked out on me."

"I'm sorry, what?" Tabby put her hand over the heart. "After all I've done for you…"

"Spare me your martyrdom today, Tabby. I have a job to go to." She pulled the door closed behind her, half-expecting her sister to open it and continue their fight to the main floor. She got into the elevator and rolled her eyes. Whatever delusion her sister needed to believe.

They pulled into the garage of an event center on the water. Staffers waited beside the minivan to help unload the food. A couple started off with Rita and the taller rolling warmers. Alice passed off trays from the van, making sure they had everything they needed. She rode in the elevator with two female servers she enjoyed.

She let them get off the elevator first. The walls of windows provided an unobstructed view of the Potomac River and Maryland. Rita already had things humming at the corner setup for them, servers plating salads and finishing the desserts. Staff from the event center set the tables. Half an hour to go.

"Are you Alice?" A woman came toward her. "I'm Cyndi."

"Really?" Alice caught herself. "Nice to meet you." She was sweet and down-to-earth, a natural beauty. Nothing like Carrie and the stuck-up sorority girls her sister spent time with. She treated Alice with nothing but kindness. They chatted before Cyndi went to do a final mic check.

The space filled up, the activity helping Alice to forget what else was going on. Halfway through the main course, Tabby stepped behind the podium. Alice leaned on the back wall, her hands sliding into her apron.

"My mother was a woman ahead of her time. In 1976, as a single mother, she worked to put herself through college while telling women they had a choice. My mother fought hard for Title IX, for equal pay, and for domestic violence to be recognized so there could be laws to stop it." Alice found her mother in the crowd. "My mother served in Congress for twenty-seven years. In her time, she fought hard for the rights of the military, for better healthcare, and to ensure you all were protected during the wars in Iraq. My mother taught me what it is to be a strong woman. You all know what it is to be a strong woman. You have to be. I started my own tech company, ready to take on a world of men that told me to sit and take my place. But I refused to listen, and in the end created the company that holds the biggest opening evaluation on Wall Street. But I don't tell you that to sound impressive. I tell you that to encourage you anything is possible. You sit here with ideas of your own. Something stirs in you, something you must pursue like I did. That entrepreneurial spirit will not be satisfied until you chase what you love."

Alice waited for the bitterness to come, for Tabby to call out those who stabbed her in the back. Instead, she kept it on point, telling the women four things she learned while starting TabiKat. For the first time she'd talked about it without any hint of hostility. Here was the passion and drive that enabled her sister to break into the tech world and do what many called impossible, that would enable Tabby to leave her mark on anything she set her sights on. If she could just let go of what happened.

Alice went back to the bakery after the event, working with the office door closed to try and get ahead of what was starting to bury her. Her cell phone rang midafternoon, Eddie's name on the screen. Alice answered, unsure why he'd be calling.

"I want to talk to you about being our chef full-time," Eddie said.

"What does that mean?" She sat back.

"Morse needs to back out. He wants to be with his wife who is dying, and then, well, as a single dad he can't travel the world on a moment's notice. What do you say?"

"Delany knows about this?"

"Of course." He laughed. "You'd be on-call for emergencies, so could still work your catering job."

A calendar of the next year hung on the wall across from the desk. The number of free weekends was declining, most of their weeknights filling up as well.

"Let me think about it."

"I just sent you an email with all the details. Look it over and get back to me."

"Thanks, Eddie." She hung up and skimmed his email. They were going to pay her how much per trip? It was more than she made in half a year with the food truck before Valencia left and would keep her from feeling one bad month away from losing everything. If it was a bad year, meaning she got called out to multiple natural disasters, she could make a comfortable six figures.

Alice reread the number, things spinning. She'd be an idiot not to take the job. Not to mention she loved the work. If the offer came before the latest fight with Tabby, she would have said yes without a second thought. Now she saw it as another way she worked for Delany, another way her career was tied to him. Once people knew they were together would anyone see her as anything other than his girlfriend gaining favors because of who he was?

Paul was waiting when she came out of the bakery. She slid into his X5, asking about his day.

"We might be getting somewhere with the case. How did the luncheon go?"

"Her speech was amazing, actually. Just wish she'd take her own advice."

The drive was quiet, Paul using the time to listen to 90s R&B and unwind. Alice threatened her brother-in-law with karaoke, Paul telling her it was her gift for their commute. Traffic stalled on the bridge into Virginia. Alice watched the water, unable to quiet the questions that started after she got off the phone. Delany's name came up on her cell. She kept the phone on her far ear, Paul lost in his song.

"Do you want to do dinner?" Delany asked.

"I'm on my way back to Tabby's. I need a night in."

"Oh, sure." He sounded disappointed. "Eddie said he talked to you."

She started to ask how, if they were dating, she could work at his nonprofit. What about the optics? Would people ever believe she made it on her own or would it all get incorporated under who Delany was? She hated that Tabby got into her head and made her question Delany's intentions. If she didn't know Delany's heart and trust what he told her since July, she might question if his pulling her into his various businesses wasn't a backdoor way of taking over her company.

"Hold on. What's going on Bobbie?" Delany's voice got further away. Bobbie must have come into his office, they started to have a conversation. Alice closed her eyes. To date Delany meant interacting with Bobbie and eating her humble pie with Carrie and socializing with those who took everything from her sister. Her heart ached. For all her bluster and hopes that Tabby might understand, she was making her career off the man who stole her sister's dream.

"Don't let me keep you." She glanced at Paul, who pulled off their exit and started to merge into the outward lane.

"Did something happen?" Delany asked.

"Just a lot going on."

"Okay." He didn't believe her. "Helene and I will be at your place around ten tomorrow morning if that works."

"I'll see you then." She thought about getting out of the trip to New York City, but couldn't bring herself to back out.

"Hey, listen, I want you to know last night meant something to me."

"Me too." He was the first guy she'd slept with since her ex left. Her head spun; too many things vying for attention. Her loyalty to Tabby told her to walk away. But she was desperate to figure out a way to merge Delany into the rest of her life, and yet realized because of how things went down certain aspects remained closed to the other. Tabby would never agree to a meal, and could she ever sit with his best friend without feeling like she was betraying her sister?

"Have a good night, okay?" Alice slowly hung up.

"You okay?" Paul asked.

Alice could only nod, hating the fear sweeping in and making her question everything.

# CHAPTER 37

ALICE PACKED HER OVERNIGHT BAG for New York. The last time she went to the city was with her ex. They went to an overpriced Italian restaurant and a bad Broadway show he wanted to say he'd seen. Their hotel was centrally located, but like always, he refused to leave. Alice told him to enjoy himself and went to see the city. She wandered around questioning what the hell she was doing. With a ring that felt nothing like her on her finger, she told herself to be happy he'd noticed her and suppress her questions and frustrations.

"Where are you going?" Paul stood in the doorway.

"A friend invited me to New York City for the weekend." Alice kept packing. Paul sat on the edge of the bed.

"You're moving out?"

She nodded. If Paul knew, Tabby did. She'd managed to muck things up. Her phone buzzed, Delany waiting. She put the last things she needed in her bag.

"Tell the twins I'll be back tomorrow."

She reached for her overnight bag and slipped out the front door. In the elevator she pushed it all from her mind—Bobbie, Nadia, Tabby, the mountain of yarn she needed to find a way to undo. For twenty-four hours it was about being with Delany and Helene. Everything would still be there Monday.

Helene waved from her open window. Alice caught her hand and kissed her fingers. Delany opened the trunk and asked for her bag. She walked back to give it to him. He kissed her hello, reaching to hold her.

"Daddy, let's go!" Helene called. Alice got into the passenger seat. It was a short drive to DCA, Alice never having flown on a private plane before. Helene claimed her favorite seat, one that gave her the best view of the city on takeoff. Alice sat next to Delany on the couch across the aisle, her legs tucked up under her.

The plane took off, Helene telling Alice to come see the view. She sat in the chair across from her. Helene pointed out things on the ground, asking if Alice could see them. Alice settled into her seat as they rose higher over the city. The flight attendant asked what they wanted to drink. While she went to get it, Helene unfurled her tray table, taking a collection of snacks out of the small backpack she'd worn on the flight.

"You're prepared for this."

"You'll learn." She went to the window again. Delany reached for Alice's hand and pulled her back to the couch. The flight attendant came back with their drinks before leaving them alone.

"And three, two, one." Delany counted down. Helene slumped against the side of the chair, passed out.

Alice laughed. "If only I could sleep that well on a plane."

"She'll be out until we land." Delany took a drink of his beer. She got up her nerve. "Did you tell Eddie to hire me?"

His head twitched as he scowled. He set his beer down and turned to face her more on the couch, resting his head on his fist.

"No. Eddie called me, asked if you might be interested. I

don't tell people who to hire." He glanced at Helene. "I want the best people around me, that's why Bobbie's sister isn't my admin and no one from the neighborhood was going to represent me. I refuse to hire my friends because it's expected. Is that what was bothering you last night?"

She debated whether to be honest. With her ex, it was about keeping him happy and minimizing getting yelled at for things when she was never sure what she did. She looked at her hands. "Kind of. I wonder if people will think I'm a good chef if we're together and I work for you all over the place."

He moved to put his hand on her wrist but stopped, his eyes downcast. She started to take it back, not wanting to ruin the weekend, but she had to know.

"Eddie appreciated your work ethic and the way you handled yourself. To be honest, I think he only called to ask because he knew you already have a job you love. I can't help what shortsighted people think, but no one who tastes what you do will ever think you get by on my name. Don't turn down something you want because of me."

She nodded, ready to move on. He shifted on the couch and reached for his drink again. Alice thought about retreating, to sit across from Helene and pretend to look at the view. Instead she rested her head on his shoulder. He put his arm across her, his hand holding her thigh.

"Maybe we can hang out after I drop her off tomorrow."

"I don't have to be anywhere until I meet my mom at my place on Monday."

"Your place?" He waited while she sat up to look at him again.

"I'm moving home. My mom offered to update things, new paint, etc. I haven't seen my apartment in over a year so don't know what needs to be done."

"So, you'll be closer to me." He beamed. She nodded. He leaned in to kiss her, Alice praying her heart was right.

She held Helene's hand as they found their suite at The Barclay Center and followed Delany inside, others already waiting. Helene slipped her hand free and ran to say hello to a girl her age she knew well. Alice stopped, Delany talking to Seth Landry, MVP of the league last year. The man was taller than Delany, more filled out. They'd played each other more than once in the Finals. Seth hit Delany in the chest, both laughing.

"Seth, this is Alice." Delany reached his arm out for her. Alice stumbled over what to say.

"It's nice to meet you." Seth shook her hand. "Now I know why you refused my offer to Cabo."

"I have an empire to run, man. Money doesn't make itself."

"Please, you can run off to save the world, but not come hang out with the misses and her friends. What do you do, Alice?"

"I'm a chef."

"Next time you're in town, we'll have you over. Alice makes the best Cuban food."

"Sold." Seth said hello to another couple as they walked in the suite. Delany kept his arm around Alice and led her to the leather chairs where Helene and three other girls chatted away.

"I didn't realize there were going to be other people here."

"That okay?" He kissed into her hair. "I want people to know you, show off my girl."

She sat in a chair across the aisle from Helene and her friends. Delany stayed briefly before going to talk to those inside. Alice felt she should go mingle, but what could she say to that level of wealth? At any other time, she'd be the one ducking in and out to refill the buffet and clean up. Everything she wore was secondhand. The only trips she'd been on in the last ten years someone else paid for. She didn't own a car, couldn't name more than a couple in the price range these people drove. Just before halftime, Delany motioned for her to come over. She exhaled, hoping she was enough. He introduced her to another player and his wife. Alice fought to get out of her head and think of something to say. Ask about their kids, what they did all day, the last place they traveled. Over the last three months she interacted with CEOs, people in Congress, donors. But it was always with her chef's coat on, always from a role in which she felt confident and in control. Did she have anything to say without her food around to give her credibility?

Delany carried Helene to their hotel room. Laying her on the second bed, he took off her skirt before slipping her under the covers. Alice asked if she could get ready for bed first. Looking in the mirror, she tried to keep the panic from consuming her. What was she doing? She came out and Delany slipped in behind her. Staring at the two beds in the room, Alice was unsure what to do. She climbed into bed with Helene who laid toward the center, her fist barely outside her lips. She hoped Tabby would find a way to get over her anger and let the girls be friends. Annie would have been all over the trip, given Alice someone to hang out with. Delany came out, asking Alice if she wanted to sleep with him.

"I don't know how that will look."

He sat on the bed. "I can stay with her."

"I'm already here. Sleep well, okay?" She put her hands under her head. Delany got into his bed and turned off the light. Alice waited for the traffic and activity outside to lull her to sleep.

# CHAPTER 38

**D**ELANY WOKE FIRST, someone in the bed with him. Helene slept alone in the center of the other bed, her body half out the covers, spread like a snow angel. Alice laid beside him, covered in an extra blanket from the closet. Maybe he should have warned Alice about his daughter's sleeping tendencies. Hopefully Helene didn't kick her too much. He rolled to face her, resting his hand on her hip, unable to believe she was there. He kept waiting for her to back out, to say she had to work. He thought what happened with Nadia might have pushed her away, instead, it seemed to have drawn her closer.

He kissed her cheek, Alice drawing in a deep breath.

"I meant to move before you woke up."

"I should have warned you. Why didn't you just climb in?" He kept his voice down, loving his daughter but wanting time with Alice who studied him, her brow furrowed.

"Has she seen you sharing a bed with women before?" It wasn't an accusation. Alice was the first one he let into Helene's life, and it came so naturally. He didn't consider how it would look to his daughter or what she might say to her mother.

"Should I have gotten two rooms?"

Alice shrugged. Hearing Helene groan, Alice slipped out and went into the bathroom. Delany laid on his back and stretched.

"What time is it?" Helene smacked her lips.

"Almost eight. Do you want to get breakfast at our spot?"

"Is Alice still here?"

She came out of the bathroom in jeans and a Liberty T-shirt she bought the night before. Sitting on Helene's bed she asked how she slept. He let them talk, going to get ready for the day. They got breakfast at his favorite place near the arena before catching a one o'clock charter back to D.C.

"Do you want to go with me to drop her off?" Delany asked on the flight down.

"Do you think that's the best idea?"

Helene colored at her seat, listening to her iPod.

"Alice, you're in my life. Nadia needs to become okay with that."

"Did you talk to her about what happened?" She seemed to sense the answer before he could say no. "How do you see this going?"

"I see it going that we're going to build something, and she can adjust. She's Helene's mom, that's it. One of us was going to meet someone eventually."

Alice started to say something, but changed her mind. He reached for her hand, turning his body toward her on the couch.

"Listen, we can drop her off and then go walk the Inner Harbor or see if there's a Ravens game." He needed to talk to Nadia, but wanted to know what Alice saw coming from things. They'd only known each other for three months, been together for a couple weeks. It felt longer. She glanced at Helene and smiled. If only a woman like Alice could be there to influence his daughter.

"Okay. I can go."

Delany kissed her softly, Helene giggling from her seat.

"You need to talk to her." Alice motioned her head toward Helene. He nodded, he would.

Alice waited in the car while he got Helene's bag and walked toward the front door. He set her bag just inside, calling for Nadia to have a good day. As they drove toward the Inner Harbor, Alice looked up from her cell phone, asking if he liked oysters.

"I love them. Could probably eat far too many in one sitting if I'm honest."

"Do you want to do that for dinner?"

"Where do I go?"

She texted while they drove, directing him to a warehouse near the water. Alice said she'd be right back and got out. A man came out of the warehouse with an apron on and his hair in a wrap, handing her a bushel of oysters in a nylon bag. They talked for a minute before Alice touched his arm and started back for the car. Delany got out and went to open the back passenger door, looking for something to put the oysters on. Alice told him to take the newspaper she stole from the plane.

"We have about ninety minutes to get these cool again." She brushed off her hands.

"How fresh are those?"

She shrugged. "Maybe caught yesterday."

They drove to his apartment, Alice making a list of what she wanted with their meal. They put the oysters in the fridge before walking to the store near his house. She already knew the layout, Delany guessing she shopped there too. Could he have seen her before and never known? The idea of her being blocks away made him feel like a rookie getting drafted. He was excited to see how things would shift without her sister hovering.

"What kind of wine goes with oysters?" He asked when she came back with bacon and fresh veggies.

"Something white, I think."

He had some in his wine fridge from the vineyard he owned in Napa. He would take her there someday, and she could make something, and they could eat on the back deck and watch the sunset.

Back at his apartment, she started to dig through the kitchen drawers. Delany asked if he could help, not wanting her to think she was stuck doing it all on her own. She motioned toward the stack of veggies to be washed.

"Do you have a grill on the roof?" she asked. He had no idea but gave Alice the keycard to check it out since she'd be able to tell if it was adequate or not better than he could. He hummed while he worked until his phone buzzed. Delany dried his hands, the text from Nadia.

*'You took the caterer to NYC w/o asking me? WTF Bulldog?'*

He closed the message and went to get a bottle of wine, unwilling to justify his choices. Alice came back and said she'd turned on one of the grills, suggesting they eat up there. That sounded like the perfect idea. He found what they would need, plates and forks and a shucking knife he had no idea he owned until that moment. Another bottle of wine and two glasses.

"I'll be back."

"Uh-huh," she called over her shoulder from the stove. When he got back, prepped bacon and asparagus waited near unshucked corn on the counter beside a red sauce, Alice working on slicing lemons.

"Did you make this?"

"Of course." She slid a baguette out of the bag and started to cut it open.

"I usually just do cocktail sauce."

She leaned into the island and glared. "Well, you're with me now. We're going to update your tastebuds."

His heart raced, Delany not bothering to hold back his smile.

*With her.* She turned to do something, but he rotated her toward him and kissed her like he wanted to since he picked her up. He started to bunch her shirt in his hands, wanting to feel her body against his again.

"After dinner." Her playful smile made him want her more. Before he could push, she stepped back and reached for a bottle of wine off the counter. His brow furrowed, not sure what Forager Wine was.

"My dad makes dandelion wine. It's not that alcoholic and can be sweet, but he made it, and I wanted you to have a bottle." She shrugged, flustered.

"Will it go with the oysters?"

"It should."

It took some maneuvering, but they managed to get all the food to the rooftop in one trip. Alice set the asparagus, corn, and baguette on the grill before closing the lid. He reached for her, but she went to see the city. He stood beside her, watching her as much as the view.

"So which rooftop is yours?"

She smiled and pointed in the direction of the Archives.

"It would be easier if the greenhouse was on this end. Not quite a clear shot for smoke signals or anything."

Alice checked what was on the grill before fishing the shucking knife out of the bag he used to bring the dishes up. "Do you know how to use this?"

He shook his head and poured her a glass of wine. Alice took a sip before emptying the dish bag. She shucked three oysters before he realized, handing him one. He drank it back, like butter down his throat.

"How much did you get?" He reached for the second one.

"Three pounds. This is about half." She turned to do something on the grill. He stood and reached for the knife.

"Tell me what to do."

She sat in a chair and talked him through it. How did the guys at the Macon picnic make this look so easy? He kept chucking until she pulled the rest of their food off the grill. They sat down, Alice facing the view. They talked about anything but Helene or work or their careers. He wanted to know what she did for fun, what she was curious about. He told her about the thoughts that never got shared, what he wanted to do with his life, why he was involved all over the place. The respect in her gaze humbled him. Somehow, she got what he was saying.

They cleaned up, Delany dumping their table scraps into the bag with the oyster shells.

"Can I take those?" Alice asked. Delany scowled. "There's a nonprofit that dumbs the shells back into the harbor. It helps."

He looked at the bag, wishing he hadn't made such a mess of things.

"I can clean them downstairs." She ducked to make sure the grill was off. He collected the trash and used plates, Alice working to get their wine glasses and the empty bottles before they started for his apartment. Alice reached for his keys and got the front door. He told her to set it all in the sink, he could clean up.

"I can help."

"You made dinner." He kissed her cheek. "This is my part."

That lasted all of three seconds before Alice helped him dry dishes and load things into the dishwasher. He wanted to tell her to relax, but enjoyed having her close. After, they went to watch the Sunday night football game. On a commercial, Alice asked how to turn on the fireplace. Delany found the remote he wanted. She reached for a blanket off the back of the couch and unfurled it in front of the fireplace. He turned the TV off and walked toward her. Alice finished her glass of wine, setting it just off the blanket.

"Tell me if I got something wrong." She held his gaze. The only light came from the kitchen and the city lights outside. He glanced over his shoulder for who might be able to see in but realized he didn't care. He got closer, Alice motioning with her eyes for him to lie down.

"This is a whole new side of you."

"Just because I have standards doesn't mean I'm a prude." She sat over him and started to undo the buttons of his shirt.

"I'm glad I meet your standards." He put an arm behind his head.

"Mr. Clare, you exceed them."

# CHAPTER 39

ALICE WAS SORTING THE oyster shells when Delany came into the kitchen the next morning. Her body warmed as her heart raced. What this man could do to her. They had cuddled on the blanket after, Alice watching the flames, unable to deny how safe she felt.

He kissed her and got a cup of coffee. Alice checked her watch, not wanting to be late for meeting her mother.

"It's my birthday this weekend." She leaned against the counter and gripped it for support, her heart racing. "We're doing a big shindig for my dad, our birthdays are only five days apart. Anyway, would you want to come?" She could barely draw in a breath, as it set a deadline for telling Tabby. Alice realized there would always be another excuse to delay. But she cared about Delany. Her sister would have to get over herself.

"You're inviting me to a family thing?" He tilted his head and took a drink of his coffee.

"At my parents' house."

"So this is more than a meal?" He walked toward her.

"It could be all weekend if you stop being a punk about it."

He set his coffee beside her, boxing her in with his statue of a body. "I can't wait." He kissed her, Alice hoping she hadn't made a terrible mistake.

She got off the elevator at her apartment. The door to her place was open, her mother talking to Suzi inside. Slowly, she walked into the space she had not seen in a year. The front door opened to the living room, a generic gray couch and loveseat in the middle, a TV on a short bookcase against the wall. The galley kitchen faced the dining nook on the right. The two bedrooms were at the back, a single bathroom between them. The walls were a generic off-white. It felt sterile, foreign, nothing like home. Maybe she'd get new dishes and furniture, a new bed. The space almost crawled with strangers.

"Birdie." Her mother came out of the spare bedroom with Suzi. "We were just talking, and Suzi thinks they can fit the reno in this week."

"Your mother is such a friend to the company." The woman slightly older than her clutched a dark portfolio to her chest. Her black hair was pulled into a ponytail, the dark red dress a perfect complement for her tan skin.

"So what are we doing?" Suzi looked at both of them. Alice glanced at her mother.

"This is your place, Birdie. What do you want?"

Alice laughed. She'd been there five minutes. "New paint, something earth toned. New furniture. Can we get new dishes?"

"I have someone coming to get everything tomorrow. It's a clean slate," her mother said.

"I can help with any of the furniture." Suzi looked at her mother.

"We might go look at Marco's," she said. "But we'll coordinate with you on pickup."

"Of course. I have some paint samples. Do you want to do anything with the floor?" They all looked at the sad off-gray carpet below their feet.

"Do you have faux hardwood?" Alice asked.

"Of course."

They spent far too much time talking about colors and the feeling Alice wanted to emote and while she would claim to have no preferences, Alice jumped in far more than she expected. Shockingly her mother stayed quiet, not trying to force her opinion on how things should look. After Suzi left, her mother took her to Marco's in Alexandria. Here Alice deferred, letting her mother pick out a new queen bed, dresser, kitchen table, and couches that matched the aesthetic they spent all morning putting together. Afterwards, they got a late lunch.

"Where were you this weekend? We stopped by for dinner Saturday night."

Alice finished the bite in her mouth. "I was in New York with Delany."

"For an event?"

"No, we're dating, I guess." She had never said it out loud before. *I'm dating Delany Clare.* She said it to herself again, the realization exciting and overwhelming. "I invited him to dad's party this weekend."

Her mother leaned into the table. "Have you told Tabby?"

"I'm going to today. He's a good man, Mom…"

She waved her off with a flick of her wrist. "I know, Birdie. I'm more concerned about you and your sister."

Alice glanced out the windows of the restaurant. "Well, she can be happy for me or not. I know what happened hurt but Delany's not who she thinks, and I won't…"

Her mother put her hand on her wrist, Alice wanting to shrink back from what she started. For the weekend, she let herself pretend there was no reason they couldn't be together and things between them were normal. But now she had to tell her sister, and Alice could only pray somehow she'd understand.

"What do I say?" Alice could barely ask her mother.

"The truth."

Her mother left her outside Tabby's apartment, telling Alice to be strong and to call her. She went inside, the hallway feeling like a walk down death row. She hoped for the best but got ready for the worse. She opened the door, her sister talking to someone. Alice left her bag on the bench before going to see who was there. Cyndi called hello from the end of the island. Taco came to see her, Alice kneeling to pet her.

"We are going to the Torpedo Factory to let the kids run around after school, do you want to come?" Cyndi reached for her water on the island.

"I need to do laundry and get ready for work tomorrow."

"How was New York City?" Tabby asked. "Who did you go with?"

Alice glanced at Cyndi. It might be better to say something with another person in the room. Maybe the need to keep up appearances would prevent her sister from going off. Or, it might be better to handle things one-on-one, only then the twins would be there, or she'd be back at work. She closed her eyes.

"Delany and his daughter."

Tabby stopped the water halfway to her lips. "Delany…"

"Clare, yes." Her heart raced.

"Why are you going to New York with Delany Clare and his daughter?"

"Who's Delany Clare?" Cyndi asked, unsure which sister to look at.

"The scoundrel who stole my company."

Alice stood. "A man who owns over two dozen companies in this town, who also runs a nonprofit that feeds people all over the world and donates millions to projects that help lower income individuals."

"What a saint." Tabby put her hand on her heart.

"He is the one who bought out Tabby's company, yes." Alice chose to ignore her sister's theatrics and plead her case to Cyndi instead. "But it was all his best friend."

"Why are you going to New York with Delany Clare and his daughter?" Tabby crossed her arms and cocked her head.

A ringing started in her brain, Alice unsure what to say. "Do you really care or are you just going to be mad?"

"No, please, tell me Alice, how did you all go from business contacts to spending the weekend together." She said the last words slowly, letting out part of the anger Alice knew was in there. "I'm presuming he's who you stayed with last night since you were not here."

"We're dating."

Tabby started several sentences, cocking her head. "Are you kidding me?"

Alice drew in her breath and stood straighter. "He's a good man, Tabby. I feel safe with him and think this could be something."

"You're so naïve." Tabby leaned into the counter and reached for her water. "At thirty you should be able to see when you're being played. Hear me, Alice, when it turns out I'm right, don't expect me to pick up the pieces of your life again."

"I'll be out by the weekend." Alice started for her bedroom, unsure why it was so hard for her sister to just be happy for her.

# CHAPTER 40

ALICE CAME IN FROM her shower and sat on the bed. She lotioned her legs and looked at the room that had been her sanctuary for the last two years. By the end of the week, she'd be back in her apartment. The idea made her want to weep. But Tabby dug her heels in, and Alice would not cower or beg or excuse her choices. Tabby could say whatever she wanted and give her the cold shoulder, Alice would not lose Delany to keep her sister happy.

Her father agreed to come in Thursday to help her move her stuff. It wasn't what she wanted but was what she thought would happen. At least Tabby knew the whole truth. Alice stood to get dressed, hoping it would be a better day.

Alice went to get a cup of coffee, the morning news on low. Tabby must be hiding out in the bedroom. It was the only explanation for why she wasn't out there rebuking Alice with the full weight of her smug superiority, telling Alice how stupid she was, and that Delany was using her for sex.

Annie put her cereal bowl in the sink, asking Alice where she'd been.

"Working." It was the easiest answer.

"Are you coming to my game Thursday? I get to start."

Alice held back her emotion, not daring to look at Paul who drank his coffee at the end of the island by the exit. Maybe she could con her parents into going too and the sisters could pretend to get along for the twins.

"Of course. I'm sorry I wasn't there over the weekend."

"It's okay. I just miss you."

Alice hugged her and prayed to hold back her emotion. Paul moved, asking Mac to turn up the TV. A helicopter flew over a three-alarm fire at a storage unit in central D.C. Alice moved closer, something familiar about the multistory storage building with its collection of RVs outside. Her breath got shallow, her throat constricting.

"Aunt A, your phone is ringing." Mac brought it to her. She answered Carver's call.

"Yeah, Carver. I'm watching the TV now."

"That's where we park the food truck, Lil."

That was not what she wanted to hear.

#

DELANY WAITED WHILE THE leadership of Macon came into the main conference room. One asked about his weekend in New York. Delany rambled about the basketball game and how much fun Helene had. He remembered the rest, his chest warming. He hid his smile behind his fist. Just let him see Alice again. He wanted to whisk her away for her birthday to somewhere warm and private. Maybe he could surprise her, surely Carver would help.

"Are we all set?" Moe asked. Delany glanced over who was

there, not seeing Bobbie. He reached for his BlackBerry, no text that he was running late. Katy lifted her hands when he glanced over his shoulder. After the meeting he'd talk to Bobbie. If it wasn't Alice, it was his place at Macon, or that Delany kept things from him, or that he felt hemmed in. Delany had no idea what was going on but he was over Bobbie's sulking.

The head of IT dimmed the lights and Moe started his presentation on Tabby's second app: BackDoor, which backed-up company cellphones on a main server, allowing leadership to access an employee's contacts, text messages, and emails if needed.

"Think of it like a digital cloud we can access," Moe said. "We are going to beta test the app on Macon's mobiles, loading it automatically as part of the next software push. We're not spying on people. This is our ability to pull and save data and information should an employee leave or be fired," Moe added. "It is added protection for our intellectual property."

Delany went to Bobbie's office, still dark. Delany thought about texting him, but didn't want to hear his excuses. He stopped by Katy's desk, who checked Bobbie's calendar and, as he suspected, there was nothing scheduled.

"Has Bobbie seemed off to you?"

Katy laughed and then caught herself. "Maybe a bit more moody than usual."

It was more than that. He'd been brooding since Delany announced he was coming in full-time. Delany went to his office, ready to focus on something else.

#

BOBBIE WALKED INTO THE cliched French bakery with a line out the door. He went to the coffee bar, asking if Alice was there. She sat at her desk, her head on her fist, talking on the phone. She sniffed and said she'd hold. Pathetic. He knocked on the door. Alice looked up, scowling.

"Can I help you, Mr. Dunn?" She tilted the phone down, her face red like she'd been crying. In the office! How had he not been able to banish this field mouse?

"I was hoping we could talk about your work with Macon."

"Well, I'm on a call and then have a lunch meeting…"

"This won't take long." He crossed his arms and widened his stance. Alice must have realized he wasn't leaving because she sighed and hung up the phone.

"Whatever," she said loud enough for him to hear. He drew in his breath to let out the anger around the mess she and her dowdy sister created in his life but no, eye on the goal. He knew about Delany taking her to New York, Nadia had texted him everything Helene said. If they both didn't need this girl gone, there was no way they'd be talking. What was the line about your enemy's enemy? They both had the same objective.

With Bulldog holding the contract for The Cora hostage, Bobbie went to the new GM who told him they wanted to hire Alice. No way in the hell that was going to happen. He was not going to lose what he'd invested getting Jonas into that space to this broad. Carrie said Alice never stood up for herself. Jonas mentioned she always cowered. Bobbie would ensure Alice couldn't work fast food in the area. And now she didn't even have her pathetic food truck to run back to.

They got into line, Bobbie pulling out his BlackBerry. A reminder came up for a meeting at HQ. Who gave a crap about Array and some stupid program?

"Do you want your usual, Alice?" the cashier asked. She nodded. "And for you?"

"A double espresso." He looked at Alice, who took a step back. The broad expected him to pay at her bakery. "Can I add a butter croissant to the order?" He reached for his wallet. Alice found a stool beside a bar in the window. He sat beside her, Alice leaning back.

"How was your weekend?" He watched the street outside.

"What do you want?"

"I just asked a question." He chuckled. Maybe things didn't go well. He did a slow once over on her. Bulldog should really take his advice on women. "How much would it take to buy Hasty Pudding?" Bobbie decided to be direct.

Alice laughed. "My company is not for sale."

"Everyone has their price." He stared at her, hoping he relayed bored indifference. "The thing is, Hasty Pudding would be better if it belonged to Macon. We could scale it, control the brand, give it credibility. We are working to broker a deal with Jonas. He'd love to add Hasty Pudding to his fleet of restaurants."

A barista put their order down, asking if they needed anything else before leaving them alone. Alice tried to reset her face, but he'd seen what he needed. The field mouse's kryptonite.

"Hasty Pudding is not for sale." Alice reached for her cup and turned to leave.

"After all we've done for you. How good Delany's been to you. This is how you're going to repay him? Suddenly you're too good for us after using us to redeem your name?" Bobbie had learned to play the bad cop, relished it.

"Apparently you still don't know the details of our deal."

A rush of anger flushed through him; Bobbie not able to stop the annoyed grunt from escaping. Alice smirked. Bobbie chuckled. He wasn't giving up. Like a cat with a mouse, Bobbie always got what he wanted. He took a bite of his croissant and rubbed his hands together.

"Nothing is free in this world, Alice. In business we call it a quid pro quo. Delany helped launch your company, so when the time came, we'd have an established catering arm to merge with Jonas' companies. Well, that time has come."

"Then let Delany tell me that. I have other places to be."

"You leave, I'll buy this building and push you and Carver out. Cooperate and maybe Jonas will let you keep catering—under his direction, of course." Surely Jonas could buy the building, this dump could not cost that much. Or Macon could if Delany let him do his freaking job! Alice shook her head and started to walk away.

"Macon won't be using you anymore anyway," Bobbie reached for his drink. "We've retained Jonas to do our events until The Cora is operational."

"Wait, Macon bought the Old Post Office building?" Her eyes went wide. He set his drink down, another pressure point. He wasn't sure why the broad cared about that stupid building, but it mattered and Jonas being there, maybe he found the wedge he needed.

"Jonas is very excited to go into the space."

"I want to hear this from Delany." She could barely get the words out.

He stood and got close, making sure he pulled his height. He'd waited three months to be rid of this pain in the ass. He pulled the boilerplate contract he'd modified from his jacket pocket and held it between them.

"I told you—you were the help. I told you not to get attached. You might think your weekend away meant something, but Delany sent me to tell you the news. He couldn't be bothered. So sorry, field mouse, your time has run out."

#

ALICE TOOK THE SET OF PAPERS and walked away, going to the office before unfolding the contract and slowly sitting. Her sister was right. What a dupe she'd been. She reached for her wallet and cell phone, taking the contract off the desk before sneaking out the back and walking to E Street to hail a cab. As the city passed, she tried to process the news: Macon bought the Old Post Office building. She told Delany it was her ideal local, and he said nothing. He let her blather on about what Jonas did and all the while intending for that man to get a flagship restaurant in the building she loved. That along with the contract he'd been too cowardly to deliver himself. Did Alice know him at all?

She took the elevator to his office. If he thought she would just let him take over what she'd fought to make. Was this always his plan? Get tentacles into every aspect of her business, tie her to him via events, being his private chef, working for his nonprofit. Make her business indistinguishable from his and then subsume it all.

Delany stood when she walked into his office. "What are you doing here?" His wide smile faded. "Alice?"

"How stupid do you think I am?" She tossed the contract onto the desk. "Bobbie came to see me this morning, told me about the Old Post Office Pavilion and Jonas' new restaurant."

"He did what?" He didn't reach for the contract.

"I thought you were different. For a moment I believed you were."

"Alice, I have no idea…"

"You let me sit there in New Mexico and go on like an idiot the whole time knowing who was going into *your* hotel." Her body heat rose, tears threatening to drown her. "I told you what Jonas did, and you said nothing."

"Alice, he isn't…."

"You think you could do all the legwork of getting Jonas into your hotel and I would never find out? How stupid do you think I am? I won't be treated like shit again."

He came around his desk and started to reach his hand out to touch her but then thought better of it.

"I don't think you're stupid. I think you're brilliant and incredible and gorgeous and worthy of every opportunity out there."

She scoffed and shook her head, reaching for the contract discarded on his desk.

"So I guess Bobbie telling me Macon was going to buy Hasty Pudding and that my services were no longer needed because Jones is now handling things was a lie?"

"What did Bobbie do?" He sat on the edge of his desk, setting the contract on the desk.

"Are you this out of touch with your own company?" She studied his eyes. Either he had no idea, or he was a damn good actor. How could a man who amassed a company worth billions not know? "Doesn't matter. I'm done. Don't contact me again." She walked out. Her heart wanted to race out of her chest, her skin hypersensitive. She got onto the elevator and pinched her eyes closed. She would not cry here. It was time to cut ties with Macon, Jonas could have it. Alice didn't want it anymore. For Delany to let her be so vulnerable, to know what Jonas did, and to say nothing even as they got closer, and she slept with him. Her chest constricted. Alice leveraged her relationship with her sister on a man who'd been a mirage.

# CHAPTER 41

DELANY HELD ONTO THE PAGES and went to get the next elevator. He followed Alice onto the street, calling her name. She turned to face him, ready for a fight. He needed a second to process, but did not want to let her leave. People often misconstrued who Bobbie was. He was a big personality, a lot like Nadia, and that sometimes made him come off gruff. There was no way Bobbie did what she said. He would not risk their friendship by going behind his back and lying to Alice. If she just told him what Bobbie said, he could help her figure out what he meant.

"I never asked Bobbie to come see you."

She scoffed and shook her head. "Then your best friend is playing you for an idiot."

"That's not...he would never..." He stopped. It would explain where Bobbie was during the meeting, why he blew off something so important. Bobbie didn't like Alice, but to go behind Delany's back. Delany sat on a bench, the world slightly off.

Alice took a long breath. His heart screamed at him to apologize and pull her close. Another part told him to remember who she was slandering and where his loyalty had to rest. But Alice could be his future. Whereas Bobbie felt more and more like a relic.

"I can't keep being the punching bag of those closest to you because you won't see who they are." She took a long blink. "You won't tell Nadia to back off. You won't call Bobbie out on his actions. You expect trips and hollow words and moments alone to make up for the fact you refuse to face what's right in front of you." She pressed her lips, a hmmm escaping. "I leveraged everything on you—my business, my reputation, my heart. What's at stake here for you, Delany? What have you lost except a bedmate?"

He stood and put his hands on her arms.

"That's not true. You mean everything to me."

"Do I? So I tell you that Bobbie came to see me this morning and threatened to run me out of business unless I agree to work for Jonas. And you go to Bobbie who says it's a misunderstanding and I took things wrong, and he'd never play you like that, Bulldog," she mocked his tone. "Who are you going to believe?" She shook her head. "What does he have to do for you to stop pretending that Bobbie is who you need him to be?" She set her hand on his cheek and kissed him. He reached to hold her, something solid to grasp hold of. When she stepped back, there were tears in her eyes. "I love you, but I can't do this anymore." She walked away and hailed a cab. Delany sat on the bench again, his head spinning. Remembering the paper in his hand he opened it, a boilerplate contract for the sale of Hasty Pudding to Macon.

His cell phone rang. "Yeah," he answered, not bothering to look at who it was.

"The bank is late—again!" Nadia said. "How hard is it to set up freaking autopay?"

"What?" He shook his head to clear his mind.

"Your child support is late." Nadia drew out her words.

"I can go to the bank later. What do you need that can't wait?" His mind tried to process what Alice said. He wanted to push it away, but something hooked in his brain and would not let up. The issues she had with Bobbie were not limited to her. He'd noticed a lot of things since starting at Macon full time.

"What do I need? Food, electricity, clothing. Do you even know what it takes to keep this girl going?"

"And the only funds you have right now come from me?" He looked up from the contract, everything off.

"Don't take that tone with me, Bulldog. Don't you dare take that tone with me!"

"I'll call you tomorrow. Use the card I gave Helene for emergency expenses." He hung up and silenced his phone. Needing to not be around people, he walked to a branch of his bank.

Plenty of people tried to warn him about Bobbie. Delany brushed off their concern because they didn't know Bobbie like he did. But the proof before him was solid. What was Bobbie's game plan here? Did he really believe Macon could acquire Hasty Pudding without Delany knowing, or that he'd be okay buying Alice out? Somehow Bobbie would have a story. He always did. How many questions had he laughed off or danced around with a "trust me Bulldog." And Delany had, blindly.

He asked the bank teller if she knew where the glitch with the funds came from. It wasn't the first time the autopay had not gone through. She clicked on the keyboard, tilting her head.

"You've double-paid a few months." The woman looked at him.

"No, the funds aren't going through."

"They're going through twice."

"That's not possible." He failed to keep the bite out of his tone. The woman told him to hold on and walked away. Delany scoffed. The woman came back with a manager, who asked Delany if they could speak in her office. She told Delany to sit in the chair opposite her desk and pulled up his account.

"You've been sending Ms. Goin two payments, almost back-to-back, on and off for over two years. Is that correct?"

"Why would I do that?"

The manager turned her screen toward him. There in black-and-white were double payments going to Nadia's account.

"She told me the first payment glitched and never went through." Close to an extra $60k into her account. He felt lightheaded. Something had to be wrong. "And none of those double payments were credited back to me?"

"Why would they be? You initiated all of them. The first are the autopays that all went through. Then a few times over the last few years, you've initiated a second payment for the same amount a day or two after."

Delany flexed his jaw, his hands fisting under the table. Nadia lied to him. She called him with that tone and accusations of irresponsibility, and he trusted she was telling the truth.

"Can you give me a printout of that, and the card attached to the account?"

The manager hit a few buttons, the printer behind her coming to life. She gave him a look of pity before reaching back and giving him the pages. "Anything else, sir?"

"Can you freeze the account, stop all pending transactions?"

The manager hit a few more buttons. "Done." She looked ready to say more, but closed her mouth instead.

"I didn't realize what was happening."

"We see it more than you think."

Delany left the office, stopping to apologize to the teller for his tone. She took a second before giving him a sincere thank-you. Delany walked outside. His mother told him a dozen times that

Nadia had a plan for their lives. If he refused to marry her, she would use Helene to milk him dry. The only reason the courts got involved at all was because his mother insisted. Nadia wanted to keep it between them, not leave a paper trail. She didn't want Helene to feel like a transaction. Delany mentioned it offhandedly to his mother who laughed and told him Nadia was not getting a penny without a court decree. Nadia went off, but after listening to his mother, it made more sense to do things the right way. He should have paid more attention to the account but how many expenses did he have in a month? He let his money manager oversee a lot of things, and the man never mentioned anything to him. He presumed Nadia would tell him about an extra $60k showing up in her account, tell him about the double payments. But why would she when she called to demand he pay her twice.

He took a cab to Macon, making a beeline for Bobbie's office. Bobbie saw him and shot up, getting off the phone. "Hey, Bulldog, where have you been?"

"Did you go see Alice this morning? Did you threaten to drive her out of business if she didn't let us buy her company?"

He chuckled and gave him a slick smile. "Is that what she told you? I told you that chick was just after your money."

"Then what the hell is this?" He handed Bobbie the contract, who licked his lips.

"Bulldog, she asked for an appraisal, told me she was tired of the hassle and wanted to sell but was afraid you'd try to stop her. Honestly, it's a more than generous assessment."

He walked out of the office, his world crumbling, Delany wondering what else he'd been content to overlook.

# CHAPTER 42

ALICE'S DAD ARRIVED AFTER Tabby took the twins to school. They loaded her father's Tacoma with the few boxes that held all her earthly belongings. Before she left, she put a note for Annie on her pillow under the panda bear, apologizing for missing her basketball game and leaving without telling her. She reiterated she loved her and hoped, maybe, they could see each other soon.

They loaded her boxes onto a flat dolly and started for the apartment. The door was open, her mother talking to Suzi in one of the bedrooms. The walls were now a pale peach on the top, a chair rail dividing it from the clay red on the bottom which contrasted lighter hardwood floors. Olive shelves in the kitchenette matched the tabletop on the new four-person table, the space expanded to allow full-size appliances. Two men slipped the plastic off a lighter green couch, contrasting armchairs still in the truck.

"Maryanne," her father called. She came out of the bedroom with Suzi who asked what Alice thought.

"It's lovely." She forced a smile. It all made her feel so very alone. Her mother hugged her, Alice resisting the urge to cry.

"Come see your bedroom." She put an arm around Alice and walked with her into the bedroom to the left. The hardwood carried throughout the apartment, the walls a light sage color. A rolled-up carpet leaned against the closet door. "How are you holding up?"

Alice shook her head. "I'm not going to apologize, Mom. She has to get over things sometime."

"Is Mr. Clare still coming this weekend?"

"I don't think Mr. Clare and I are together anymore." Her chin shook.

"Do you want me to stay tonight?"

"No." She had to make it on her own someday. Alice stacked her boxes from Tabby's on the new twin bed in the guestroom to deal with later. She didn't need to be in the apartment while her mother directed the furniture placement and final touches with Suzi. Being idle with nothing to do but think about what she'd lost would drive her batty. So she went to the bakery and lost herself in prepping for her dad's birthday, hoping to use it as a thank-you for all he'd done for her. In tiny ways she paid homage to his foraging roots, wildflowers in the salad, wild honey in the vinaigrette, and dessert from locally sourced berries.

Needing to not think, Alice contacted Harry, the one person who wouldn't make her talk about what was going on. Harry agreed to meet at a bar in Georgetown. Alice got through what she needed to do, leaving enough time to shower and change. She walked to her apartment realizing she had been hiding away since her ex left. It was time to get back out there and make friends, create a life for herself outside her family. Her mother and Suzi set up everything—new towels in the bathroom, dishes on the shelves in the kitchen. The movers laid out the rest of the furniture. It was an apartment ready for a magazine, which might be why it felt so hollow. She went to get ready for the night. *Don't think, just keep moving.* She found a short black-and-white dress she had not worn in forever and the only pair of heels she owned.

Harry waited, several shots already on the table. Alice slid into the other tall chair and shot one back.

"You're looking mighty nice, Lil. To what do I owe the pleasure?"

"I get why you never told Tabby about the sale." It was the easiest thing to focus on.

"She found out about you and Macon?"

"Yeah, and she's pissed." She downed the second shot.

"Salut to making your own way." He downed his shot.

"I need to get drunk tonight." Get drunk, forget all she lost, and figure out a way to deal with things tomorrow.

"Then you called the right guy." He kissed her cheek and went to get drinks from the bar. Alice pushed her thumbs into her eyes and sniffed back her tears. She would survive this. She had to.

#

DELANY WAITED IN HIS financial manager's office, taking deep breaths to stay calm. The man came in, asking how he was. Delany showed him the printout, wanting to know how the repeat charges could happen. The man apologized but had only been instructed to ensure that account stayed at $50,000. If Delany wanted him to monitor it for odd activity, he would be more than happy to do so, but Delany never asked him to do that. It was how things had been since he set up the account after deciding to stay in Helene's life. Something else in his life he let run on autopilot while he played and never bothered to look at after he retired.

"Do I have any recourse?" he asked.

"That would be a question for a lawyer."

He left, wanting to tell Alice she was right and that he was sorry, and that if she gave him time, he'd find a way to make it up to her. He stopped by the bakery midmorning, Carver telling him Alice took the day off to move home. Delany ordered a London Fog to go. Before he left, he sat at a stool in the window and called Jonas to ensure he knew he was not getting The Cora.

"Does Bobbie know about this?"

"This isn't Bobbie's decision. It's a Macon hotel, it's my choice."

"You'll regret this." He hung up on him. *Add it to the list.* Bobbie called again, Delany ignoring the call. He needed something solid but had isolated the one person who made him feel like he could make it without those he grew up with. Unsure what else to do, feeling like if he stayed still he'd shatter, Delany drove until he found an empty basketball court. He got a ball from the trunk and shot. It was a rhythm that kept him sane. Yet, he hadn't played since he decided to retire, barely had a ball in his hand in the last year. He left his tie and dress shirt on the bench and turned his mind off.

Since he was twelve his life had been about one thing. His mother encouraged his philanthropic work to keep him grounded, to remember life outside the game. Macon came almost by accident. He'd been talking to the owner of another team who ran a holding company during an All-Star weekend. The man asked why Delany didn't invest in the opportunities he saw around him, not via a loan or a partner but by acquisitions. It would give him more money, the flexibility to be generous, and let him have a part in businesses he agreed with. The man walked him through the process of starting Macon, the business taking on a life of its own.

He never imagined working in an office. Never imagined being a dad either. Since retiring, a lot happened that he never imagined. Agreeing to come in full-time might have started to keep the board chair happy, but now he found himself with a daughter whose curiosity he only wanted to cultivate, businesses that only had the chance to grow, and a woman he was crazy about who loved his little girl. He never would have set it up this way, but the life he'd fallen into was remarkable.

Delany always knew someday the lights and fame were going to fade. Someday he was going to become that guy who used to hoop. Instead of being there to transition to this next phase together, Bobbie was trying to undermine him. Delany's question was why. He went home, Alice's comment about Bobbie's screwups lingering. He sat on the couch with his laptop and a glass of bourbon not sure what he was looking for, but something that told him just how big of a sucker he was. Logging in, he went to Bobbie's phone backup from Tabby's second app. While the data loaded, Delany tried to think of a possible explanation for Bobbie's actions, something that could be cleared up.

He clicked on the email icon, seeing one from Jonas after Delany's call that morning.

*Delany just called. I'm out of The Cora?! I am tired of getting the runaround from you. Can you deliver on what we agreed on or not? How can I trust you'll get the hotel when you cannot even do this? My investors are getting impatient.*

*Bobbie: I am handling it. Let me get rid of Gibson. You will be in The Cora, own it by the end of next year. Give me time. I have money tied up in this too.*

He did a search for Tabby Black, finding an email exchange between Harry and Bobbie discussing not telling Tabby about the sale. *Don't let her guard her hand*, Bobbie wrote. He told Harry to keep Moe in line. *He can't sell his shares.* Then the Monday before the merger: *Bulldog on board, keep TB in dark.*

Over the course of an hour Delany found hundreds of emails showing how Bobbie had undercut Macon deals, gone against his stated preferences, or worked to use Delany and his company to further his own pocketbook. There were emails of Bobbie telling others to not bother Delany with ideas Bobbie then came in and claimed as his own. He used intimidation, the threat of lawsuits, or saying the person owed Macon because of what Delany had done for them. It was the opposite of what Delany believed. Unsure he wanted the answer, he clicked on the backup of Bobbie's texts. Bobbie and Nadia hated each other, and yet had been communicating almost nonstop since Olive's wedding about *the caterer* and how to get Delany away from her. Nadia let out her full anger after the weekend in NYC. Both seeming at a loss at how to get him back in line.

Delany sat back. His best friend of twenty years played him. All those warnings not to trust outsiders—all the while he'd been the plant in the locker room. Delany called the head of the finance department who agreed to come in before the office opened. Delany needed to know how deep things went. Looking at the screen, Delany realized he had lost almost everyone he thought he could trust.

# CHAPTER 43

TABBY GOT BACK FROM taking the twins to school, the apartment quiet and tranquil. Leaving her purse on the bench, she went to cleanse Annie's room of her aunt's presence. She thought about moving Annie's things, a happy surprise for when she got home. But somehow Annie would not see it that way, and Tabby wasn't sure she could keep from going off on her little girl. Instead, she went to pull the sheets and pick up the clutter her sister left behind. Turning on the light, she found the bed bare, nothing left on the floor. A note on the end of the bed told Tabby everything was in the washer.

The sight of the empty room made her heart ache. She wanted to call Alice and tell her to come back. The twins enjoyed having her close. Who else would cook with Mac and help defuse Annie's energy? But Alice deceived them, choosing the scoundrel over them, making a name for herself off the man who killed Tabby's dream. She chose that man over the twins and all Tabby gave her. Crinkling the note, Tabby went to do something else.

Paul called her name when he got home that night. She

answered from the bedroom where she worked to fold their laundry. With nothing but the rhythm of folding to distract her, Tabby thought about the now empty bedroom and set her jaw, still unsure how her sister could lie to her for so long. Paul gave her a quick kiss before he went to take off his suit, asking about her day. She told him the generics of what was becoming her new routine that left a bitter taste in her mouth.

"The twins are asking about Alice." He leaned his knee onto the bed.

"What did you tell them?" Tabby tilted her head. Paul started a couple sentences. "Are you defending her?"

"I'm not defending anyone. I get that you feel betrayed…"

"Don't say it like that! I *was* betrayed. My little sister built her business off the man who stole mine and lied to me for months!"

"But how would you have felt if she came to you in August and told you what was going on?"

"I would have expected my sweet little sister never to get involved with that man."

He paused. "So you expected her to walk away from an investor?"

Tabby reached for a stack of clothes and went to put them in the closet.

"There were plenty of men who wanted to invest in my business that I walked away from. It's not that hard. There will be others."

"We're going to see her this weekend at your parents' house."

Her father's birthday. She forgot. She finished putting the clothes away and went back to the bedroom.

"I don't want her near my kids."

"Well, that's not your choice." He gave a slight laugh.

"Not my choice?" She took a step toward him, her heart ready to beat out of her chest.

"You are not going to push Alice out of the twins' lives. I get that you feel betrayed, but she's too ingrained."

She started and stopped several sentences. How could her husband be so cavalier? Surely if someone sabotaged his precious big case, he would not be so forgiving. It was unacceptable that he was defending her sister.

"Maybe I won't go." Better than having to stand there and pretend things were okay. Someday, Alice needed to face what a weak and passive woman she was. There had to be some way of getting revenge for what she did.

Paul scoffed and shook his head. "It's been four months, Tabby. When are you going to let things go?"

"I built that place from nothing with my blood, sweat, and tears! I told you those Stooges were only going to stab me in the back. Maybe if you believed in me more, I'd still have my company and be doing something that mattered."

He said "wow" to himself and stood. "What about our marriage, Tabby? Or the kids? Don't they matter?"

"Of course…"

"Because I've tried to be patient and understanding. I've tried to be there. But you are consumed with this. Aren't you tired of carrying all this anger and bitterness? I know I'm tired of hearing about it. Look at what this is costing you. Look at who you are now." He walked out of the bedroom. Her own husband ready to stand with those who stabbed her in the back. He was acting calm about things. Maybe he knew about Alice. What else was he hiding from her?

She reached for his phone on the bed and tried his pin. He changed his passcode. She went through her pin, their birthdays, the twins'. Nothing. If he had nothing to hide from her, why did he change his passcode? He was trying to shift blame like Alice, put her off his trail. Was there no one in her life she could trust?

She held onto Paul's phone and walked to the kitchen. The twins sat on their stools, Taco eating her dinner. Sounds didn't register as she laser-focused on Paul. Tabby leaned on the counter close to him and held his phone in her hand.

"What's the passcode?"

He reached for his phone, but she held on. "Tabs."

"You changed your passcode. Why?" Her skin felt like it was on fire, every hair on edge. Her heart raced. He pulled it again, meeting her gaze.

"There are things on here about the case you can't see. I am tired of taking the brunt of your anger because you won't deal with things." He slid his phone into his pocket before turning to set dinner in front of the twins. Tabby reached for the bottle of white wine and started back for her room.

"Is Mom okay?" Mac asked.

"I don't know anymore, bud," Paul said.

He came in after dinner, Tabby watching TV. He sat further down on the bed and waited for her to look at him. "I would never cheat on you."

"You really expect me to believe—"

"I get that losing your company hurt. But there are healthy ways to grieve. It's been four months. You should not be this irate. Either get some help, or I'm leaving. The kids and I don't deserve to be your punching bags anymore." He walked out.

Tabby studied where he had been, feeling like she was coming undone. She felt so alone. She wrapped her hands around her wine glass, but didn't lift it to her lips, unsure who or what to trust.

# CHAPTER 44

ALICE DROVE TO HER PARENTS' HOUSE, dreading the weekend before her. She rubbed her forehead, still recovering from the previous night. They stayed at the bar before Harry took her to an oyster place in Georgetown that did something with rum where it came out as pearls that burst when she shot an oyster down. It made her feel lovely. Harry got them a bottle of sake. That was the last thing she remembered. It took her a minute to place where she was when she woke up, her apartment foreign to her. She didn't remember getting home. At least she woke up clothed and alone.

She pulled it together enough to walk to work and load the van. Carver made her an extra strong latte and gave her basic carbs to eat. Fortunately, the desire to throw up had subsided. Her sunglasses did little to combat the sun, her head feeling like someone dropped an anvil on it. Hopefully if she kept drinking water and focused on what she was doing her mother wouldn't figure out what happened. She didn't need a lecture.

In the morning light, she had no idea what she lost Delany over. There was no way he asked Bobbie to deliver a contract for her business. To do so would go against everything she knew about him. The fact he didn't mention The Cora hurt. That he would let someone like Jonas have a restaurant in a hotel he owned was beyond what she could comprehend. If she had listened, maybe he could have explained what was going on. Except Bobbie was his blind spot, just like Nadia. Someday he would have to see the truth. Alice backed the van up to the kitchen door and went inside. The house was pristine, a setting for ten on the table in the kitchen. Bing Crosby crooned over the speakers. She didn't call for her parents. Instead, she opened the side door to the van and started to unload.

It would be best to cut her losses and move on. Rita could oversee the Macon events as they transitioned them out. On Monday, she'd call Eddie and tell him she was not taking the job at Comida. Steps from what she wanted, and it all got taken away—again. Macon had felt like a lifeline, but look what it cost her. She should have been upfront with Tabby, but knew her sister would make her pick and she wanted to be near Delany. He was everything she never thought she'd find in a man. Now she'd lost him and her sister; nothing was worth that.

Her mother came into the kitchen. "I didn't hear you come in." She did a slow scan of the counter. "You've been here for a while. How are you holding up?"

"Fine."

"She was going to find out sometime, Birdie."

"Not today, Mom. Okay?"

"I think the best thing for both of you is to just let it go and move on." She went into the living room. Alice scoffed and shook her head. Of course, her mother found this trivial considering whatever consumed her time. Tabby wouldn't speak to her, and she had never felt so alone. Just move on! What did that even mean?

Needing to get out of the house, she took a basket from her dad's greenhouse and went to see what she could forage. He called her name as she opened the side door. Alice waited, her dad joining her a moment later. She asked about his latest book, letting him ramble as they went to the wildflowers on the edge of the property. Finding a patch of Virginia spiderwort, she knelt.

"What's going on, Birdie? Is it the move?" Her dad dropped nasturtiums and calendula into the basket before crouching close to her. Alice sat on the ground and told her dad everything—losing her food truck, meeting with Bobbie, fighting with Delany, walking away.

"I'm back at square one, Dad." Only now she didn't even have the food truck. The insurance company held up the money, something about possible arson. The police told her they found an accelerant on her truck. She had yet to tell Valencia what happened. Just let her go back to the spring and sit in the food truck and listen to Valencia sing and not have her heart trampled again.

Her dad put a hand on her arm, waiting until she looked at him.

"Are you sure about that? Cause from where I sit, you've found a nice niche."

"I know I'm a good chef, Dad. That's never been the issue." She tore a blade of grass between her fingers.

"No, believing in yourself has been. Remember what you asked me before—what if you take this opportunity and fail? Have you? You've come into your own, Alice. You're fighting for what you want, chasing it. So Delany gave you a hand up. The rest is your doing, all of it."

Maryanne called out for him from the house. Her father pushed himself up, groaning.

"Now it's time to pretend I enjoy this half as much as your mother." He started for the house. Alice looked at what was around her. For everything else she wanted Delany there that weekend. She wanted him beside her, meeting her parents' friends, getting to know the twins, being a part of her life. She'd lost the best thing in her life because of her fear.

# CHAPTER 45

TABBY RESTED HER HEAD on her fist, the Maryland scenery flying by as Paul drove. She set her jaw. It was time for him to get over himself. She had done nothing to deserve his ultimatum. He was taking the stress of the endless trial out on her. He didn't appreciate all he'd asked her to do since they got home. It was easier to defend her sister than see she was miserable and floundering.

Annie watched the world outside her window. She had barely spoken to Tabby since they told the kids Alice moved out. Tabby was being polite in telling Annie her aunt moved home because of her job, not that she was a liar and unworthy of her time.

Her parents' house came into view. Before Tabby could say anything, the twins were out their doors and running toward the other kids playing in the backyard.

"Can we pretend for the weekend that you still love me?" Tabby asked Paul when he started to get out of the car.

He stopped moving and sighed. "If you cannot see I love you

dearly, then I have severely miscommunicated why I want you to get help before you push all of us who care away." He got out of the car. Tabby got her emotions under control before she walked into the house overrun with people, the conversations overwhelming. Any other time, Tabby would have been all over this scene. Network, check in, be her mother's junior hostess. Alice would be hiding out in the kitchen or with the kids, leaving it to the real adults to make their guests feel welcome. Instead, she got a soda and went to find her aunt who lived near Lancaster and always had fun stories to tell. Most times she found her father's sister's life too simple, but today she needed the uncluttered.

She sat with her aunt and let the morning pass. Paul talked to some friends, forcing a smile. Her mother fluttered in and out of the room. She would only land for a moment and yet people would claim to have her undivided attention. Tabby still didn't know how she did it.

A group of kids ran through the house on their way to a cooler of juice boxes, small waters, and sodas set up just for them. Her sister walked through the kitchen, not in a jumpsuit for once, but in loose plaid pants and a white blouse. Tabby rolled her eyes and asked her aunt what was going on at church.

Alice came back in, telling Mac she had to work as a van pulled up beside the house. Carver and a younger man got out and propped the back doors open, carrying trays of food into the kitchen. Her mother had set the table for the thirty adults invading the house. The kids were set to eat in the living room, Tabby desperate to join them. Not that her kids were speaking to her. Tabby had told her mother about the twins' behavior on the phone, who chuckled and said karma usually got the last laugh, as if Tabby was ever this insolent growing up. Tabby wanted to call her daughter out on her attitude, but then Annie would ask why she sent Aunt A away and Tabby could only tell her it was for the best. No one seemed as miffed by it all as she was. Even her mother—Ms. Remember Every Offense Ever—seemed okay with Alice lying to her.

She went to get another drink from the kitchen where a line of dishes waited on chafers, the room rich in butternut and garlic. Alice tore leaves and flowers she'd collected from their father's garden, fresh honey in a jar beside her. Carver moved around her, slipping something into the oven. In the corner, the younger guy worked to set up a small cocktail bar. Tabby had never seen her sister in action except the wives' luncheon, Alice truly in her element. Something had shifted in Alice since the summer. She was freer, happier. There was a light in her eyes. Her sister seemed to be at peace, whereas Tabby felt lost in chaos.

Her mother asked if everyone could come to the living room. Tabby went to find her aunt again. Alice leaned in the entry, Carver just inside the kitchen. Her father stood next to her mother who slipped her arm through his and kissed his cheek, her father smiling. Tabby never remembered her parents fighting; never remembered her father speaking ill of her mother. Her mother could look at her father across the room and everything else would fall away for him. She remembered the discussions when her mother was trying to decide whether to run. As a woman in 1979, what right did she have to try? Her father told her to get out there and let people see her passion. He'd fallen in love with her at a feminist march—that Maryanne Gibson could change the world. And she did.

Tabby looked at Paul across the room, unable to deny the sadness in his stance. How had they lost each other? What happened to the magic of Europe? She had been half-alive until she met Paul. Her mother cut her off after she graduated USC, saying it was time for Tabby to sink or swim. She used her mother's connections to land a job doing marketing for a beef association and hated every day. She lived with five other women in a house on The Hill who were all so excited to be making it, but Tabby knew what life in D.C. should be like.

She started sleeping with a married exec at the beef association whenever he was in town. He gave her a credit card and keys to his company apartment. Tabby knew it would never last, but she wasn't eking by anymore. A friend set her up with Paul. He was dorky and quiet, unlike anyone she ever thought she'd be attracted to. Then he confessed his favorite movie was *Three Musketeers* (hers, too!) and he loved R+B (her too!). He treated her in a way no other man had. He saw her and pushed her to dream big and chase it, just like her father did for her mother. But the one time she needed him to be in her corner, he told her to let things go. She didn't need counseling; she needed someone in the trench with her.

"Thank you all for being here," her mother said, "for my husband's sixtieth birthday."

The group hollered and cheered. Her father raised a hand, hating being the center of attention.

"I met this man in 1974, working the phone bank for our House rep. He impressed me with his kindness, his ability to get even the staunchest opponent to listen. We moved to D.C in 1977, so I could work on The Hill. Less than two years later I ran for my own seat." She looked at her husband. "This man helped raise our daughters, got them to school and helped with their homework, all the while finishing his Ph.D. and finding ways to connect in our community. I often get the credit for seeing those around us, but I tell you it's only because James saw them first and helped me to see the right thing to do. You are my light and my true north. I am so grateful for all these years with you. Thank you for being my compass and my best friend. I love you." She kissed her husband, who rested his fingertips on her cheek. Tabby dabbed the tears off her cheek before she applauded with the rest of the room.

"Thank you for being here," her father said. "Many of you have been there for Maryanne and me since the start. I am humbled by your friendship and continued support. Life is not what we do; it's who we have around us. My wife tells me I was a lone ranger when we met. I didn't think I needed anyone else. I've been blessed to pursue what I love and sit here today richer in friendship and community than I ever felt possible. To my daughters, Tabatha and Alice, you are my greatest joy. I am blessed to be your father. You are both so much more than I ever could have imagined."

"To James!" a voice called out from the crowd. The rest of the group repeated the sentiment. Her mother motioned for Alice to come out and placed her between the two of them. Her father hugged her from the side and kissed her cheek.

"Today's meal has been prepared by our culinary genius, who has come into her own this last year. I wish I had a thimble of your talent, maybe we wouldn't eat out so much. But then again, we must support our local economy." She raised her first finger, people laughing. "What are we having today?"

"We have a fresh greens salad with a homemade honey vinaigrette, a butternut and goat cheese side. There is a wild rice and shiitake mushroom sauté I learned in New Mexico and cannot stop making. All complemented with seared beef tenderloin seasoned with rosemary, garlic, and horseradish."

"Bon appétit!" Her mother said in her best French accent.

Carver played bartender in the corner, the younger man bringing people their drinks. He handed Tabby another cucumber mojito. Paul sat next to her talking to her father, the men laughing. She took a long sip. Alice brought another round of platters of food to the table. Every seat at the table taken. Alice would eat in the kitchen with Carver and their staffer.

Alice walked past the main door, carrying a tray of grilled cheeses to the kids' table. Tabby waited for her to walk by again, but she must be taking a minute with the kids. Surely the twins would want to keep her close. Tabby didn't try to get into what was happening around her, instead she sipped her drink and waited for the meal to be over.

With the plates cleared, her father's favorite, wild berry pie with homemade vanilla bean ice cream, was served. Carver stood at the head of the table explaining the berries were locally sourced, and he'd made the cassis using a local vodka. There was more at the bar if anyone wanted a full cocktail. Alice leaned in the door rolling her eyes, a smile on her face.

Tabby believed her sister could have gotten to the top without Delany Clare's help. It didn't make any sense that he would ask for nothing in return. If Alice told Tabby about the offer, she could have helped her see no one just opens their network. Everyone acted like he was a saint, but Tabby knew who he was.

At the end of the night Paul stayed with the twins to watch a movie in the living room. Tabby reached for a bottle of her father's dandelion wine and went to their room. She loved the tiny balcony off the tall windows, her secret place. One summer night Paul tempted her onto it after everyone else was asleep. It was hot and illicit and happened many times since. They'd lay a blanket down and he'd push into her. She loved her husband's body, how it felt when he was with her, how he'd tell her how beautiful she was and what he loved doing to her while he got her body to melt. Let them go back to those easier times when she knew who she was, and things made sense.

Her mother called her name. Tabby took another drink; just leave her alone.

"If you're going to ignore me, at least pull the blanket back so I can't see it." Her mother's head came out of the window before she worked her body through. Tabby took a long drink of her wine. Her mother took the bottle and smelled it, pulling back.

"Not his best year. But it does the trick, I see."

"Can't this wait, Mom?"

"No, it can't. You're a teakettle, Kitty Cat. I am trying to avoid you blowing your top."

"What did my sweet sister say in her defense?" She looked into the darkness, wishing her mother would give her the bottle back.

"I'm more interested in yours. Don't you think this is a bit long to carry this torch?"

Tabby gasped and looked at her mother, ready to let her have it.

"Wake up, Tabatha. It's time to stop feeling sorry for yourself."

"She lied to me!"

"I don't care what your sister did or did not do, I'm talking to you. You and Paul have not said three words to each other all day. When are you going to let this go?"

"Let it go?" How her mother could say such a thing. If her mother's rival did some underhanded trick to win an election, would she be so quick to forget? She remembered far too well when her mother wanted revenge. After Alice's ex went off to elope with his pregnant side hustle, they donated all the overpriced furniture in his apartment, cleaned it out. He came back to an empty apartment and a broken bottle of his family's mead on the floor. She heard her mother conspire against those who screwed her on The Hill like a bad TV drama.

"If you lose Paul, I don't want to hear you complain. That man is the best thing in your life. If you don't get over yourself quick, there won't be very many pieces left for you to collect." She moved off the porch. Tabby looked for the wine, but her mother must have taken it. She pulled the blanket closer. The flicker of anger she tried to stoke blew out under the weight of what she was getting ready to lose. For the first time since losing her company, Tabby pulled her body close and wept.

# CHAPTER 46

TABBY WATCHED THE SUNRISE come to the valley outside her parents' house. For the moment, things were quiet, most of the party guests gone. She and the kids would leave after lunch to give Paul a chance to get some things out of the apartment. All weekend they barely spoke to each other, slept on other sides of the bed. He moved around her, Tabby unsure what to say.

If she admitted she was happy for Alice, wasn't that agreeing Delany Clare was okay? If she got the help Paul demanded, didn't that make her weak? She was not weak, and Delany Clare was a scoundrel. She wanted to be happy for Alice—but what about what Delany did to her? He gave Alice the opportunity to soar while clipping Tabby's wings and sending her crashing to earth. To just move on from the summer, to stop trying to reposition herself in the tech world, to admit maybe there might be something else she could do, didn't that negate everything she went through?

"Morning, Kitty Cat," her father said from behind her. "You're up early."

"Did you get Paul to the MARC okay?"

"He caught a ride back with Alice."

"She left already?" Tabby looked over her shoulder.

"Paul said he might stay at her place, and I think she has an event tonight." He took a drink of his coffee. She looked at the view again. He started several sentences. Tabby rolled her eyes.

"It's fine, Dad."

They had never been good at talking. He found her abrasive and impatient. She wanted him to get to the point. And yet, it was the better qualities about her father she loved most about Paul—his patience, his lack of judgment toward others, his belief in her. Her dad got her into coding, told her to pursue it when her mother thought all that time looking into a computer screen would ruin her eyes.

"She didn't tell you what happened, did she?"

"What do you mean?" She faced him, her father walking into the greenhouse. Tabby sighed and followed him. Why couldn't her father just tell her what was going on? She leaned on a worktable and let him check his vines and adjust his grow lights.

"Bobbie came to see her last week, told her Macon wanted to take over Hasty Pudding." Tabby started to say she was right, but her father held up his hand. "Alice thinks it was a lie, an intimidation tactic." He set his arm on a workbench and leaned into it. "Did you know her food truck burned last week in that three-alarm fire?"

"She didn't tell me that," Tabby said softly.

"I know you're mad at Delany, but I think you've missed something in all of this."

"What is that?" She crossed her arms.

"Your sister is happy, really happy. And it's not just Hasty Pudding." He rested his hand on her forearm, Tabby watching a spot on the wall. "He's a good man, Tabby. Alice trusts him, that should tell you something." He kissed her cheek and went into the house. Tabby let out her breath. Yeah, she'd seen it too. Her sister smiled more, was lighter than she'd been since before she met her ex. Tabby suspected a man was involved somewhere. She wanted to hold onto her anger, but she couldn't justify denying Alice what she herself was getting ready to lose. Real, honest love.

Annie walked into the living room of the apartment, Tabby looking back from the TV. They came home before dinner, the kids needing to get ready for school the next day. Tabby told the twins their dad was working on his case. He'd been gone enough in the last two months that neither questioned her. She dreaded trying to sleep without Paul there, the apartment uninviting without him.

"What's up?" Tabby asked. Annie sat on the couch and crossed her legs, a notebook in her lap.

"How do you code?"

"How do you code?" Tabby laughed. "Why?" She reached out and fluffed Annie's hair, getting the part in the middle again before she pulled one side behind her daughter's ear.

"I want to make a game."

"You want to make a game?"

Annie giggled. "Are you going to repeat everything I say?"

Tabby laughed too. "I don't understand what you're asking."

"I was working with Aunt A on this idea for a game." She opened her notebook and kept talking over Tabby's objection. "And I thought since you were such a great coder, you could help me."

"You think I'm a good coder?"

"Yeah, I mean Aunt A said so. Said you were a top coder who could change the world."

Her throat constricted; Tabby desperate not to cry.

"What's your idea?"

Annie scooted closer and opened her notebook. It was a rewrite of Sleeping Beauty, because how stupid that all she did was lay there while the boy got to have all the fun. She wanted to rewrite the trope, as Aunt A called it, and do a game where the girls get to kick butt, while the boys wait. Tabby reached for the notebook and glanced at the storyboard while Annie talked.

"You've seemed sad. I thought maybe this could cheer you up."

She looked at Annie. "You know I've been sad?"

Annie hung her head and played with a nonexistent spot on the sofa. "Since you lost your company, you've been sad and kind of detached."

"That's a big word for a ten-year-old." Tabby narrowed her eyes.

"I asked my teacher what the word was for someone who seems to be separated from everyone else and not doing what they used to love. She said it was detached."

Tabby nodded. How blind she'd become to her own children.

"So do you want to learn to code, or do you expect me to do all the work?"

Annie's eyes got big, and she smiled wide. "You can teach me how to code?"

"I would love to, around your homework. Maybe we can work on this over the weekend? Now go to bed."

Annie hugged her and kissed her cheek before walking out of the room. Tabby reached for the notebook, full of pages of ideas and storyboards. Some of it was crude, but there was something there. Annie had a list of characters and scenes and how a person progressed from one chapter to the next. Tabby found a notepad on the base of the coffee table and began to work out the details. Her little girl was onto something.

# CHAPTER 47

DELANY RAISED HIS HAND and weaved through the tables toward Collins. Collins folded the paper, asking Delany about his weekend. What to say? Helene was with her mother for the week, giving him time to figure out what to do. He unfroze the account, needing to keep Nadia in the dark. His financial guy knew to call him if anything happened.

"Mr. Clare?" Tabby Black walked toward his table. "I thought that was you."

He stood. "Mrs. Black. This is…" He started to introduce Collins.

"I don't particularly care. This won't take long. Are you proud of yourself?"

"Mrs. Black, I want to apologize again…"

"It's not what you did to me. It's how you treated my sister, strung her along. You opened your Rolodex and then slammed it shut when she demanded better from you!"

"That's not what…"

"No, it is. Both of us went against your crony and lost. Both of us dared to take a stand against the irrefutable Bobbie Dunn and have nothing left to show for it. My sister—she pours her heart and soul into every dish she makes." She talked over his objection, Delany deciding to just go silent. "She worked hard to get to the top of Cornelia's kitchen, and when he died…" She stopped. "You men are all the same. I'm glad my sister still owns her company. I guess she's the lucky one."

"If you're talking about Bobbie's…"

Tabby laughed. "Do you know, I can't get an interview because of Bobbie. He told firms not to hire me because I stood up to you. He's lied and said there is a non-compete clause or if they hired me, he'd freeze them out of the area. I don't understand how someone who is so connected into the community and longs to help the little guy as much as you pretend to can tolerate someone like him. Surely the bro code doesn't go that far. I'm sorry Alice lost her food truck. She might need it at the rate Bobbie is going."

"What happened to her food truck?" Delany asked slowly. Tabby crossed her arms.

"There was a fire at the place she stored it, burnt to a crisp. She's devastated."

There had been a text on Bobbie's phone from an unnamed number about something burning. He felt ready to throw up, only wanting to hit a wall from what he had been so blind to.

"Mrs. Black, I didn't know…"

Tabby laughed. "Save it. My website, the business you stole—it was my Hasty Pudding. Bobbie Dunn cut me out, lied to keep Moe in line. Your little takeover never would have happened if Moe could have done what he wanted and let me get over 50 percent."

"I never meant to hurt you or your sister."

"That doesn't mean much now, does it? Enjoy your lunch."

She walked away. Delany paused for a moment before he sat down, apologizing to Collins.

"She's right, you know. Bobbie called to tell me to back out. I guess there was some guy you grew up with he wanted at the hotel. He said he'd hate to see me move my family from Miami for nothing."

Delany knew who Bobbie was thinking of and wouldn't hire him if his life depended on it.

"Well, thank you for saying no."

He got outside the restaurant before slipping his trilby on. He looked down the road, the city feeling different. He called Katy and asked her to set up a meeting with the head of finance and Macon's chief lawyer at an off-site location. It was time to do something about Bobbie Dunn.

#

TABBY SET HER BAG on the bench and slid off her heels. She looked at where Alice usually put her bike, missing her sister. In the kitchen, her mother helped the twins with their homework. She thought getting to say everything she wanted since losing TabiKat would make her feel vindicated. She thought seeing Delany's guilt over her jabs at his integrity, being able to call out his henchmen, making him look her in the eye as she told him what his acquisition did to her, would liberate her from hating him, instead she just felt hollow.

"Am I holding onto things?" she asked when her mother came to say hello. Her mother leaned against the counter and loosely crossed her arms.

"You're mad over losing your company, fine, but be mad at who you need to be mad at. Call Carrie and tell her she's a self-involved snot. Go see Harry and hold him to account. You've been firing cannonballs at everyone around you instead of facing what happened and finding a way to move on."

"I worked so hard on that website." She looked at her mother.

"I know you did. No one will deny you made that business. I get it. I poured my heart and sweat into bills that died for political convenience. I gave my district twenty-seven years, and the party nominated a man I cannot stand. It's part of being in the fight. But you need to learn to separate your disappointments from those around you. You need to start letting what's bothering you be what bothers you, and stop making it about Paul's job or your sister's career or the PTA." Maryanne put her hand on Tabby's cheek. "Alice should have told you. We told her to tell you. I won't excuse her actions. But she is not the issue here, is she?"

"How do I let go, Mom?"

Mac got Annie laughing at something, their homework forgotten.

"Don't make my mistake and lose sight of your real legacy." Her mother kissed her cheek and started to load the dishwasher. Tabby watched her children laugh. All along she'd been denying these four walls held what mattered. Paul's absence and her children learning to function without her made her realize she did not want to become replaceable. Growing up she wished her mother would give the girls half the attention her district got. They were second, or tenth, behind poll numbers and backdoor deals. Tabby felt overlooked, desperate for a crumb of her mother's day. How had she repeated the mistake with her own children? Nothing was worth doing if her family—the four of them—weren't in it together.

"Can you stay for a little longer?" she asked her mother, who told Tabby to go. Tabby thanked her and went to the garage. She got into her car and drove into the District. Fear threatened to stop her, but she refused to listen to it anymore. Nothing—not her pride or her need to be right or the grief that felt like a noose—was worth it if Paul wasn't with her. She hated the idea of pouring her soul to some nosy nelly counselor, but maybe her family had a point.

She knocked on Alice's apartment door, praying her sister was at an event. Paul opened the door in jeans and a Wizards T-shirt.

"Can I come in?" she asked, having no idea what to say. He stepped back and she moved inside, the TV on, Paul's work spread across the dining room table. "Is Alice here?" she asked. He reached to mute the TV and shook his head. Tabby nodded. The updates looked good. Her sister would never have gone for boring colors, and hardwood was a good choice. Her mother picked out the furniture. She glanced in the second bedroom, unmade twin bed, Paul's suitcase open on top of a generic light brown dresser. Paul said her name, impatiently.

"You were right," she said. Paul crossed his arms and waited. "I have been using you as my punching bag. I've been wallowing and seething, and it's not healthy. I let my company become the most important thing in my life, assuming you and the kids would run on autopilot. Then I lost everything. I kept thinking you all could exist on fumes."

"You haven't lost everything yet, Tabby." He shook his head and looked towards the ceiling, sighing.

"That's what I hadn't figured out. I let myself become wrapped up in TabiKat. I let it tell me who I am and that I was doing something worthwhile. I took you for granted. I took what we have for granted." She stood before him, her hands on his arms. "Europe should have told me that all I need is you. If you and the twins are there, things will be fine. Alice should have told me the truth. But you were right, I wouldn't have heard anything positive in it for her. I was jealous and took all of that out on you. I am sorry, Paul."

He hugged her and pulled her in. Tabby rested on his chest, able to hear his heartbeat.

"I've let it go." She looked at him. His lips were pressed, his eyes full of doubt. "It's true. There's something else out there for me, and what good does hating Delany Clare do? Maybe he's just as duped by Bobbie as Mo Mo was."

"And what about Alice?"

She drew in a deep breath. "I'll come see her, let her tell me what happened. I can't believe she'd lie to me, but I can see why she did. I'll talk to someone, but will you go with me?"

"Of course." He kissed her, Tabby grabbing the front of his shirt. "I'm with you, you know that, right? I'm in your corner, and I believe in you. I've hated seeing you in this much pain."

She studied the blue eyes that had come to mean safety and love. She would look into those eyes after the twins were grown and all they were doing now ceased to be important. Let them sit together and hold hands like her parents did. Let her never take the love in those eyes for granted again.

"You got a great little setup here by the way."

"What? It works for me." He glanced over his shoulder into the bedroom.

"I never did see your bachelor pad, did I?"

"No." He laughed. "And for good reason. Man, you would have walked away if you had seen the near squalor of that place." He held onto her forearms when she reached to hold him.

"Come home."

"Gladly." He kissed her again.

TABBY LOOKED AROUND THE RESTAURANT, unsure why she was there. Delany's admin called that morning and asked if she was available. Really, what else needed to be said? Tabby wasn't going to cower before his version of events, and she didn't care about his justifications or how Bobbie spun things for him. She was over hating him and blaming Bobbie and caring if Array failed or not. Letting go of her hatred toward Delany opened her eyes to the host of other options—like Annie's game. Ideas swirled in her head, but this was her little girl's project. They were working on a presentation for an event at her school later in the week. Who knew, maybe she'd get into gaming after all.

Delany pulled out his chair. Tabby sat up more and pressed out a line in her skirt. He ordered a sidecar when the waiter arrived, Tabby asking for a cucumber mojito.

"Alice did one of those for an event, put vodka and frozen honeydew balls in it. It was good."

"Why am I here?" Tabby asked. "Surely after our last encounter…"

"You were right, Mrs. Black, I'm an idiot."

Tabby sat back and tapped her foot hanging over her knee. She was going to enjoy this. "About what, Mr. Clare?"

"Everything, apparently." He leaned into the table. "I am hoping for some trust on your behalf. I have no right to ask for it, but I hope it shows I'm serious."

She studied him, her curiosity piqued. "I'm listening."

"We screwed up the acquisition of your company. *I* screwed up the acquisition of your company. I wanted to come to you directly." He paused while the server put their drinks down and took their orders. "Bobbie met Carrie at a party, got talking about TabiKat. She told him about the app and your other ideas. He told me. We just acquired Chip-Pixel and wanted another tech company to merge them with. I thought you'd run Array. I was going to talk to you about it at the party, then Bobbie told me he had it. As things went further along, something shifted in how he talked about you. I kept asking if you knew about the sale, he kept saying you did. I should have asked more questions. I should have talked to you before the merger, and I apologize for not."

"Thank you." She cleared her throat. She had been too nervous to take a drink while Delany talked and now took a bit more than she should have, having to focus to swallow without coughing. If Delany realized, he didn't say anything. Instead, he sipped his drink, keeping his hand around the glass on the table.

"I let Bobbie fool me into thinking this was a simple merger, and it wasn't. I got into this to help people not amass an empire."

He sat back and waited while the server put their meals down. Tabby finished her first drink, ordering another round. To hear the words she'd wanted for months, to have him acknowledge that losing her company meant something. Part of her brain told her to remember he was a scoundrel, and this must be a ploy. But she didn't believe that anymore. Her parents were excellent judges of character and only had the best things to say about him. She'd asked her mother about what was going on with him and Alice and it sounded almost storybook. She chose to believe he was telling her the truth. She forgave him for what happened, realizing in some small part that hating him only allowed Bobbie to keep him in the dark for longer.

"Why am I here, Mr. Clare?"

Delany put his sandwich down and wiped his mouth. "I want you to come be my new Chief of Initiatives."

She laughed before she could stop herself. Delany let her, reaching for his water.

"You're serious. Why?"

"Because what you did at TabiKat is remarkable. You care about the little guy, and something tells me you have an eye for finding that diamond in the rough."

"What about your current chief of initiatives?" She had only heard that stupid term once. Men and their need for titles that stroked their egos. Delany dropped his gaze and shook his head. "Oh." She was taking Bobbie's place. Adrenaline flooded her body, her skin tingling. She didn't know whether to laugh with joy or faint with disbelief. She put her fork down. "What happened to Bobbie?"

"He won't be working at Macon much longer. That's the piece I need your discretion on."

"Of course," she said, slowly processing. "One condition." She leaned into the table. Delany reached for his sandwich, his gaze telling her to go on. "I want to oversee the projects for Array."

"Of course. I think Mr. Manuel will be relieved." He put his food down. "I never meant to imply I did not believe you could code. I was given bad intel and…Work on whatever makes you excited like Welcome Note did."

Tabby smiled, able to think of one project already. "I do have one more question."

"Just one?" He reached for his drink.

"What are you going to do about my sister?"

Paul called her name when he got home that night. She pushed dinner onto a cold burner before going to see him. She kissed him and pulled her body close to his. He held her and breathed deep, a small moan escaping.

"What's got into you?" he asked.

"Thank you for being patient with me."

"How did the meeting go?"

"He offered me a job—Chief of Initiatives. I'd help determine what companies we take on and can oversee apps being developed."

"And you said…" He slipped off one of his work shoes before pushing off the second.

"How can I not take this job? The salary is incredible. He said I could work at home sometimes. He gets needing to be out of the office for the twins. I want to do it."

"I think you should." He undid his tie.

"And that's not weird, after everything…"

"Tabs, this is your chance to leave the mark you want. What does your gut say?"

"I'd be an idiot to not do this."

"There you go." He kissed her again, Tabby smiling on his lips. Mac called her name. She went to sit with her kids at the island and help with their homework. After dinner, she worked with Annie on her coding. Her girl a natural.

She kissed her daughter's head. They could be her legacy the same as a job could. What if she poured into them like she did her company? Maybe she'd offer to take Mac rock climbing or to a parkour gym. Once things settled, he could see Alice and cook. Both of her kids held passions she wanted to cultivate. They'd become their own people while she was busy trying to find her identity somewhere else.

"Hey, string bean," she said. Annie looked up at her. "I'm sorry for being so mean and detached these last few months."

Annie shrugged. "I'm just glad you're back. I like having you around more." She went back to her work. Tabby kissed her head. She would not lose sight of her family again.

# CHAPTER 48

DELANY OPENED THE DOOR to the bakery fresh off his lunch with Tabby. Carver raised his hand hello, Delany asking if Alice was there. Carver told him to come on back. Her laugh floated out of the kitchen. She stood at a mixer with the guy from the basketball event, whose hand rested on the table as he faced her, Alice laughing.

"Hey, Mr. C," the boy said. Alice looked over her shoulder, her smile fading.

"What do you want?" she asked.

"Can we talk?"

She led him into the office. He knew what he wanted to say—he was sorry, he loved her. He'd been an idiot and if she would trust him one more time, he would be the man Alice thought he was. The man he'd been too scared to acknowledge was waiting to be called out, one that could make it on his own, one that wanted to be open and engaged with the world around him. One more chance and she'd never have to take Bobbie or

Nadia talking down to her again. He saw it now. Things were different. "Your sister told me what happened with your food truck." He had practiced what he was going to say. If she didn't want to be with him, he at least wanted her in his life on a business level. She had put too much into things to walk away because he was too blind to see the truth.

"Tabby told you that?" Alice crossed her arms and shifted.

"I saw her the other day. What are you going to do?"

"I don't know. The police think they have a suspect, but I can't get the insurance money until things shake out more."

"I'd like to replace it for you, give you the best of what's out there. Let you be able to work events. Make it so Carver doesn't have to drive separately."

"That's not necessary." She slid her hands into her back pockets.

"It's not a big deal. I'd love to…"

"No. I mean I won't take it. I don't want it from *you*."

He hoped this would go better. The level of pain radiating from her was more than he expected. But if he'd been in her place, put down by those closest to her, had his name disparaged for jealousy and self-preservation, he might not be that congenial either. Still, with what was coming, it would be so much easier if she stood there with him. It only felt doable if Alice was in his corner. He hoped Tabby mentioning her might be a sign she was open to seeing him. Now it was obvious the sisters had not talked. Whatever sweet reunion he hoped for faded under the reality of where their decisions placed them. He would never regret offering to help her, that decision changed everything for the better.

"I was talking to Collins, and we'd love for you to take the restaurant at The Cora."

"You want me to what?" She drew in a long breath. "I won't work for Jonas." Her voice heaved with pain. He'd never ask her to do that. How could he? Just let them go back to that night in his apartment when existing became living. He finally found the one he loved.

"No. It would be yours. Executive Chef. Cook whatever you want. State of the art kitchen in your favorite place." He waited. Something moved out the corner of his eye. Carver stood outside the open door, eyes wide, nodding at Alice.

"You don't have to do this." She sounded so defeated.

"I know I don't have to." He moved around the desk. Alice pulled her hands free and tried to step back. Delany reached for her upper arms, pulling her to him.

"You deserve this, Alice. Come on. I'm sorry." He stopped himself from saying he loved her. She said it to him, and he'd been too lost in things to hear it. She loved him. Loved. Now Delany saw that that door was closed.

The restaurant should have been hers the whole time. It was the only thing he had left to give. To make her happy, he'd give up his dream of living there and helping it come back to life. He'd back out of the hotel and own it in title only, watching her soar from afar. He'd never go on another Comida trip. Just let her do what she was meant to.

"I can't. Find someone else." She backed away and walked out of the office and straight through the rear door of the kitchen. Carver started to say something, the sound catching in his throat. Delany walked into the kitchen.

"She'll come around," Carver said.

"I don't blame her for not."

"Listen, don't give our events away, someone from this company will be there. Have your admin call me." Carver gave Delany his card.

"Will do. Have a good day, okay?"

"Yeah." Carver let him leave. He walked into the daylight and flagged down a taxi. It was a short ride to his lawyer's office. The man shook his hand and asked how he was. Not good. They went over the paperwork. Delany failed one woman he loved; he would not fail his daughter too. She deserved to be raised around women who did not take and lie and steal. How had he missed it for so long? He shook the thoughts away and focused on what was before him. Something new was coming.

# CHAPTER 49

ALICE WALKED TO THE END of the alleyway before she glanced over her shoulder, willing Delany to follow her. Just call her name and let them have one of those cheesy scenes from the movies. Only he wasn't there for her. Whatever they had wasn't more important than his pseudo-brother. He'd come to settle their business accounts, to make-up for Bobbie's stunt, to rebuild what she'd lost in the fire. He acted like they could just go back to how things were before New Mexico, as if the time since meant nothing. Only, why he was talking to Tabby didn't make any sense. Knowing her sister, she got mad over something else and, without Alice there to kick, called Delany to yell and tell him what a scoundrel he was. Maybe if she'd gotten it off her chest in June, they'd all be better off.

Needing to move, she walked around the block. The last week hurt. She lost the best thing in her life and didn't know how long Tabby would choose to ignore her. But she'd rebuilt her life once before; she could do it again.

Things were quiet when she got back, Carver working in the office. She reached for her messenger bag, ready to head home.

"You're letting your fear dictate things again," he said. Alice knelt on the chair across from the desk. "We're not dropping the Macon events."

"That's fine. Rita can keep taking the lead on them."

He sighed and leaned into the desk. "Why are you doing this? He's offering you everything you want."

"Because it's what I should have done in June." She stood. "Have a good night." She walked home, keeping her head down. Of course she wanted The Cora. It was her dream. Knowing Delany bought it assured her it would stay a D.C. treasure. But she didn't want it as some consolation prize. She couldn't work for him and not be with him. If Alice had any hope of moving on, she had to get Delany out of her life entirely.

The doorman welcomed her, Alice stepping on the elevator. The apartment felt quiet and sterile again. Paul moved home the night before, leaving Alice a note that simply said he and Tabby talked. She grabbed her notebook and leftovers from one of their events and went to eat on the rooftop, sitting where she couldn't see Delany's building. Her father's comment lingered. She had come into her own. Hasty Pudding's reputation and success were because Alice cooked her way. Delany opened the door, but Alice's ingenuity turned her business into a premiere catering company.

That article all those years ago that called Alice a chef with a vision who could change the culinary reputation of D.C. could be correct, if she stayed true to who she was. What Carver did not see was the base they had. Macon accounted for only half their events, and they turned down other clients to accommodate them. The decision to walk away was doing what Delany always said he wanted to help her do—soar on her own.

Alice had taken time over the week to visit local farms, walking the fields and talking about ways they could partner. She met with oyster farmers, fishers, and ranchers, who could accommodate the volume Hasty Pudding required. After she finished eating, she reached for her notebook. She was tired of cooking boring food for people who did not get it. It was time to niche Hasty Pudding as local flare, with a foraging and creative twist. Losing the food truck hurt, but she didn't want one replacement—she wanted four or five, a fleet to go out to company events and schoolyards and festivals. Carver might not get it yet, but Alice saw a way forward that aligned with who she was as a chef and let them have fun with food, while subtly challenging the way people ate.

THE NEXT DAY, Alice parked the catering van at the twins' school and went inside. Cyndi called earlier and asked her to do the food for the students' entrepreneurship event where Annie was presenting her gaming idea. Alice donated the payment for the event back to the fund to pull more girls into STEM. She decided to attend the rehearsal to hear Annie's practice run, not wanting to risk Tabby's ire by showing up for the main event.

She brought two boxes of cupcakes for the students, sliding them onto a table in the back. A student came over, asking if he could have one. She opened the second box as more students made their way over.

Annie stepped onto the stage. She cleared her throat and nodded. A female avatar came onto the screen with a green tiara and short teal jumpsuit, her hair a messy pixie cut.

"This is Princess A. She is here to save the prince, who can't seem to wake up to his alarm." While she talked, a mix of stills and basic videos from her game played behind her. "She needs him to be ready to go for the basketball tournament to decide who will rule Mac-Land. Their opponents are The Stooges, a duo of tricksters hellbent on stealing what Princess A has built." A few adults in the room for the practice run booed and hissed as the tricksters flashed on screen. "It's only by believing in herself and facing her fears that Princess A can reach the prince and get them both to the game on time."

Alice knelt and waited while Annie ran to see her. She hugged her close. "I am so proud of you!" Alice met her gaze. "That was amazing."

"My mom thinks maybe we can make it into a real game."

"I think you will have a room full of people tonight ready to buy it." She rested her hand on Annie's side.

"Are you okay, Aunt A?"

How to answer that. It was hard not seeing the twins all the time; they had been such a bright spot in her life after her ex left and Cornelia died, and she pieced herself back together. Annie's room was a sanctuary, but only for a time. Now she needed to stand on her own. For once, she wasn't in anyone's shadow. It was scary, but also freeing.

"I'm getting there, sweetheart. Maybe your dad can bring you on Sunday to see me?"

Annie nodded. Her teacher called for her to come on. Alice left behind what they would need for the night, two staffers coming back for the actual event. She drove the van back to the bakery and walked to her apartment.

She unlocked the door and rested her messenger bag on the short table by the door. Her parents came by earlier in the week to start the process of getting her name on the deed. She had a place of her own. Still too quiet. The twins weren't there, Taco wouldn't come and sit on her bed. She couldn't hear Tabby and Paul banter in the kitchen. New accessories and paint did not change how alone she felt.

She looked up and let out an expletive, her hand on her heart. Tabby sat on the chard-colored sofa against the wall, her legs pulled under her.

"I told Mom peach was much more your color." Tabby pointed to the painted walls.

"We put new locks on the door."

"Please. Mom gave me a set before they left town. You think dad's going to drive three hours when you lock yourself out when I am here to take care of you?" She put her hand on her heart.

Alice went to the kitchenette, a bottle of red wine on the counter beside two glasses.

"Did you go through everything?"

"I tried to find your diary. Then I realized your life is just as dull as it was in sixth grade so gave up and reorganized your closet instead. You don't have as many jumpsuits as you once did."

"Maybe I'm growing up." Alice finished her first glass.

"Don't drink the whole bottle before you even sit down. I'm not that horrible."

Alice sipped her second glass and went to sit beside her sister. Tabby poured herself a glass and hit it against Alice's.

"What are we toasting?"

"My little girl's presentation tonight. Cyndi thinks you might get some appointments from it."

"Don't worry I'll give the STEM club the 30 percent I promised."

"Thank you for doing that." Tabby took a sip. "Not just her event, but her idea. I didn't know she was into all that." She leaned further back onto the couch. "I really checked out there. You were there so I didn't have to engage my children and felt free to pursue other things. Feels so horrible to say."

Alice stayed quiet, taking another sip. Her sister was there for a purpose.

"So, thank you for being there for my kids. I am sorry for what I said to you. I overreacted."

Alice finished her glass. "I didn't know how to tell you. I got the Macon gig before I knew who he was, and then he came to the food truck, and I needed the money. I thought it would be a gig or two. I never intended for it to go so long. I should have told you, but I was getting my chance and if I admitted it to you then

I had to recognize what I was doing and…" She was rambling. She shook her head, running the stem of the glass between her hands. "I never meant to hurt you."

Tabby scooted closer to her, putting her hand on Alice's knee.

"You were right. Paul was right. I was wallowing. I was angry and full of self-pity. I lost sight of what was important. I understand why you took the job and why you didn't tell me. It still hurts, but I forgive you."

"Thank you." Alice could barely get the words out. Tabby hugged her from the side before she reached for the wine and refilled their glasses before hitting them again. "Are we toasting making up?"

Tabby shook her head and finished her sip. "That is for my new job," she said. Alice repeated the line back to her. "I am the new, oh what did he call it? We are going to have to rework the title, 'Chief of Initiatives'. Only men think of stupid titles like that."

"Chief of Initiatives?" She only ever heard that stupid title given to one person.

"At Macon. Delany asked me to lunch yesterday, cleared the air as it were. He told me he was firing Bobbie and wanted me to take his job."

"Wait, Delany fired Bobbie?" Alice faced her more on the couch.

"Can we stay on me, please?" Tabby dropped her jaw and playfully scoffed. "He's a lovely man, Alice, not at all like I thought. I can see why you love him."

"I do not…" She stopped and closed her eyes. "You're such a pain in the ass."

Tabby laughed behind her wine glass. Alice met her sister's gaze.

"You deserve this, Tabby. I'm proud of you."

# CHAPTER 50

DELANY WALKED INTO HIS OFFICE. Today was the day. He nodded to Katy, who bit her bottom lip. A backup of Bobbie's desktop and phone waited on his desk. He sighed. He could do this. His best friend did this to himself. Bobbie used their friendship to get rich and hurt other people, presuming Delany would keep being naïve and in the dark, and he might have been. That was one thing Alice gave him. She removed the blinders and helped him see what his fear of others cost him.

Katy came in with his paper and coffee, setting them on the edge of his desk.

"I owe you an apology," he said. "You tried to tell me who Bobbie was, and I blew you off. Gave him a pass. I am sorry for not doing my part in seeing what was going on."

Katy took a moment, her mouth ajar. "I appreciate the apology, Delany. Thank you."

"Thank you for staying with me."

She smiled. "You're not getting rid of me any time soon."

The lawyer came in and Katy left pulling the door closed behind her.

"It's wiped clean," the lawyer said. "Bobbie wiped his hard drive and his phone."

He suspected something. Not hard given Delany had been avoiding him since the encounter in his office, not taking his calls, pulling other people in on his projects.

"I have it." Delany handed him the backups.

"Here's the paperwork you asked me to draw up." The lawyer handed him a file, Bobbie's termination settlement. His stomach tightened, Delany fighting the urge to throw up. His palms were sweaty. Let him wake up and find this all a bad nightmare.

"I'm sorry, Delany."

Bobbie came in midmorning, creeping toward Delany's desk. Delany did one more scan of his emails, still no word from Tabby.

"How are you doing?" Bobbie sat across from him. "Everything good?"

"Why do you ask?" Delany looked at him. Bobbie tried to play it cool, but sweat lined his top lip and he fidgeted more than normal. He gave Delany too wide a smile.

"You haven't been returning my calls."

"What did you see coming out of your conversation with Alice?"

Bobbie started to stumble and give an excuse. Delany raised his hand. He didn't care. "Today is your last day at Macon. Today is your last day in my life. I know about the deals you made with companies we merged with, how you bullied people into giving you what you wanted, and went behind my back. I know you lied to me. I know you were working with Nadia to keep Alice out of my life. I know about the deal you made with Jonas for The Cora. I know you set Alice's food truck on fire. What I don't know is why, but I guess I don't care."

Bobbie's face twitched. He watched Delany, choosing his words. "Bulldog…"

"I hate that nickname. I have always hated that nickname. And maybe that should have been a sign to me of how big a jackass you are. It's not outsiders I can't trust, Robert, it's you."

"You can't prove any of it," he said after a moment. No denial, not an apology or any sign of remorse or accountability, only the arrogance that he'd covered his tracks and would get by scot-free.

"The police have a copy of your hard drive and phone from last week. You can thank Tabby Black for that little innovation. I was going to offer you severance, make it so you were okay." He took the pages out and tore them in half. "But now I want you gone. You will never use my name to further your life again. Let's see who wants you when you have nothing but bravado to back you up."

"Delany—I'm your oldest friend… It's that woman… They're lying!" He stood.

"Emails and text messages and eyewitnesses tell a story of how you played me for a fool." He stood and leaned into his desk. "You're lucky I'm not suing you for all the BS you pulled here— those trips, all the favors you extorted. You're lucky I am not full-court press. I defended you against your old company, paid for your legal fees, and you lied to me! You've been using my name to garner favors and support since we were kids. You think your father would be proud of you? You think this is how J.R. got by, why everyone in our community revered him?"

"Don't mention my father!"

"He is rolling in his grave, Bobbie. Your father was not slick. Not manipulative. Somewhere you know this isn't how he'd want you living your life."

Bobbie took a breath before resetting his tie and standing fully. "You'll regret this."

"My only regret is ever trusting you."

Bobbie stormed out of the office, security waiting. Katy stood from her desk. Delany sat and put his head in his hands. His door closed a moment later. One down.

He drove to Baltimore that night. His mother reached for his hand; he could do this. He nodded weakly. It was the right thing— the right thing. His mother waited in the car while he knocked on Nadia's door. Helene opened it and ran into his arms. He breathed her in. For his little girl. He told her to go see her grandma before he went inside and called for Nadia. She came out from the kitchen in her pajamas and fuzzy slippers.

"You fired Bobbie?"

"Why are you two still texting? Alice is gone." He hoped to catch her off guard, but she just smirked and raised her wineglass.

"Good riddance, I say. That man has been leeching off you since we were kids. I'm glad you finally saw what Bobbie is." She stepped closer and took a long drink.

He removed the tri-folded collection of papers from his jacket pocket and handed it to Nadia. "These were filed in Baltimore yesterday; I am going for primary custody of Helene. She's going to live with me, and you can see her on the weekends. Also, I am suing for the $240,000 you owe me in overpaid child support."

She laughed and slid the papers back into his jacket pocket, holding him.

"We should celebrate getting Bobbie out of your life. My mom can keep Helene. Aruba is lovely this time of year. Bali. We don't have to leave the room." She went on her toes to kiss him, Delany taking a step back.

He reached for her wrist without the wine and slid the papers into her hand. "Nod, listen. I'm asking for Helene to come live with me."

"You can't take my daughter." She set her glass on the table and skimmed the pages.

"Our daughter, Nadia. She's both of ours. I am not going to let you use her to fund your lifestyle anymore."

She pouted slightly. "Bobbie told me you came to your senses with the caterer. I know we didn't get along, but I think you'll come to see I was right." She held out the pages for him.

"I'm serious."

She chuckled. "Give it a few days and you'll realize this is a mistake and the best thing for all concerned would be for you to come home and us to be a family."

It was the same look Bobbie gave him, the one that said he'd been a sucker for twenty years and this little showing of backbone didn't mean anything. He ran his hand over his mouth, widening his stance.

"We're not a family, Nadia. We have never been a family. It's over. I'm not your ticket to the Gucci life. Go to Aruba on your own dollar because you are not getting any more money from me."

That seemed to break through, Nadia recoiling slightly. "Don't start what you can't finish, Delany. You have no idea what I can take you for."

He got closer to her and pulled up to his full height. "Don't threaten me. We both know I have better lawyers and a mountain of evidence."

Nadia stepped back and cocked her head. "I see your game. Two can do this. You wait, I will take you for everything you have. I am going to get total custody of my little girl, and you will give me every penny I ask for and more! You hear me!" She kept raging. Delany reached for Helene's bag and walked out. She sat in the back of his car, laughing with her grandma. The evening felt warmer somehow, the breeze on his face a reminder that he could do this.

# CHAPTER 51

ALICE WALKED TO WORK the next morning, unable to believe what Tabby told her. Delany fired Bobbie. He saw who Bobbie was and cut him off. It almost made her giddy. If he saw the truth about Bobbie, there was hope he'd stand up to Nadia.

Tabby's burden was gone. She had a light in her eyes and smiled again, looking toward the future. Alice could never have orchestrated that moment for her sister, but was grateful Tabby let go and moved on to a position that seemed perfect for her.

Alice walked into the overly crowded bakery, raising a hand hello to the staff behind the counter.

"Are you proud of yourself?" Jonas' voice bellowed behind her. Alice paused as activity in the bakery stopped. "You think you can do this—run a restaurant of such esteem? You're nothing, Alice. That restaurant is the score of the decade. I worked too long and too hard to lose it to you!"

Alice sighed, unsure what this buffoon could want. Any other day she would have cowered to this man who did nothing but tear her down. But she saw it now—it wasn't that he didn't believe she could cook, but that he knew he could not. She was a beacon of what he would never be. She laughed once and turned, meeting him full on.

"I'm not the fraud here. I am not the one who relies on their staff to cook and then takes the credit. I am not the one who tried to intimidate a girl in her twenties into a sexual relationship so I could steal her ideas and build my brand off of someone else's work." She stepped toward him. Jonas glanced around, Alice refusing to back down now. "You can't stand that I remade myself and built something on my terms, and you are not even a footnote in my success. That I didn't bow before you and climb into bed with you and let you get by on what Cornelia taught me. You exist on money, pomp, and intimidation. But hear me—you don't scare me anymore. I earned my place at this table, and I did it by my talent and creativity. We both know your talent is like your restaurant, cold and devoid of anything real."

"I will get that restaurant," he said through clenched teeth, his face red. Alice wondered why this man ever scared her, why she ever let him hold her back for so long.

"Okay." She stood straighter and shrugged. "Go for it. Call Collins and make your best appeal. We're not in competition here, Jonas. We're not even playing the same game." She stepped back. "You've spent your entire career in D.C. trying to erase Cornelia from the industry because you know you will never match up. You can take his restaurant, but you can't cook his recipes. You can intimidate his staff, but you can't force us to work for you. You can manipulate his co-owner into perpetuating your lies, but you can't cover up for your extreme lack of a palate. I don't know what you expected to gain from this, but I'm done giving you any more time. Move on, I have." She turned, having forgotten they were in a crowded room. Carver stood beside the pastry case, his elbow resting on the top. The cashier asked the next person in line what they wanted. Alice went to the kitchen not looking back. That was the last time she considered what that man thought about her. He would never define her or her career again.

A staffer came back midmorning to tell her Derek Collins was there. She took off her apron and walked to the front. He stood from the café table he sat at.

"Ms. Gibson." He shook her hand before they both sat. "I wanted to come ask you to manage the restaurant at The Cora. I've tried places all over this town, and, well, what you do is what we want."

"Mr. Collins…"

"I know there's been some miscommunication, but I've been given the authority to bring on who I think would best serve what we want to do. And that's you."

"I accept."

"We can pay…I'm sorry, you what?" He chuckled. Alice smiled and laughed.

"I'm in. The Cora is my dream. I've wanted to be in that building since I was a little girl. It would be my honor to work with you."

He sat back and smiled wide, letting out a sigh of relief.

"Mr. Clare will be so excited. I can call him right now." He reached for his cell. Alice leaned forward and put her hand on his wrist.

"Let me tell him, please. It would mean a lot."

"Of course. Maybe we can get together next week, and I can show you the space."

#

THE ELEVATOR CLICKED THROUGH the floors, Tabby fighting off the memory of the last time she was there. She spent all weekend picking out what to wear, finally deciding on dark green slacks and an off-white blouse with a tie at the top. Annie said it felt like the first day of school. In many ways, it was. She hoped people would be nice to her, and she'd figure out where to go. She debated for an hour whether to wear her hair up or down and finally went for her power look—a high ponytail, natural make-up and her favorite coral lipstick. Alice came to see the twins on Sunday night, reassuring Tabby that Katy was amazing, and Delany was empowering, and she was going to kick ass.

Paul kissed her goodbye when she dropped him off at the EPA. Tabby pulled into the building and parked where Katy had told her to. Katy waited when she got off the elevator.

"It's nice to see you again, Mrs. Black. I'm Katy O'Toole, welcome to Macon. Mr. Clare is this way." She led her to Delany's office, who stood when he saw her.

"Welcome." Delany shook her hand. They went to talk at the conference table in his office by the windows. Tabby glanced over the view again wondering how he got anything done. A schedule of meetings was on her open portfolio, next to the list of things Tabby wanted to do. Delany reiterated that he and Katy were there to help however they could. He stood, Katy waiting with all the forms she needed to fill out.

"Where is Moe's office?" she asked.

"I can take you," Katy said. They chatted while they walked, Tabby unsure what she was going to say. Katy showed her the open door and told her to take her time. Tabby let her walk away before running a hand over her blouse and knocking on the door.

"Hey Tabby," Moe stood slowly. "I saw the email from Delany…"

"I owe you an apology, Moe." She refused to chicken out. "You were a good friend and did a lot for me. I'd never have gotten TabiKat off the ground without you. I know what happened wasn't ideal and faced with those three, not easy. But I want you to know I'm sorry for taking your friendship and talent for granted, and I hope we can find a way to work together."

He moved around the desk to hug her, Tabby slowly closing her arms. This was their second chance to do what they talked about at her kitchen table when TabiKat was getting started.

"Welcome to the team," he said. She met his gaze and nodded.

"What do I need to know?"

He motioned for her to sit. They spent the rest of the morning talking, her ideas only getting bigger.

#

KATY KNOCKED ON DELANY'S door mid-afternoon.

"How is Tabby doing?" he asked.

"Like she's been here forever. The foreman called. They have some questions with things at The Cora. He wondered if you could stop by."

He sighed, wanting to go home and watch the game and forget. But they were behind schedule and every day cost him money.

"I'll go by after I leave."

He went to check in with Tabby, her office dark. He rode the Metro, needing to call Collins to see what the game plan was now that Alice said no. Anyone else would be a step down. Maybe in time he'd stop comparing whatever they cooked to what Alice could do.

The building looked dark, a note waiting at the service entrance in the back.

*Follow the path.'* An electric candle flickered on the ground just inside the fence. He found the next one, the path leading him to the entrance for the elevator exclusively for the tower which opened, a candle inside. The doors closed and Delany pushed the button for the only other floor the elevator went to. He faced the glass enclosure, the elevator rising into the dark. It opened on the 10th floor to another candle. Now he was curious.

"Hello?" He went into the illuminated landing, an arrow of candles pointing him toward the door to the observation deck. The chill from the open deck hit him as he stepped outside. He started around the lower deck, Alice looking over her shoulder.

"Have you ever seen the view up here at night?" She faced him in the dress she had worn to Emre.

"No. I can't say I have."

She turned toward the Washington Monument, the lights of Virginia shining in the distance. He stopped behind her, taking off his jacket and putting it over her shoulders. She pulled it closer.

"Pretty remarkable, right?" she asked.

"It's amazing." He rested his hand on her far side and pressed a kiss to her hair, the moment still sinking in.

She faced him and reached for his hand. "I got a new gig this weekend."

"Yeah? Where?" His heart dropped; please don't say she was leaving town.

"Collins came to see me."

"Wait, so when he asks you to do it?" He tilted his head, Alice smiling. It took all his restraint not to just kiss her, things needed to be said.

"I never talked to Tabby about my decision to work for you and took my guilt out on you. I convinced myself that what I felt wasn't enough when really, I've never cared about anyone as much as I care about you. You and Helene, you're home to me."

He squared his body to hers, running his knuckles down her face. "I love you," he said. "And you were right, I was being played. But I'm getting primary custody of Helene, and I spoke to Tabby…"

"I know. I helped her pick out an outfit. It's a whole new day for you, mi amor."

"That is so much better than Bulldog."

"I thought you might like it." She smiled as Delany put his arm around her. He leaned in, Alice going on her tiptoes. He kissed her, pulling her closer. There was nothing between them now, Delany grateful for those drinks over the summer and the woman who never left his mind. She led him to a picnic she set up on the upper deck with her infused Cherry Blossom gin and tonics and his favorite dessert. They sat there and watched the lights. Delany able to see a lifetime play out before him, humbled.

# CHAPTER 52

ALICE PUT THE FINISHING TOUCHES on the platter before the server could steal it. She looked around her kitchen, double the size of the one at the bakery. A butcher block prep table just after the main doors enabled her to double-check orders and add finishing touches. A lower wall and a shelf beyond the table let those at the stoves and friers pass plates up. Fridges and other prep stations lined the edge of the main room, Alice wanting to be able to invite a station chef over to help with a dish or add their unique twist. The dishwasher was tucked into its own alcove, with the freezer at the far end.

The Cora opened in a few days, the event tonight for friends and family. On the desk in her office was the latest issue of *The Washingtonian* with Alice standing before The Cora—*D.C.'s Top Chef Gets New Home*. The story talked about Alice's plans for 'Rassasy', meaning to be satisfied by a great meal. Rassasy promised to be a home for the multifaceted history of D.C. cuisine with a foraged twist. The best of what the local area produced, including edibles, infused with the multicultural fare Alice, and those she met with Comida, were becoming known for.

Alice ran her hands over her apron, another tray on its way out. Carver came to see if she needed anything. They renovated a space next to the restaurant for a second location of his bakery with an entrance to the street. His flagship store in Chinatown would continue to oversee his wedding business, but this location let him play and be creative.

"I have something for you," he said. Alice took the bag from his hands lifting out the purple chef's coat, *Alice Gibson Executive Chef* embroidered on the left chest. She ran her fingers over the lettering, speechless.

"Cornelia knew you'd get here. He told me once he was afraid you'd figure out you were bigger than what he could teach you. I wish he was here to see this."

"Thank you." She could barely get the words out. She handed Carver the coat and took off her apron. He held the coat open and slipped it over her shoulders. Alice buttoned it and turned to face him.

"Looks good on you." He laughed when Alice hugged him.

"Thank you for believing in me." She let go. "I couldn't see that chef for a while."

She told the staff she'd be back, going to check on things in the main room. Servers in jumpsuits moved through the crowd offering a selection of samples from Alice's spring menu. The space itself opened to the skylights ten stories above. Muted-turquoise half-walls held planters filled with local edibles. Seating centered around a series of long farmhouse tables in the middle, booth seating along the perimeter. Art on the wall highlighted heroes of D.C.'s culinary past silenced because of their race or gender.

Across the room, Valencia spoke with Alice's parents. She had taken over the day-to-day operations at Hasty Pudding, whose menu tied into what they served at Rassasy, enabling Valencia to cover when Alice went out with Comida. She brought back a host of ideas from her time in Spain. Together, they were ready to keep changing the idea of what was possible with food.

Tabby talked to Moe and his fiancé. Back to being Tabby's right-hand man, he oversaw Array and developed apps, the company about to announce higher than anticipated earnings for the quarter. He was back to his sweet spot with coding. Tabby used her position at Macon to work with smaller tech firms to get a leg up, not by selling their companies, but by training and financing for specific projects. It was a whole new avenue for Macon to pursue, another way for Delany to impact the communities around them.

Alice's father moved to say hello to Coretta and Olive, who was due any day now. Annie chased Helene around the space. Mac stood with Paul talking to Collins and his family, his daughter the same age as the twins. Alice leaned against the wall and tried to capture the moment. The previous year felt like a blur, but at the end waited something precious and better than she ever imagined. She looked up, wanting Cornelia there. But he'd prepped her for this, given her everything she needed to succeed. All Alice needed was the courage to see it.

Delany reached for her hand as they rode in the elevator, Helene asleep against his shoulder. She was thriving at Delany's charter school, taking up the trumpet, a seeming natural talent. She moved in with Delany, her life transitioning down to D.C. more and more. He tried to keep her from the custody battle drama. A gossip columnist had picked up the story and went looking for dirt, obtaining copies of the court filings and writing about Nadia's using funds meant for her daughter to take lavish trips. It wasn't what Delany wanted but, like Bobbie, Nadia had made her bed.

Bobbie moved to South Carolina, Carrie choosing to stay in D.C. The kid he hired to torch the food truck took a plea deal, Alice deciding not to pursue a civil case. Delany stayed quiet, not defending his former best friend but not adding fuel to the gossip mill. It was on Bobbie to decide how he wanted to live and the legacy he'd leave behind. His mother kept calling Coretta to get Delany to help Bobbie out, but Delany had given him all he was going to.

The elevator opened to the top floor, Delany handing Alice the keycard to his apartment. She went to look at the view while Delany put Helene to bed. He came back and they went through a side door to the tower. Alice opened the door to the observation deck. For so many years, she walked this route to stare out over D.C. and imagine what life would be. She never saw it being this sweet or her feeling so content.

Delany opened a bottle of champagne and poured Alice a glass. She took a sip and drank in the view of the city lights. Delany hugged her from behind and told her he loved her. Alice smiled. How much she'd been willing to walk away from. Yes, Delany gave her everything, but she wasn't a footnote in his career. Few realized Macon owned The Cora, and Hasty Pudding succeeded because of her cooking and vision. It was her work within the community that people were talking about. And Alice was just getting started.

# ACKNOWLEDGEMENTS & AUTHOR'S NOTE

This book would not exist without the love and never-ending belief of my husband, who created space for me to chase what I love. He is my biggest supporter, holding onto the flicker of my dream when I want to snuff it out and give into my fear. Thank you, David, for believing in me and giving me the opportunity to tell stories that matter. I love you.

To those who read the book along the way: Sharon R., Janna R., Melissa S., Trillian S., and Hope B. I am indebted to how you each made the story stronger. Thank you for pushing me to go deeper, to be truer, to make the characters more real, and to write with courage. This book would not be what it is without each of you.

To my best friend, beta-reader, co-adventurer, and fellow creative—Tisa, thank you. You have walked so much of this creative dream with me, not just *The Caterer,* but life! Thank you for repeatedly lending your input, letting me bounce ideas off you, being there to vent about this thing called the creative endeavor, and all around just being in my corner. I would not be here if not for you.

To Diane and Becky, thank you for your constant support and encouragement to get my words into the world, for being there to help me find the way, and for believing in me when I wanted to shrink back.

Meghan and Drake, you have made my life brighter and fuller. You have taught me about love and strength and believing in myself. I am blessed to have you in my life. Thank you for allowing me to become part of your family. To my family, my parents for supporting me, my sisters for being great cheerleaders, and my nieces and nephews for teaching me so much. Thank you for shaping me and helping me become who I am.

I started this novel in 2021 while my husband and I were living outside of D.C. We watched the documentary *We Feed People*, which tells the story of José Andrés and World Central Kitchen (WCK). Shortly thereafter, David and I visited The Anacostia Community

Museum's exhibit on food insecurity, and learned how gentrification affects communities, including the mom-and-pop food markets people rely on for the foods they know and enjoy.

Those experiences shaped many of Alice's ideas and attitudes towards food. Food is necessary for life. It has the ability to foster community and to comfort. Many of us don't have to think much about our food, so it can be a humbling and rewarding experience to put ourselves in other people's shoes. *We Feed People* is a great place to start. I also recommend WCK's James Beard Book Award winning cookbook, which features stories and recipes from chefs all over the world.

My stepdaughter Meghan introduced me to foraging. We have walked around D.C., Philly, and Colorado Springs, Meghan pointing out what is around us that we can consume. As I've learned more, I've added dandelions, stinging nettles, and calendula to my garden. If you want to know more about edibles around you, there is likely a foraging group in your area!

A big yard or a green thumb is not required for a garden: all you need is a bit of sunlight and some love to give. Research edible flowers and plant some on your patio. Find a local nursery and pick up a few herbs. Shop at local farmers' markets and enjoy what grows seasonally in your area. One of the best (and simplest) things we can do for our planet is to eat locally with the seasons. The more attune we become to what grows around us, the more we care about what we consume.

I've been a storyteller since before I had letters and words to utilize. Seeing how the pieces of this book came together, how it went from being about two sisters, one given the chance to fly by the same person who denied the other their dream, to what you hold in your hand is something only God could have orchestrated.

I believe that heaven is fields of picnic tables, where those who love to cook will do so with joy, and those who enjoy decorating will make it gorgeous while musicians play, and children run around, and mixologists combine the best flavors available in our return to Eden. I strive to create longer tables where all feel welcome. I hope Alice's journey stirred you a little and piqued your interest somehow. Mostly I hope you take away that we can all do something where we are, with what we have, and who is around us.

# ABOUT THE AUTHOR

Amanda Lunday is a lover of cultures and a history buff. She spends her days creating mysteries and drama for the people in her head to maneuver through. Writing has been an outlet since she was a child when she read out loud to her grandmother the gibberish she wrote on her typewriter. Having lived in D.C. twice, she strives to write about the city in a way that shows the treasure that exists outside the grime of politics. She took a circuitous route back to what she loves, completing a bachelor's in international affairs and a master's in nonprofit management before realizing she exists to tell stories that matter. She now lives in Colorado with her husband and two precocious beagles, and enjoys being close to family while continuing to write stories with characters you can (hopefully) relate to. You can find her online at www.amandalunday.com. *The Caterer* is her debut novel.

Made in the USA
Columbia, SC
15 October 2024

43827294R00212